JOHN DERRY

The story of Britain's first supersonic pilot

BRIAN RIVAS and ANNIE BULLEN

Foreword by Neville Duke DSO, OBE, DFC, AFC

Haynes Publishing

First published in 1982 by William Kimber & Co. Limited
This new edition published by Haynes Publishing in 2008
Copyright © Brian Rivas and Annie Bullen 1982 and 2008

A catalogue record for this book is available from the British Library

ISBN 978 1 84425 531 3

Library of Congress catalog card no 2008922575

Published by Haynes Publishing,
Sparkford, Yeovil, Somerset BA22 7JJ, UK
Tel: 01963 442030 Fax: 01963 440001
Int. tel: +44 1963 442030 Int. fax: +44 1963 440001
E-mail: sales@haynes.co.uk
Website: www.haynes.co.uk

Haynes North America Inc., 861 Lawrence Drive, Newbury Park,
California 91320, USA

Designed and typeset by James Robertson
Printed and bound in Britain by J.H. Haynes & Co. Ltd., Sparkford

CONTENTS

LIST OF ILLUSTRATIONS

44. John and Eve with Carol and Jo and the dogs at Greensleeves.
45. The SS *Hebrides* in the Western Isles, May 1952.
46. John, with 'onion seller's' beret, and Eve on board the *Hebrides*.
47. John, Eve and Jo on holiday in Cornwall, July 1952.
48. Ann Todd and David Lean chat with John and Eve outside the test pilots' tent.
49. John Derry and Tony Richards (white overalls) with ground crew.
50. Stills from the Gardner cine film showing the break-up of WG236.
51. John Derry and Tony Richards
52. 'In memory of the few and those that have come after them.'

FOREWORD

by Neville Duke DSO, OBE, DFC, AFC

Aviation is probably unique, and test flying in particular, in generating a flame, which flares into life for a short but brilliant time before it flickers and dies. Such a phenomenon was John Derry whose brilliant contribution to aviation was cut short in spectacular disaster when technology failed him in his prime.

He lived in dangerous days when we lost thirty-two of our best pilots in five post-war years and his work was in the most hazardous field of all – transonic research. You will read of his courageous high-speed tests in the DH108 – all of which crashed, taking with them three of our most valued test pilots. Whilst his flying was aggressively bold it was matched by strangely gentle pastimes – and when the time came his courage, too, was matched by his wife, Eve, and his family.

Neville Duke

ACKNOWLEDGEMENTS

First Edition – This book could not have been written without the generous help of the following:

John Derry's family – Mrs Eve Derry, Dr and Mrs Duncan Derry, the Rev Hugh Derry, Mrs Jo Laurie-Pyle.

Friends and colleagues – Russ Bannock, G.R. 'Jock' Bryce, Mr and Mrs Les Colquhoun, Grp Capt John Cunningham, Eddie Dissat, Sqn Ldr J.S. 'Fifi' Fyfield, Jeffrey Quill, Wg Cdr R.R. 'Bob' Stanford-Tuck, Sqn Ldr Denis Sweeting, Mr and Mrs John Wilson.

War years – Wg Cdr H. 'Poppa' Ambrose, C. Thomas, L. Tanner, D. Tyler, Kent Walton, Wg Cdr Bill Wood (RAF Museum, Hendon), Public Record Office, Kew.

General assistance – Denis Goode and Brian Kervell (Main Library, RAE Farnborough), F.H. Jones, M.J. Goldsmith (Divisional Managing Director, BAe Hatfield), J. Scott and M. Brown (Public Relations, BAe Hatfield), members of the Photographic Dept at BAe Hatfield, C. Burnet, R.M. Hare, R. Jones, Eric B. Morgan (Library, BAe Weybridge), Sqdn Ldr J. Potter, the Rev J.D.R. Rawlings, Richard Riding (editor *Aeroplane Monthly*), C. Martin Sharp, E. Short, J.P. Smith, Ann Todd, M. Turner-Bridger, J.C. Wimpenny (BAe Kingston-upon-Thames), Alec Lumsden.

Foreword – Sqn Ldr Neville Duke.

New edition, 2008 – Barry Guess and Mike Fielding (BAe Systems, Farnborough), Nick Stroud (*Aeroplane Magazine*), Bruce Gordon (de Havilland Aircraft Heritage Centre), Richard Gardner (Farnborough Air Sciences Trust).

Grateful thanks to Jonathan Falconer, Senior Commissioning Editor at Haynes Publishing, for his enthusiasm and dedication in launching this new edition.

PREFACE

When John Derry made the first supersonic flight in Britain in 1948 it was a proud and memorable moment for the country. And even now, after all these years, the term 'sound barrier' still carries an evocative resonance of those skilled and brave test pilots of the early jet age, many of whom lost their lives on flights into the unknown. Even in that select company, John Derry stood out for his skill, courage and professionalism and was respected equally for his personal qualities. Once a household name, Derry's tragically early death shocked the nation, but he was never forgotten by those who knew or worked with him. This biography tells the story of an outstanding pilot and a greatly loved man from the pioneering era of supersonic flight.

B.R.

Only the air spirits know what lies beyond the hills, yet I urge my team farther on, drive on and on, on and on.

Greenland Eskimo song from *Rasmussen's Across Arctic America*

INTRODUCTION TO
NEW EDITION

It was a warm April evening in 1948. The radio masts at the BBC transmission station at Brookmans Park in Hertfordshire stood starkly against the setting sun. All was quiet and peaceful. Suddenly the silence was broken as a strange looking jet, flying very fast and low, whistled past; an aircraft that would look futuristic even today.

It was the little swept wing tailless de Havilland DH108 in which test pilot John Derry was about to set a new 100km closed circuit record at more than 600mph. Waiting by the runway for his return to de Havilland's base at Hatfield were scores of reporters, photographers and television cameramen. Derry was already well known for his superb demonstration displays and on landing he was greeted like a hero.

Even though we were in the austere years after the war, these were exciting and heady times for aviation. Rationing still existed, food was basic – a chicken was considered a luxury – and values and behaviour were very different from today. Televisions were small-screen black and white valve designs in the homes of the few who could afford them. The age of instant global communication was many years away. But in spite of the hardships, the wartime spirit remained and there was huge pride in Britain's technological achievements, especially in the aircraft industry where new and extraordinary shapes appeared in the skies from companies such as de Havilland, Hawker, Vickers Supermarine and Gloster.

And the Press were talking of a strange phenomenon they called the sound barrier, a term that had immediately captured the country's imagination – especially after Geoffrey de Havilland Jr died in a high-speed break-up of another DH108 in 1946.

There was speculation in the Press that perhaps the aircraft broke up because Geoffrey had reached the speed of sound – even that he might have been making some 'death or glory' attempt to do so.

The dangers and difficulties of flying near the speed of sound had already been encountered: during the war Spitfires and other high performance piston engined aircraft began to run into compressibility effects in high-speed dives in which control became difficult and sometimes impossible. There could be severe buffeting, wing drop, a feeling of increasing nose heaviness and other alarming phenomena. Small wonder that flying at or beyond the speed of sound seemed like an impenetrable and hazardous barrier.

It was against this background that John Derry, who had a distinguished and brave war record flying Hawker Typhoons and had already done some test flying, took over the high speed test programme of the 108, extending the performance envelope very gradually and reporting his findings accurately. And on 6 September 1948 he achieved lasting fame by becoming the first pilot in Britain to exceed the speed of sound in the little aircraft. This book, first published in 1982, has been reissued to commemorate the 60th anniversary of that historic flight.

These were extremely dangerous and hazardous times in the air; in the five years after the war we lost thirty-two test pilots in accidents. That would be unthinkable today. But Derry remained cool and analytical, even in the face of extreme danger and fear, and he quickly established himself as among the first of a new and necessary breed of test pilot. Transonic flying was the biggest challenge ever faced in aviation and in the absence of telemetering equipment or computers the responsibility of noting and reporting everything accurately, often unexpected events in very quick succession, lay with the pilot.

After his first supersonic flight, Derry became a household name, along with other pioneering test pilots such as Neville Duke, Mike Lithgow, Dave Morgan and Bill Waterton. How different from today when very few people could name a single test pilot. And the country was treated to a sound never heard before: sonic booms.

Throughout the test programme, and later on the de Havilland DH110, forerunner of the Sea Vixen, Derry continued with his remarkable displays at air shows and other functions, and he took this aspect of his work just as seriously as his test flying. He was soon regarded as the country's foremost exponent of the art in jet aircraft, and his focus was firmly on showing the aircraft's capabilities rather than his own – but the accent was always on safety.

Derry was not only admired by all who knew him for his outstanding qualities as a pilot, but equally for his warmth, kindness and charm as a man. He loved his work, but he was a devoted husband and father, and in moments of relaxation he studied nature and wildlife. He kept a diary of his holiday in the Western Isles in 1952, which you will read in this book. In the light of what was to happen so soon afterwards it is a touching and moving account of what was a very special time for him. His widow, Eve, always said that to find out what he was like as a person, all one had to do was read this diary.

It remains a terrible irony that John Derry, ever mindful of safety, was to lose his life at Farnborough on 6 September 1952 when his aircraft failed him and broke up in front of a crowd of 120,000 spectators. Not only did Derry and his flight observer Tony Richards lose their lives, but 29 spectators were killed when one of the engines from his DH110 crashed into the dense crowds. The tragedy was witnessed by Eve.

This book is as much about Derry the man as Derry the test pilot. When it first appeared many of his relatives and contemporaries were still alive and had the warmest memories of an exceptional man as well as an exceptional pilot. Without those people, many of whom have now passed on, this story could not have been written.

And yet the legend of John Derry still lives on nearly sixty years after his death, thanks in part to the internet where memories and views are shared. He lived in a golden (and often hazardous) age of experimental flying when he and his contemporaries were heroes, and without whose skill and courage supersonic flight would not be what it is today – something so routine that it is done without a second thought.

B.R.

Chapter 1

THAT ELIZABETHAN
SPIRIT

*'In John was reincarnated that Elizabethan spirit which has made
our country great.'* Wing Commander C.D. North-Lewis

The penetrating throb of an aeroplane engine disturbed the clear blue skies over a Canadian lakeside garden, where a tall blond boy sat lazing in the sun.

'Tomtit,' he observed, without looking up and he turned to grin at his brother and sister-in-law, who were just getting used to the phenomenon of a seventeen-year-old who could identify an aeroplane or a motorcar simply by the noise it made.

Duncan and Alice Derry were enjoying the process of growing to know their young relative who had come to spend his first holiday with them in Ontario during the 1939 summer break from Charterhouse, his English school. John, on the verge of manhood, was tall and well built, with corn-blond hair and clear brown eyes, which crinkled easily into friendliness. He had scarcely recognised his older brother, Duncan, on his arrival in Canada, as the two of them had rarely seen each other during John's childhood at Haslemere in Surrey, but the brothers formed an immediate warm friendship during that summer, despite the fifteen years that separated them.

Right now they were planning a shooting trip to James Bay, in the north of the country where they would find duck, geese and ruffed grouse and would camp in the open in wild, rugged countryside. This was exciting enough for a young man with an adventurous spirit but the best part of the trip was to be the flight up there. Duncan laughed at the youthful idealism of his younger brother whose enthusiasm for aeroplanes was boundless and who refused to contemplate any career for himself except one that involved flying, but while he teased John he realised that this boy with a charm and maturity beyond his years, was singleminded in his steady determination to learn to fly and his passion for the air was more than a mere boyhood craze.

Alice helped the brothers to plan the trip, but before John and Duncan could set out, there came the radio broadcast with the news that they had all been expecting and dreading; Britain and her Commonwealth were at war with Germany. John forgot all about the disappointment of the cancellation of the shooting trip in his determination to sail back home on the next boat so that he could join the Royal Air Force. The day before, Canada, with the prospect of hunting trips, swims in the lake and days of freedom in the autumn sunshine, had seemed to be the best place in the world; now the young man fretted impatiently as he thought of the queues of hopeful pilots enlisting at home in England, while he was separated from any hope of doing so by the wide gulf of the Atlantic. John had been hoping to go to the RAF College at Cranwell when he left Charterhouse at eighteen but the coming of war meant that now he would take a short cut into the Air Force.

He walked alone along the shores of Lake Ontario to think about his plans. Suddenly, here was the culmination of a childhood passion for aircraft and a boyhood spent 'plane spotting, collecting books and magazines on aircraft, cutting out pictures and photographs of the machines for his scrapbooks and making models and paper aeroplanes in his spare time. The conception of the spirit which was to urge him on in his search for knowledge and mastery of the air was made early in his life and now was the time to realise his ambition. John decided that he must make his apologies to Duncan and Alice and take the next boat home.

But that was not so easy. All John's impatience wasn't enough to secure a passage when shipping plans were suddenly thrown into confusion and he was just one of hundreds of people trying to get home across the Atlantic. Duncan and Alice, upset at the prospect of saying goodbye to John just as they were all getting to know each other, persuaded him to wait patiently for a sailing and to make the most of the last week or so of his holiday with them. Duncan, a successful geologist, had left the family home in Surrey when his younger brother was a child of four and because of his job, which took him all over the world, had made only four visits back in thirteen years. In view of the separation, which loomed now, there was a lot to be said and much family news to be discussed before John found his way back to England and the Royal Air Force.

John and the three other Derry children had been brought up in a strange, scattered way. Duncan and John were the oldest and youngest sons of Dr Douglas Derry, a brilliant man, who became Professor of Anatomy at the Royal Egyptian University at Cairo, and whose name became known to the world when he was called upon by Howard Carter and Lord Carnarvon to unwrap and examine the Mummy of the boy king, Tutankhamen, and to write the chapter on his findings in Carter's book about the discovery.

Douglas Derry must have seemed a stern and remote figure – remote in the geographical sense as well as the spiritual – to his youngest son who was brought up in a comfortable English home, hundreds of miles away from his father, whose visits every summer often disturbed and upset him.

The anatomist's own upbringing had been a strict one and he had made his way in the world largely through his own effort and determination to succeed, characteristics that his children inherited. He was one of fourteen children of an accountant who was also a strict Plymouth Brother. Douglas and his brothers and sisters all received a good education – and they all had to attend what often seemed like endless religious services at the insistence of their parents. Although none of the children stayed with the Plymouth Brethren when they were old enough to decide for themselves, the upbringing and the early way of life gave each of them a particular directness of manner which was sometimes taken for abruptness and a way of viewing life in simple terms which meant they were able to reach a goal or an ambition without cluttering the way with complications.

Douglas left school in his mid-teens but at that time money was short and he knew that he wouldn't be able to go to university. So he worked for a year or two for a tea company but, like his youngest son many years later, he knew that there was only one path for him in life and that, one day, he would take it. He bought medical textbooks and saved as much money as he could so that eventually he could fulfil his ambition to become a doctor. In the meantime a brighter prospect than that offered by the tea company presented itself to him. His brother-in-law, Charlie Holland, who had married his eldest sister, Kathleen, owned some property near Bulawayo in the recently settled African colony of Rhodesia and he wanted the eighteen-year-old Douglas to run it for him. So Douglas and Charlie left England in 1892 for Cape Town. The trip was by no means an easy one. The newly built railways only went as far as Pretoria and that left 400 miles to be covered to the little six-acre farm, east of Bulawayo. A long and tiring but exciting journey followed in a bone-shaking cart drawn by oxen across wild country, where lions prowled and game of all sorts roamed the plains. Douglas stayed there for several years (three of his brothers and a sister went out later) and survived the often tough life, including the horror of the Matabele rebellion, when he and other property managers had to hole up in besieged Bulawayo.

He never lost his desire to train as a doctor and, during all this time, he read medical textbooks and stored his savings, which were to be spent on his university education. Family legend has it that he was sitting in a railway carriage one day, reading one of his medical books, when a stranger, sitting opposite, asked if he were a doctor. He had to say he wasn't and he told the man his ambition.

Amazingly, it seemed that the man understood and he offered to lend young Douglas the money to return to England and study medicine. This may only be a family story, but there is no doubt that he did manage to borrow the balance of the money he needed and in the late 1890s he enrolled at Edinburgh University as a medical student and he graduated in 1903. He stayed in Edinburgh and worked at the University as a demonstrator in anatomy until he met and married Margaret Ramsay. Their eldest child, Duncan, was born in 1906 and soon afterwards the whole family moved to Cairo where Dr Derry became Assistant Professor in Anatomy at the University. During this time he had a taste of a life of adventure again when he joined an expedition up the Nile, to Nubia, as medical officer.

The family returned to London and when the First World War broke out he joined the staff of a base hospital in Boulogne and then, in his early forties, entered the Royal Army Medical Corps, earning the Military Cross on the Western Front, in Belgium. By this time his other son, Hugh and daughter, Helen, were born and, after the war, the family again moved to Cairo, where he was offered the Professorship in Anatomy at his old department.

Duncan and Hugh were at Rugby and the Dragon School, respectively, so that the only child with Douglas and his wife, who was affectionately called Daisy, was young Helen. But on 5 December 1921 she had a little blond brother who was christened John Douglas. It soon became apparent that John's mother was becoming very ill and not long after his birth in Cairo, he and Helen were sent, with a nurse, on the long journey to England to live with an aunt at the Derry family house, which Douglas had bought before leaving for Cairo for the second time. John was never to see his mother again, for although she did not die until some years later, she never recovered from a severe illness.

John and Helen were greeted at Meadfield by Aunt Connie, their father's younger sister, who was looking after the family home and keeping an eye on Duncan and Hugo (as the second brother was known) in their school holidays. She was a true eccentric in that everything she had to cope with in life was, to her, perfectly straightforward and uncomplicated and she failed to recognise difficulties raised by others. She adored John and all the large family and she was the one who looked after him for the greater part of his childhood.

Aunt Connie, unmarried, short and stout, with a head of curly hair and an unadorned stern face, which would break into the most devastating smiles, was an unusual custodian for a small child. She was an innocent who trusted people, even if they abused that trust and, above all things, she loved John and indulged him. Connie had fallen, early in life, to the usual fate of unmarried daughters of large families – she had spent many years looking after an old lady, which was a thankless task for a young woman. This chance to run her brother's large comfortable house and to look after her nephews and niece when they were there must have made a welcome change. But the opportunity to look after John, who was little more than a baby when he arrived at Meadfield, was something that she welcomed eagerly and the little boy with bright blond hair, the pointed ears which stuck out at an angle from his head and the clear 'Derry' eyes with a downward slant on the upper lid, became her whole life. She did her best to see that he had all the material things he needed and she arranged treats and, later, outings for him. But, try as she might, she was unable to fathom the workings of a small boy's mind. Clear and uncluttered as her own brain was, the complicated reasoning and the demands made by a child were often lost on her. John loved Aunt Connie dearly but as he grew up he was often lonely, feeling the need of someone to talk to about the things that worry and puzzle all children.

He soon learnt to become, if not emotionally independent, at least detached where his feelings about anything that hurt or upset him, were concerned. Later, when he was a young man of twenty-one, he met his future wife, Eve, and it was with a great flood of relief that John realised he was able to talk to someone about the things that pleased and hurt him – probably for the first time in his life. But the childhood practice of detaching his mind from immediate fears and worries stayed with him and often stood him in good stead when his work demanded it. Diving in an out-of-control aircraft from great heights at speeds approaching that of sound until the machine would at last respond to the controls and the terrifying rush would be manageable, John was able to tuck his fear away and methodically and calmly start to note aspects of the aeroplane's behaviour that would be of value to the scientists and engineers on the ground. He would never deny that he often felt afraid – he knew that only the foolhardy pilot never felt those sharp twinges at the pit of the stomach – but throughout it he was able to note, record and analyse and to act rationally. Today, test pilots are trained to do this; with John it was instinctive and natural.

If as a boy John was often lonely, he would look forward to the family gatherings at Meadfield in the summer. Duncan, fifteen years his senior, was making his own way in the world and didn't have the time to come home often although John enjoyed the few visits he did make.

Hugo, a young man who loved books and the stimulation of an intellectual discussion, wasn't that much help to John when he wanted to talk about cars and aeroplanes, but he would always give his younger brother a lift to the motor races at Brooklands. He would leave the small, excited boy in the milling crowds at the race circuit and head off to find a peaceful spot in a wood or by a river, where he could read in peace. When it was time to pick his younger brother up, Hugo would wonder, with a sinking heart, how he was ever going to find him in the crush, but he always managed it somehow.

Sometimes both Hugo and Helen would bring their friends home and the large comfortable family house, set in grounds of several acres, would come to life in the summer when Douglas Derry shut up his department at the University in Cairo, which closed for four months every year, climbed into his little Singer, and motored home to England, which was no mean feat in those days. He did this with a little help from the Automobile Association, who must have been mildly surprised each year when Dr Derry would write to them for an up-to-date itinerary – from Cairo to

London. But they never failed him, and he and Helen, who sometimes accompanied him on these journeys, would travel along appalling roads, suffer several breakdowns which were, somehow, always repaired and often have accidents, including the time the Singer left the road and ended up at the bottom of a steep bank, having knocked down a peasant's precious pear tree. They were only helped, dazed and bruised as they were, after they had reimbursed the outraged man for his tree. But they saw beautiful scenery and visited wonderful cities, full of life and colour.

All of the Derry children inherited their father's adventurous nature, in some measure. It led Duncan to remote parts of the world to seek his fortune and Hugh, later a Church of England priest, faced the rigours of life in distant parts of Africa, as a missionary. John's search towards the unknown compelled him to press on to the ultimate goal for a pilot of his time – a way through the aptly named 'Sound Barrier'.

John and his father were outwardly glad to see each other at these summer meetings but there was constraint on both sides. Dr Derry had a manner that seemed abrupt and blunt and, in some obscure way, he blamed his youngest son for his wife's illness and the boy realised this and resented it. John would go to the houses of school friends, see the companionship that existed in a conventional family and feel the lack of it in his own life. It was only after the war when he was working as a test pilot that he and his father were to get to know each other properly and a deep friendship and relationship was established between father and son.

It was at Meadfield that John developed an interest in the wildlife around him. The grounds were full of birds and animals and the small boy, often on his own, spent hours crouched in the woods or hidden up a tree watching the birds, or crawling along a hedgerow to see the rabbits come out to play in the evenings. He learnt to be patient, to wait until the bird or animal he was watching for came into view and he learnt, by careful slow observation, the different song of each bird. He noted that the rabbits came out of their burrows in response to a call from one of the big bucks and, after weeks of careful practice, he was able to reproduce the sound – and found himself ringed by startled rabbits.

When he grew older and got to know his brothers better, he found that they too were particularly interested in wildlife, especially birds, and letters between them mention any rare species they had seen and carry descriptions of unusual aspects of bird behaviour. John liked to do things thoroughly and to find out facts the hard way, so, if he could fool Aunt Connie, he would slip out at night when he had the chance and sit quietly in the woods until badgers or foxes came out. He never thought it unusual that he should do this and after his marriage to Eve often climbed out of bed in the middle of the night, or very early in the morning, to watch the nocturnal creatures.

As a young boy John could name any bird by its song but he could also tell you the make of every car on the roads and every aeroplane in the sky – he could do this before he was able to read. He wanted, more than anything else, to learn to drive, and his excitement when Aunt Connie, badgered to take him to the 1929 Schneider Trophy race at Calshot, bought a baby Austin, was intense. Poor Connie, who was over fifty by then, decided that she would have to learn to drive, but it cannot be said that she was an unqualified success behind the wheel, although she was never apparently unnerved by any of her driving experiences. There were several occasions when she would turn up at a friend's house for tea with a white and shaking passenger tottering along behind. During the tea time conversation it would transpire that the car had turned over in a ditch on the way.

There was the time that Connie, blithely ignoring all the rules of the road, had sailed out of a minor turning in front of a column of heavy Canadian Army trucks. She was very offended when they made rude gestures at her. Connie always remained unruffled, even on the day when she got out of the car, which she had stopped on a hill. It started to slide backwards towards a small lake. Connie realised that it was too late to do anything and gave it an affectionate pat on the bonnet as it gained speed.

'Off you go,' she said as it slowly disappeared in the murky water.

John thought driving with Aunt Connie was a wonderful treat. One day he and Helen were out for a spin with her when Helen unwisely remarked that the carpet near the gear lever was becoming frayed. Connie immediately bent down to look. The car mounted the nearside bank, stayed upright by some sort of a miracle, and turned round in the road, across the traffic, facing the way it had come.

'That was fun-do it again!' said John from the back seat. He was eight or nine at the time and, like most small boys, knew exactly how a car should be driven. In fact he probably knew better than most others because Connie, who could never understand that motor cars could possibly present any danger to anyone – she'd never been hurt, after all – used to let him drive in the grounds at Meadfield and sometimes, illegally, on the roads.

But it was Connie who drove John to Calshot to see the Schneider Trophy races. Two in succession were held there in those pre-war years – 1929 and 1931. The former was won for Britain by Flight Lieutenant Dick Waghorn in the Supermarine S6, that only the night before the race had seemed as if it would not be able to compete because of piston failure. But the British fitters managed to get a new cylinder block in position, working through the night, and Dick Waghorn flew the seven 50km laps at an average speed of 328.63mph, beating the keen Italian opposition.

Enormous amounts of money were poured into these races, which were theoretically held annually (because of the tremendous organisation, some years were missed) and were generally fought between British, French, American and Italian teams. They were for seaplanes – or hydro-aeroplanes as they were then called – and the trophy was first presented by Jacques Schneider, a pilot and air enthusiast, in 1912. The early meetings were often very badly organised and dangerous affairs, but they were always tremendously exciting.

Young John, who was transferring his early passion for motor cars to anything that flew, heard that the contest was to be held in Britain and demanded that he should be taken to see the races.

He and Aunt Connie climbed into the little Austin and, after a hair-raising journey to the south coast, which John thoroughly enjoyed and which Connie was oblivious to, John scrambled out of the car and rushed to Calshot beach to find the best spot for spectating. The narrow spit, cramped by the high tide, was crowded with good-natured enthusiasts who let the eager little schoolboy through. He hopped up and down with excitement, a broad grin splitting his face, as his heroes skimmed over the water.

He disregarded everything else and poor Connie just had to wait patiently until the last aeroplane had flown. Once back at Meadfield, out came John's scrapbook and he pasted in carefully cut out pictures and photographs of the machines and the men who flew them.

John was lucky in 1931, when the contest was won by the British for the third time in succession making the winning country the outright owner of the Trophy. The enormous silver and bronze vessel, mounted on dark marble and showing the Speed Spirit kissing the Water Spirit on a breaking wave, came to England to be displayed for posterity in the Royal Aero Club in Pall Mall. Flight Lieutenant John Boothman was the winner this time, in a Supermarine S6B. What John didn't see was the new world air speed record which was set up a few days later, at the end of September, when Flight Lieutenant G. Stainforth, using the S6B with a specially prepared Rolls-Royce sprint engine, exceeded 400mph on a measured run. Seventeen years later John himself was to establish a world record over 200mph faster than this.

By the time John was nine or ten, his interest in aircraft was intense and it was to develop over the next few years until it became part of his life. He was determined to go for a flight and he saved every penny that came his way until he had enough to go for a 'joy ride'. His sister Helen was at Meadfield and John decided that she was the one he should wheedle for this little outing. He told her of an airfield at Croydon, where he had heard that they would take you up for ten shillings a time. Helen, with a good dose of the pioneering Derry spirit, agreed to take her starry-eyed younger brother, even though it was a filthy day, gusty and wet. They arrived at the airfield and saw the little biplane, which looked frail, and the open cockpit (they were to sit in front of the pilot, Helen realised with horror) was cold and uninviting.

But John was thrilled and he climbed in eagerly. The pilot then offered them each a hat, as it would be bitterly cold once they were airborne. Helen was already wearing a white woollen cap, which she pulled down well over her ears, and John also refused the offer.

'I've brought my own,' he said and he pulled out of his coat pocket an old leather flying helmet, which he had somehow acquired, and proudly put it on.

The next stage was to get Connie into the air. When she told John, now a pupil at the Dragon School, Oxford, that they were to spend a holiday on the Isle of Wight, he decided that they must fly there. He was about twelve at the time, and he got his way, although Connie's feelings about the flight aren't recorded. She probably enjoyed it immensely. When they reached the island, they had a car for the duration of the holiday and John, on new territory, decided that he was going to be the driver. No one would realise that he was under age if he sat on two cushions (he was tall for his age, anyway), tied a scarf round his neck and put on the old hat which had been left in the car by Hugo. No one did. He spent a lot of time at the wheel, exploring the island, with Connie by his side. The locals were probably a lot safer than if Connie had been in charge.

John's upbringing, slightly unconventional and unhampered by tight family restrictions, must have nurtured what was essentially an independent spirit.

There is no doubt, though, that he missed the closeness of a proper mother and son relationship and that the constraint, which existed between him and his father when he was young, upset him as he passed through adolescence. He was helped in some measure in his teens, when he formed a close relationship with the mother of one of his school friends. Guy Daniels tragically died in his teens and 'Duchess', as Mrs Daniels was known to all her friends, looked on John to fill the gap that her son's death had left. John, for his part, responded and the friendship that she showed him helped him through the awkward years of adolescence.

But there were other influences. Throughout his childhood he had the advantage of regular contact with a large and interesting assortment of relatives, without feeling the suffocation of identity that can happen in big families. There were letters from Egypt, describing cities, journeys and expeditions and he also heard from Duncan who was forging a career for himself in Canada as a geologist and doing a lot of bush flying to remote places, which made his younger brother green with envy. Helen divided her time between Cairo and England, sometimes bringing friends to Meadfield, and Hugo joined a monastery. He never took his vows, because when war broke out he decided to join the Army as a stretcher-bearer. His friends were horrified, but it was a very brave act for someone who couldn't reconcile himself to warfare. Hugh and his fellow stretcher-bearers saw a lot of front line action and had shattering first-hand experiences of the horrors of war.

These were the influences that surrounded John in the twenties and thirties, which were good times for the child of a well-to-do family. The depression had no real effect on the Derrys and life was exciting for a boy who was interested in cars and aeroplanes. Technological change and development meant that there were new machines on the roads and in the air all the time, and, while going for a drive was exciting (even more so for John when he was the driver), the hope of a flight was a dream sometimes to be fulfilled. Home was large and comfortable and surrounded by large grounds and the countryside full of the wildlife in which he developed such an interest. A diary, kept later, when he and his wife, Eve, were holidaying in the Western Isles of Scotland, shows an expert knowledge of the many birds they saw, while people with whom he worked in the RAF and as a test pilot remember going with him to watch birds or to make midnight forays to watch and sketch nocturnal animals.

Although he worried about the looseness of family ties, he was lucky to have a huge variety of interesting relatives. Both his father and his mother had many brothers and sisters, and the aunts and uncles were a constant source of family diversion. Meadfield was the central meeting place for this scattered family and their friends, who always found a welcome from Connie. John would spend his school holidays at Meadfield with Connie and other aunts, sometimes Helen, and any school friends who had come home with him. Sometimes he would go to stay at friends' houses and some holidays were a little more adventurous.

There was one occasion when John, not much more than nine, decided that he and a young friend wanted to go camping and it must be by a river. He said it wasn't to be too near home, and eventually Helen and Connie, with plenty of misgivings, agreed to let them pitch their little tent on the banks of the Hamble. They were well equipped with frying pans and plenty of sausages, but when Helen drove away they looked very young and small, standing by the tiny tent, waving goodbye. They were both very subdued when she went to pick them up the following day but John always maintained that he enjoyed this first taste of true independence.

Another memorable holiday came later when John was in his mid-teens and he and Helen, together with a German friend of Helen's whom she had met in Cairo and who was trying to escape the surveillance of the Nazis, decided to take a caravan to Scotland. Helen, who wasn't nearly as indulgent as Aunt Connie, insisted on doing all the driving herself and they motored to the south of Edinburgh, to the family home of John's mother. They parked the caravan in the large grounds of the house that was to be their base. But the family butler clearly did not approve and both John and Helen were reduced to giggles when he stalked into the drawing room one morning, holding at arm's length a silver tray, with a jug balanced on top, and gloomily announced:

'Milk, madam, for the people in the caravan.'

John was always a likeable child and, although he had been indulged by Aunt Connie, whom he could twist round his little finger, he was never demanding or conceited. He was extremely energetic, physically very strong and always full of plans, but invariably very diffident about his achievements.

His school days were unremarkable, but before he went away to his preparatory school in Oxford he decided that he had had enough of the small local day school. So he took advantage of Aunt Connie's absence to tell Aunt Nell, who was looking after him, that the school was closed because the teacher was ill. He somehow contrived to let the school know that he wasn't well and it was only when John and Aunt Nell met a crocodile of children hustled along by a very healthy looking teacher, that Nell realised she had had the wool pulled over her eyes. It was soon after this that he was sent away to the Dragon School, where both his brothers and Helen too, for a short time, had been. He was very happy at this famous prep school, making several good friends and spending a lot of time experimenting with the construction of paper aircraft, which he would make by the dozen.

He went on to the great old public school, Charterhouse, at Godalming, in Surrey, as his brother Hugh had done. Duncan was sent to Rugby and was a little put out at the time that his brothers were going to a soccer school. John was less happy at Charterhouse than he had been at the Dragon School. He was an extremely good-looking boy, blond and athletic, and he hated the attentions of the older boys, which his appearance seemed to attract so easily. He was in the school shooting team but this was the only subject at which he excelled, although he had a good all round record. The aptitude for Maths which he developed as a test pilot to make quick and accurate calculations was not apparent and there was nothing outstanding about his achievements.

But Carthusians will never forget him, for, during the seventies, an enormous work building 'The John Derry School of Technology' was endowed in his memory at the school. In the entrance hall of his old House, Hodgsonites, hangs a large picture of John standing in front of the little de Havilland 108, the tailless research aeroplane that turned him into every schoolboy's hero overnight, when he became the first pilot in Britain to fly faster than sound. He was a popular boy at school where he acquired the habit of mixing easily with all types of people, and in the school holidays Helen discovered that her younger brother was actually good fun to go out with despite the difference in their ages. They would go out with a crowd of friends and John, eight years younger than Helen, would keep all her more worldly friends amused for hours with his talent for mimicry.

Later, when he joined the RAF, he would bring people home on leave with him. Helen was very moved one day when a tough, hard-bitten airman, who was stationed with her brother in Iceland and who didn't seem, she thought, John's type at all, took her aside and told her how much John was respected by the men he worked and flew with.

'He's one of the best there is,' the man told her.

When John went to Canada in the summer of 1939, to stay with his brother and sister-in-law, it was his openness of character and easy frankness that captivated Duncan and Alice and their friends. Knowing that Aunt Connie had indulged John, Duncan was dreading the arrival of a spoilt, namby-pamby young man. But John greeted everything in Canada with energy and enthusiasm. Freed from the discipline of school, he thoroughly enjoyed himself on the boat trip over and he discovered that his good looks and easy manner were irresistible as far as several girls on the ship were concerned.

In fact he was so busy that he only had time to write one letter – which he sent home as a 'circular' to be passed to everyone who was waiting to hear from him. When he reached Duncan's home he wrote to England to apologise and also wrote a letter to

'Duchess' to explain that he really hadn't had time on the crossing to send everyone a letter each. He apologised disarmingly to her about the circular letter and described Duncan's home and the wonderful holiday he was having:

'It's a grand spot, right on Lake Ontario . . . and we bathe before breakfast. It's grand. We're having marvellous weather and quite hot. About 80 in the shade. There's a big exhibition on in Toronto which they have every year. We've been twice. Yesterday went to a circus affair there and saw a crowd of unmitigated hooligans doing crazy things with cars they crashed head on and drove on two wheels etc. It was a very exciting performance and was called (this is copied from the programme) "Lucky Feeter's hell drivers, madmen on wheels, automotive fury". There (sic) were all of that.'

The exhibition he mentions is the Canadian National Exhibition, held every year in Toronto. He closed the letter by saying that he would arrive home on 29 September on the *New Mauretania* (these plans were, of course, altered, as the letter was written four days before war broke out) and tells her of his scheme to miss a few more days of school:

'With any luck I shall be able to pop up to Donington for the biggest race of the year. Not a word about this, though, because it might get round to the school and then they would make be (sic) return before Sunday.'

When the hunting trip to James Bay was cancelled, Duncan's boss detailed him to go to a remote property in Manitoba to examine the area for signs of copper and other base metals that would be needed in the war effort. So they switched their plans and packed provisions and sleeping gear for a different sort of trip to the wild. The property wasn't far from the mining centre of Flin Flon in part of the great pre-Cambrian shield.

The trip was a long one and they packed plenty of food, which they supplemented, once there, with the duck and ruffed grouse which they shot. The journey was sheer delight for John. They travelled to Winnipeg in a Trans Canada Lockheed Electra and this was followed by a longish train journey out to Flin Flon. Then came another flight by bush plane to the rough landing strip alongside the old log cabin, which was to be their base for the next few days. These flights by bush plane were all in a day's work for Duncan and he took them very much for granted, as his job frequently entailed travelling to very remote regions to prospect the area and the only means of access was by these little aircraft. But it was all new to John and he was thrilled by the flight.

He was also very enthusiastic about living rough at the cabin, which was set in rocky country, the bareness made beautiful by a sprinkling of small lakes and great thickets of pine, spruce and poplar which housed a wide variety of bird life. Both Duncan and John spent a lot of time watching these birds and they also tracked moose and beaver and observed their behaviour.

The two brothers also got to know each other better. Duncan was relieved to find that John wasn't at all the spoilt boy he had feared and found he had a brother to be proud of. He was surprised at how well informed the boy was on a wide range of subjects and how articulate he was in speaking of the many things that interested him. John especially enjoyed hearing Duncan talk about his bush flying experiences. Despite the age difference and the fact that they had hardly known each other before the visit, there was no difficulty between the two brothers in establishing a relationship, which was only broken by John's tragic death, thirteen years later.

The two returned from the camp firm friends and John was full of the birds and animals they had seen and of the life they had led. But he was beginning to worry again about finding a passage home. Much as he was enjoying himself with Duncan and Alice, and much as he was growing to love the vast scenery, the wildlife and the open spaces in Canada, he was thinking all the time of the situation back home and of his own future. He planned to enlist in the RAF and hoped to be accepted for pilot training as soon as he arrived in England. But there was still no news of a boat and, to stop him fretting, Duncan and Alice arranged for him to go to the lovely lake district of Muskoka for the weekend, with some friends of theirs who had a holiday cottage at the lakeside. John went off, flying the 100 miles, and while he was there word came through that a boat would be leaving for England from New York in the next few days. He was off like a flash, first to Toronto, to pack and make his farewells to Duncan and Alice and then down to the States, to New York to start his journey.

As soon as he was back at Meadfield and had told Connie and Helen news of the Canadian branch of the family, he contacted his great friend John Lowe, who shared his love of aeroplanes, and the two of them asked Helen to take them to the RAF recruiting office in Reading. Connie was busy with her own war efforts. Since most of the staff at Meadfield were being called up, she decided to do a bit of social work and arranged for a succession of unmarried mothers and their babies to come and help her run the house. This idea was not an unqualified success. Helen, who was making her own arrangements to join the WRENS, agreed to take the two Johns to Reading, but she suffered a pang as she looked at their eager faces and thought how young they both were.

The boys rushed into the office full of hope, but only a few minutes later they came slowly out, looking utterly crestfallen and dispirited. They had been told to go back to school until they were eighteen and old enough to join the Force. They went back to Charterhouse, reluctantly, but John had only a couple of months to wait until his eighteenth birthday and in December he tried again. He was accepted this time, but again disappointed when he found that there was no chance of immediate pilot training. However, he joined up as a wireless operator and, full of high spirits, he and another friend from Haslemere, Ken Beckett, stayed overnight at a dreary hotel in Reading before starting the long business of becoming competent members of His Majesty's Forces.

Chapter 2

FLYING

'If you don't like the idea of flying, you've come to the wrong place!'
John Derry, 1940

The first three days at Uxbridge did nothing to damp their high spirits. Ken Beckett, who was later to change his name and to achieve fame as radio and television personality Kent Walton, was not as interested as John in learning to fly, but he and young Derry were masters in finding out where any fun was to be had and making the most of it. During the weeks before they joined up, they had become the nucleus of a group of young people, all restless and excited by the sudden change that the declaration of war had brought to their lives. Parties, spectacular drives in whatever motor cars they could muster and huge gatherings at local pubs had been the order of the day. Local landlords, knowing that most of the young men were waiting to be called up, were sympathetic – and enjoyed the good business engendered by the sudden surge of the 'let's live for now' restlessness which affected so many people at this time.

Ken, then in his early twenties, had already started a show business career and he and a young woman called Dandy Nicholls, also destined for the limelight, were on the point of staging a new production when war broke out and his plans had to change. When he returned home to Haslemere, he was surprised to see the difference that the last few years had made to John Derry, whom he remembered as rather a quiet small boy with a passion for aircraft. The families had known each other in Cairo – in fact Ken had been delivered by John's father – and the children were expected to play together during the school holidays. Ken had often been in the annoying position of playing nursemaid to young John, keeping a stern eye on him as they rode their bikes around the small town, knowing that he would be accountable to Aunt Connie if anything happened.

The boy was now a self-possessed, good looking young man, game for anything and still passionate about aircraft. He was also great fun to be with and Ken realised with relief that his nursemaid days were over.

The two of them, unawed by the countless rules and regulations of Air Force entry procedure, doubled up at each other's efforts to learn to wear the awkward forage cap which had to sit impossibly on the side of the head; they refused to be cowed by the often overbearing NCOs whose sole aim seemed to be to make the raw recruit feel as small as possible. John learnt his number – it was 915444 – and he soon realised that although the NCOs couldn't remember his name, they never forgot a number and when they yelled: 'Ere you, that triple four, what do you think you're doing?' they were shouting at him.

Kitting out over, they were both posted to Morecambe to start their training, but on the third day there, John came into Ken's hut looking ill and flushed. He started scratching his chest and it only took a brief examination to see that the red spots covering him were chicken pox. After three weeks' sick leave he came back and soon caught up in time for their new postings. Ken was to go to a place in Scotland whose name he could never remember. John, groping for the improbable sounding 'Lossiemouth', inventively christened it 'Lithergussie', and from that day Ken Walton couldn't think of it by any other name.

The two of them met up again when they went to complete their training at Yatesbury in Wiltshire; rather they met at Reading railway station where Ken was waiting for his connection to Wiltshire. He looked up as his train steamed in and there, strolling down the platform ready to board the same train, was John Derry.

The months at Yatesbury were marked by routine wireless training, learning to send and receive Morse messages, punctuated for John and Ken by a series of escapades involving Ken's precious little MG car. Aircraftmen were not allowed to have cars at camp, but Ken discovered that the friendly woman at the café just up the road was quite happy to let him keep the MG 'round the back'. So at weekends he and John would slip down to the car, roar past the camp with their heads well down and drive off home to Haslemere to see their girlfriends. This was all very well, but to get back to camp in time for roll call at 10.00, they had to leave Haslemere by 6.30. At least they did until Ken put John behind the wheel. To Ken's utter astonishment, John's extraordinary ability to drive fast and well, even with the headlamps narrowed to slits with the Hartley masks which all cars had to use in the blackout, meant that they could say goodbye to their girlfriends at a pub on the outskirts of Haslemere and make the journey back through Surrey and Hampshire in half the time. Ken's admiration for John's split second reflexes grew on these trips and the dexterity with which he would weave the car unerringly through the crowds of returning airmen and WAAFs as they neared the camp, never failed to excite his passengers.

One night they were returning to camp with a friend, clutching a case full of bottles, in the back. Ken was in the passenger seat and John was speeding along with a large sandwich in his right hand and the wheel in the other (he was naturally left-handed). Suddenly, as they raced down a hill, a car in front braked hard and started to turn right, into a driveway. There was no room to pass on the nearside, so John, in mid-bite on the sandwich, put his foot down hard, shot in front of the turning car, driving up the bank as he did so, and carried back on course, finishing his mouthful and talking in the same level tones as before. The backseat passenger untangled himself and the bottles from the floor and they arrived back on time, as usual.

On another occasion John was driving his own car, a Hillman, on official weekend leave in Haslemere. With him was his girlfriend, a very tall, good-looking girl, whose own driving was good enough to rival John's. They had arranged to meet some friends for a drink that evening at a local hotel and were on their way there, driving down a winding road called Polecat Lane. Rounding a left-hand bend, they saw, outlined in the narrow strips of light from the Hartley masks, a figure in uniform lying prone across the width of the narrow road. There was certainly no time to stop and no room to avoid the man, so John, putting his foot down hard, wrenched the wheel round to the right and carried on so that the offside wheels left the road as they passed. He stopped the car and they ran back to the man whom they found unscathed but still sound asleep. With some difficulty they woke him up and discovered that he was a sailor who had spent the last few hours making a thorough exploration of all the pubs and hotels in Haslemere before unwisely choosing a roadway as the best place to sleep off the effects. He was rather shaken when he learnt what had happened and he went with John to the police station where he was found to be none the worse for his experience, although by now he was inclined to grumble about the faint tyre marks made by the wheels passing lightly over his clean uniform jacket.

Although the course at Yatesbury was only designed to qualify the aircraftmen as ground wireless operators, part of the training involved taking and sending messages whilst airborne in one of the RAF's de Havilland Rapides. John was delighted but Ken, who didn't like the thought of trusting himself to a pilot he didn't know and who, he said, might have had a row with his wife that morning or even a rotten hangover, grumbled about it. John was astonished:

'If you don't like the idea of flying you've come to the wrong place,' he said.

At that time some Polish airmen were arriving in Britain, and several of these brave fliers were sent to Yatesbury. John and Ken were in the NAAFI bar on the night the Poles arrived and, feeling sorry for their isolation and admiration for their courage, the pair of them went over to the tight little group of solemn-looking men, hoping to give them some sort of a welcome. Although there was a language problem – at that time the Poles spoke no English and John and Ken certainly had no Polish – they got by with a little bad French and a lot of sign language. Many entertaining evenings were spent in their company; one of the Poles had perfected an alarming party trick which fascinated the British airmen when he pushed a steel hatpin through his lips and tongue without apparently feeling any pain. John Derry, who had a gift for mimicry, would amuse everyone with his monologues à la Jack Warner and the lugubrious Horace Canny. He had the whole bar in stitches one night after a pay parade where everyone waiting for their wages had to line up in ranks in alphabetical order. Derry was there when a particularly nasty NCO spotted one poor little aircraftman creeping in, late:

'You – come 'ere,' he bellowed.

'Sir!' saluted the quaking aircraftman.

'Wassyername?'

'Phillips, sir,' was the reply.

'Get with the bleeding 'F's then,' yelled the officious NCO who couldn't understand why the whole parade suddenly appeared to be choking with suppressed laughter.

It was probably the same NCO whom John, with a sinking heart, spotted when he was trying to slip out of camp unnoticed one day. He had a satchel with him containing his clothes, was trying for a bit of unofficial leave and had no business at all to be where he was. There seemed to be no escape from the man who was still some way off along the long rows of huts and who hadn't yet noticed John.

Suddenly, Derry spotted a ladder propped up against one of the huts, and three men hard at work painting the roof black. In a couple of seconds he had whipped his jacket off, stuffed it and the satchel under the hut and was on the roof, earnestly wielding a paintbrush, when the man marched past. It was then an easy matter to slip out of camp when he was out of sight.

Just before the end of their course, John and Ken applied for the newly designed air gunner wireless operator training, which meant that they would qualify as aircrew rather than ground operators. Although this didn't further John's ambition to be at the controls of an aircraft, it did at least mean that he would see service in one. They were both accepted, but saw no more of each other during the war as they went to separate gunnery schools.

John finished his course at Sutton Bridge while Ken was sent to Scotland and both passed out eventually as wireless operator/air gunner. John would have been interested to know that when his first Service posting came through, to 269 Squadron in Wick, Scotland, Ken was sent to join the crew of a Wellington squadron. Wick, perched on the north-east tip of Scotland in Caithness, only a few miles away from John O'Groats, is exposed to the full force of the weather blowing across the vast tracts of the North Sea, and John discovered that the dozen or so Hudsons from 269 flew daily across these grey seas, acting as escorts to the many convoys and single vessels travelling around the tip of Scotland, making thorough reconnaissance missions and, increasingly, waging war against the many submarines nosing around in the cold northern waters.

Like so many aircrew members, John was still very young; at nineteen he first crouched in the freezing rear compartment of the twin-engine Hudson which was a converted American passenger aircraft. The rear gunner had a little Perspex 'bubble' canopy so that vision was theoretically good, but all too often the weather was freezing and foggy. Most of John's contemporaries at Wick were experienced airmen, used to easing the hard biting edge of the northern winter with the comforts of the whisky bottle. John found himself joining in heavy drinking sessions – and suffering for it. After that period he could not bring himself to drink whisky again for a long time and even the smell of it made him feel ill.

Coastal Command never had the same glamour in the eyes of the public as the daring image of the men of Fighter Command, or the bomber pilots, but the work they did was just as valuable and dangerous. They were out on patrols, day after day, in dreadful weather conditions over icy waters. If a Hudson was shot down or came down in the freezing seas because of engine trouble, the length of time for survival for a man in the extremely low temperatures was literally a matter of minutes, and many aircraft and their crews were lost when they were at odds with the elements as well as the enemy. Derry once found himself being ordered to bale out over the sea when the Hudson he was in got into an uncontrollable spin and the pilot told his crew to leave. But John's chute was inoperable – it had somehow become unpacked – so all he could do was to crawl forward from his gun position, flattened back by the increasing g forces of the dive, to try to help the pilot, who was doing everything he could to level out. After seconds that felt like hours, the pilot, with Derry helping to pull on the apparently immovable stick, managed to regain control and they landed safely.

Six months after his posting to 269, the squadron was ordered to even more remote parts and the Hudsons were soon operating from Kaldadarnes, in Iceland, where their work was extended to establishing the extent of the miles and miles of pack ice, besides the investigation of any suspicious objects in the steel-grey waters (including the occasional whale), escorting convoys for part of their journeys and dropping torpex and amatol depth charges on the U-boats for which they kept a constant and vigilant lookout.

John liked the clean austerity of Iceland. The coastline, with its strange and complicated rock formation, looked to him as if it had been 'scrubbed with a giant brush' and its remote nature attracted him. He also found in his off duty hours that at least half the population (the female half) was prepared to welcome the British airmen, even if the other half wasn't so happy about the influx of the RAF.

By his twentieth birthday in December 1941, he had learnt to accept with equanimity the knowledge of the suddenness of death and to take in his stride the fact that death in war, when it came to pilots and aircrew, seemed to strike impartially. Later, when he led a fighter squadron in Europe, Derry was quick to realise that a good pilot must possess a great degree of thoroughness and care to switch the odds in his favour in wartime. Later still, as an experimental test pilot in peacetime, he knew that fear, which must never be allowed to rule, must nevertheless be accepted as the pilot's governor and must teach him to fly to his limits, but to keep within those limits, however near to the margin he may venture.

The knowledge of the instability of life during the war meant that young people grew up quickly and John Derry was no exception. As a gunner his aim was good – he'd excelled in shooting at school – but he learnt more during his first two and a half years with the RAF than the mechanics of operating wireless equipment and guns. He learnt the discipline of working with others and taking orders, and the necessity of accepting that his life was in the hands of the other crew members, just as, to a certain extent, he was responsible for theirs. The crew spirit counted for much in what could be essentially dispiriting work, and while many crews in those hard regions flew into such dreadful conditions that they didn't come back, those who returned safely carried on, because that was all they could do.

By Spring 1942, John, an old hand after nearly eighteen months with 269 Squadron, was sent to Silloth, in Cumberland, on rest. While he was at the RAF station that was perched, bracingly, on the wide banks of the Solway Firth, he was spending this time away from active service as an instructor – and still hoping to be selected for pilot training. Before he was commissioned as a gunnery leader in the early summer, he would spend some of his off duty time enjoying a drink in the sergeants' bar at the Golf Club with his friends. One day, a casual glance out of the window grille made him put down his beer and lose the thread of the conversation. He saw a tall, dark young woman, very beautiful he thought. He stared, absorbed, until she was out of sight, but didn't say anything. Casual enquiries later revealed that she was the young wife of a flight lieutenant also on 'rest'. John, who had enjoyed a variety of female company since he had joined the RAF, nevertheless still kept in regular touch with his girlfriend in

Haslemere; but the girl he stared at, surreptitiously, still kept occupying his thoughts.

To his mingled relief and disappointment, the flight lieutenant was posted away from Silloth during the summer and his wife, naturally, went with him. John tried to put the tall dark girl out of his mind. As the weeks went past, he was becoming increasingly restless at what he felt what his own lack of participation in the war and he was also irritated when he realised that he was no nearer to the controls of an aircraft than he had been in 1939; if anything, this long period of training and instruction meant that he wasn't even getting the chance to serve as a member of the aircrew.

In this mood, he went down to the little café in the village one brisk November morning with a crowd of friends who also felt like a break from the atmosphere of the camp. He flung his cap onto the table, turned to sit down and was completely taken aback when he saw, walking over to the other side of the room, the young woman he had watched through the grille of the sergeants' mess, six months before. She only looked up briefly and then sat down, speaking in low tones to her companion, a girl of about the same age. John sat, quiet amongst the noisy banter of his friends, trying to decide what to do. Every time he looked across the café he felt exasperated as the other girl caught his eye.

Eve was the name of the girl whom Derry was determined to know. She had hardly noticed the noisy young men from the RAF station, wrapped up as she was in her own problems. She had married at twenty and now had a young child, Carol, a daughter of eighteen months. After less than three years, her marriage had gone badly wrong and she had left her husband and was keeping a roof over the head of her baby and herself by housekeeping for a friend. The future was uncertain and the prospect of any sort of a settled life seemed remote.

Suddenly Eve realised that it was time to go back to the house to prepare lunch. She jumped up and hastily left the café. By this time, John couldn't bear to see her disappear again and perhaps never speak to her, so he did the only thing possible and chased after her. Eve turned round in some confusion when she heard the pursuing footsteps and was listening to him, half amused and half bewildered, when she looked up the road and gasped in horror as she saw her little mongrel bitch, Wendy, hurtling towards her in terrified flight from a pack of chasing dogs. John, summing up the situation, rescued Wendy, who was on heat and had somehow escaped from her safe refuge in the house. After that it didn't seem too hard to get to know Wendy's mistress.

John decided that he would take Eve to the ball at Silloth to see in the New Year, 1943. After a few meetings with her he knew that his first reaction had been the right one and he was going to cut through all the difficulties and objections with typical straightforward simplicity to make sure that he and Eve could be together. There could be no doubt about the obstacles, but John calmly decided that they could be dealt with as they cropped up. Eve was a married woman of twenty-three with a young child; he was only just twenty-one with no very bright prospect for the future; their respective families were bound to recoil in horror from any relationship they might form and moreover John was, if not officially engaged to his Haslemere girlfriend, at least committed to her on a more than casual basis. To John, normally level-headed when it came to any sort of romantic entanglement, none of these objections mattered at all.

Eve pledged her silver fox furs to a friend for the money to buy a dress for the New Year's Eve ball and John went with her to London to choose it. They went to a club to dance after dinner and there they met a high-ranking RAF officer from the Air Ministry who listened sympathetically to John voicing his frustrations about his own part in the war. John's application to be trained as a pilot was constantly under review and the officer could do nothing about this. But he told John that he could arrange a posting to Egypt in his present capacity as an air gunner. Eve was upset, although she didn't show it. Egypt, the country where John had been born and where his father still lived, seemed alien and menacing. She thought that if this posting came through, she would never see him again.

But John had to be on active service. He told Eve, who kept her fears from him, that they would be together when he came home on leave and there was nothing she could say. So they both prepared for the parting when, at the eleventh hour, John had news of another posting which cancelled the Egypt trip and seemed to him to be too good to be true. He had, at last, been selected for pilot training and, after an initial period at Brough and Torquay, would go to Canada for six months. Eve was delighted for him and although she regretted the parting, it was only for a short period and Canada was certainly a safer place than Egypt. John was thrilled. At last he would be in sole charge of an aircraft and was to have the training, which would have been his three years earlier if war hadn't broken out. Canada was the country where he had first tasted independence and freedom from school. He would be no stranger in Canada and, with some luck, he would see his brother, Duncan, who was by now a Navigation Instructor in the Royal Canadian Air Force.

Before the parting came a period of initial training at Torquay and, by a little coincidence, a lot of manipulation and some luck, Eve managed to move there too for a while, to stay with the parents of the girl she had been living with at Silloth. John's admiration for Eve and his attraction to her was growing steadily and they took the opportunity to go out often together during John's evening leave.

One day a German bomber, patrolling the south coast of England, came low over Torquay. Its main weaponry exhausted, a stream of tracer fire peppered civilians and houses in the street where Eve was living. John, on duty at the time, heard about the casualties and was frantic. He knew that Eve had planned to take a bus that morning and should have been standing at the stop, directly in line of fire, at the time of the attack. He was desperately worried but could not even get to a telephone. As soon as he was off duty, he rushed round to the house. Eve, who was to go out with him later that evening, was upstairs, getting ready. She had caught an earlier bus that morning and knew nothing of John's panic. The door was opened by the owner of the house who was confronted by a pale and gasping John:

'Is Eve all right?' The next minute, overcome by the worry, which had been building up all day, he slid to the floor and had to be helped to a chair and revived with brandy. It must be put down on record that this is the only time that he ever panicked in the face of the enemy.

John and Eve parted in the summer of 1943 when he went first to Monkton in Canada and then on to Neepawa, in Manitoba, for his elementary flying training in a de Havilland Tiger Moth. Duncan, by now stationed at Rivers, only forty miles away, was delighted to be able to meet up with his brother on several occasions when they talked of their wartime experiences.

The year 1943 was when the British Government, becoming concerned over the loss of pilots, decided to train a huge batch of experienced aircrew who had expressed a wish for pilot training and John had been one of the lucky 500 to be selected. One of the other pupils in this intake in Canada was Scotsman Gabe Rob 'Jock' Bryce, later chief test pilot of Vickers Armstrong, and a friend of John's in his test flying days, although the two didn't meet during their training.

From the time he first went solo in the Tiger Moth, to his first flight in the Harvard trainer, John and his instructors knew that his longings to fly had been totally justified. He passed out at Calgary, one of the star pupils in a large batch of trainees, with the knowledge that he had a natural feel for the controls of the aircraft and the perfect co-ordination of hands and brain which makes a good pilot super-sensitive to his machine. His letters home to Eve showed how happy he was to be in the air at last.

Chapter 3

A WIZARD BALE-OUT

'Flying Officer Keith Goddard was hit by flak but he did a wizard bale-out
from 2/3,000ft (YES) and got away with it.'
Operations Record Book, 181 Squadron, 11 February 1945

Eve and Carol had moved to a little cottage in a tiny Devon village, with the dog and a cat that they had acquired. Eve and John wrote to each other, but the letters were somehow unsatisfactory. John was only twenty-two, extremely attractive and with a friendly, outgoing nature. His open character, honest to the point of naivety, had something of Aunt Connie in that he never suspected the worst of anyone, and he had no doubt that when he came home he and Eve would be together again. But it was not so easy for Eve to be certain, disillusioned as she was by the failure of her first marriage. Wartime England, even in rural Devon, wasn't a comfortable place to be and it was not so easy for her as for John, achieving his ambition, in Canada. Her job, in a canteen, was undemanding to the point that her mind was free to rove over the obstacles to a stable relationship with John. She knew that both of the families would be sure to object. Eve's parents were very well-to-do Scots of the old school, to whom the word 'divorce' meant nothing less than a scandal. John was still the baby of the more cosmopolitan Derry family who were sure to see Eve as a scarlet woman out to trap an innocent young man.

Even though the letters kept coming, Eve worried about the future. And then, at Christmas time, came the telegram: 'Terribly happy, coming home. I love you. John Derry.'

This caused speculation at the little village post office where

Eve was known by her married name but she didn't care, especially as John arrived shortly after.

Then followed a strange interlude of life together, isolated from the war and the events and people around them. Carol, who spent some time in comparative safety with her grandparents, was in Scotland. Later on, when John was flying Typhoons over enemy-occupied Europe, destroying German lines of communication and equipment to clear a path for the advancing Allied Forces, he was to look back on his periods of leave with Eve in rented cottages or digs as interludes of perfect happiness – even though the days together were sometimes interrupted by alarming events.

One of these, about which they were to laugh a lot later, happened suddenly and without warning.

They had been to the cinema at the nearest town and caught the last bus back to the village. The conductor, who knew Eve by name, came up to her uneasily and told her that her husband had been to the cottage while she had been out. Neither of them said much on the brisk walk back from the bus stop. It was a dark, cold night and John opened the back door of the cottage with some trepidation. The place was dark and quiet. Eve's dog, with her newly born puppies, lay peacefully in her basket in the kitchen, but the door into the hallway was open although John knew that he had closed it before they left. John reached out and switched on the hall light and there, framed in the doorway, stood Eve's estranged husband, surrounded by an uneasy posse of special constables looking sheepishly at Eve, who knew them all in their everyday capacities as village tradesmen. Their spokesman explained apologetically that they had to ask John to leave the house as he had no legal right to be there if Eve's legal husband wanted him to leave. John argued bitterly with them, but they were insistent, if embarrassed about the whole business. So he left while Eve barricaded herself in the bedroom with flasks of tea and a pack of cigarettes to see her through the night.

John didn't go very far away. Although it was a freezing night, he stationed himself in the porch and spent an extremely uncomfortable few hours sitting on the icy doorstep, wrapped in a blanket. Eve crept down in the morning to let him in and the charade ended after the three of them ate breakfast together in a very uneasy fashion. Eve's husband, seeing that there was no way that he could force her to return to him, left the cottage.

The next few months saw John and Eve make no fewer than six moves around the country. These postings soon took on a pattern; the order would come, the three of them (Carol's stay in Scotland was now over and she was at home with her mother and John) would pack up and travel to a new town and look for somewhere to live for the next month or two. There was no question of RAF quarters as they were unmarried and so often it would have to be a hotel for the first night. Then, when John reported for duty at the airfield or RAF station, Eve, with Carol in the pushchair, would traipse around the town, trying to find a temporary home for them.

First they went to Harrogate and then to Prestwick. At Peterborough, which came next, they had particular trouble finding somewhere to live and Eve became so tired that she collapsed miserably into the pushchair while John and Carol, hand in hand, went to inspect yet another set of lodgings. When they came out she was still there – unable to move, stuck fast in the tiny seat. John, convulsed with laughter, had to make her stand up, with the pushchair still attached, before he could pull it off.

When they eventually found somewhere to stay in the crowded town, they shared their lodgings with an assortment of people, including a conscientious objector. John was invariably polite and courteous to this man, respecting the stand that he would never have taken. So perhaps it was natural that their fellow lodger should offer John, home after a day's work at the RAF station, a large perch that he had caught whilst fishing that day. It was very big and coarse and Eve cooked it for him that evening, although she didn't have any herself. It tasted muddy and unappetising and it was all John could do to stop himself from choking when the fisherman told him that he'd pulled it out of the local sewage works.

Petrol was of course rationed and John and Eve had no car, so when John got hold of an old motorbike he worked on it and doctored it until it would run on paraffin. By this time they had moved to Hawarden, near Chester, and the motorbike proved invaluable for getting to work during the day and was transport if he and Eve wanted to go out during the evening. The only problem was that the lights on this old boneshaker were so unreliable that when they drove over a bump they were plunged into darkness.

Life for John and Eve at this period was a real hand to mouth existence. Both had been brought up in comfortable homes with everything they had needed, so the constant living out of suitcases, often in extremely uncomfortable lodgings with a very small child to look after, was something new for both of them. Hot water in most of the digs was a luxury, rats commonplace, and very often there were not even knives and forks to go round, while cooking arrangements could be primitive and, at times, dangerous. One set of digs did not even have a lavatory – not so much as a bucket in the yard – and this meant waiting for the pub on the corner to open. They did not stay there long.

There was another set of rooms with a leaky roof so that they would have to take it in turns to sleep on the side of the bed with the ceiling which dripped when it rained. But they were young and the pleasure to each of having the other to share the surprises and the horrors which they encountered, meant that they nearly always ended up crying with laughter as they moved from place to place. There was another bonus. Carol was by now a lively, very intelligent, three-year-old. She and John, who was young anyway to be a father, had established a strong bond which was to deepen into a special relationship during their short years together as father and daughter. Any implied criticism of Eve angered John very much, as did the suggestion that Carol was anything less than a daughter to him. It was John to whom Carol turned later if she was in trouble at school and it was John who taught her to ride and swim and took her flying with him at weekends. At Minchinhampton, near Stroud, John was delighted with Carol's precocity when she suddenly climbed onto her chair while the three of them were eating rice pudding at Sunday lunch time and proceeded to wave her spoon in the air and to repeat a garbled version, with whole words and phrases intact, of the sermon they had heard that morning at the village church service.

The three of them formed a closely-knit little unit in wartime England where time was very much out of joint for so many people. This situation would not be extraordinary today when no one worries very much about couples living together without marriage, but in the early forties their declaration for each other was a brave act on both sides.

Eve felt this all the more keenly when, after a spell with 3 Group Support Unit, John, by now a flight lieutenant, received the news that he was to be posted abroad to a fighter squadron, flying Hawker Typhoons on close support duties.

The Typhoon – Tiffie to her pilots and detractors alike – was a single-seat interceptor fighter and fighter-bomber, which aroused strong feelings. In the early part of the war the Tiffie's 24-cylinder Napier Sabre engine was notoriously unreliable and there were an alarming number of disastrous incidents when Typhoon tail sections had broken suddenly. The fault seemed to lie in the rear fuselage transport joint and the appropriate strengthening was carried out, but although there was some improvement the trouble was never completely eliminated and the final diagnosis, towards the end of the war, was elevator flutter caused by fatigue in the mass balance weight.

The Typhoon was not an easy aircraft to get out of in a hurry and pilots knew that engine failure at low level – not uncommon – meant an almost certain plunge to death unless you were quick thinking enough to use the last traces of momentum to get up to about 800ft where you stood a chance of baling out. When Derry reported for duty with 182 Squadron at Eindhoven in Holland on 13 November 1944, he found the Tiffie an incredibly noisy machine which could be utterly deafening on take-off.

But, on the credit side, she was one of the fastest wartime

aeroplanes at low level, with a maximum speed of over 400mph and renowned for her superb handling and turning capabilities which were essential when manoeuvring over enemy territory and liable to attack from both the air and the ground. Her performance was not so good, however, at altitude. Originally designed as a replacement for the Hurricane, her role switched to that of ground attack fighter when it became clear that her virtues did not assert themselves at any sort of height. The Tiffie was a very strong aeroplane, and a good pilot could see to it that a badly damaged Typhoon would limp home safely. Another characteristic was her suitability for steady gun aiming and, with up to eight rocket projectiles, she proved deadly against enemy supply targets.

Both the Typhoon and the Tempest, which was a development from the former aircraft, excelled in their close support roles, and in the earlier part of the war they had inflicted heavy damage on the German fighter-bombers as they intercepted the enemy attack. They were also instrumental in spotting and destroying the deadly 'doodlebugs', the terrifying little pilotless exploding craft which were directed from the Low Countries over England's south coast in their hundreds. Later on, rocket-firing Typhoons wreaked havoc among enemy shipping and supply lines and they played a big part supporting the Allied land forces in Europe during 1944. One of their interesting attacking roles was the 'Cab Rank' patrol, when they flew at about 10,000ft over the battle area, ready to be called down by the land forces when they were needed to initiate the attack. It was in this close support role, spearheading the Allied attack on the enemy in Europe, and clearing a way for the advancing Armies by attacking German supply lines, bridges, convoys, trains, trucks and weapon dumps, that 182 Squadron and its fellow squadrons in Europe were to play a part.

John was greeted at Eindhoven where several squadrons were living in an enormous building which, before the war, had been a monastery, by Squadron Leader G.J. Gray, who was in charge of the thirty or so pilots under his command.

He was also welcomed by another young man who was to play

an important if unobtrusive role in the welfare of the whole squadron. Leading Aircraftman Des Tyler was, at twenty-four, just a few months older than John, and, before the war, he had worked for a large men's outfitters shop. He had liked the retail trade and he loved order and tidiness. Before the squadron moved to Europe, he was with another Typhoon squadron, 181, looking after the Mess and the stores and generally keeping things in order, a job which suited him down to the ground.

He had just become engaged to a very pretty girl and he knew that he and Anita would miss each other when he went overseas. He was not much looking forward to living under canvas or in hastily commandeered quarters, but he was a conscientious and efficient young man, and he soon found to his surprise that he was enjoying looking after a bunch of high spirited pilots who were daily risking their lives. Des and his fellow batman, Albert Ward, took their work seriously and they saw that the wartime spirit meant a lot in this squadron where no one seemed to feel that he was any better than the next man. The two of them made it their primary task to see that the pilots were as comfortable as possible under the circumstances. When they were on the move and under canvas, they slept on camp beds, in long rows, rather like a school dormitory and at Eindhoven the pilots again shared a long room while Des, Bert and the ground crew slept in little cubicles. When they arrived at the monastery, the first thing to worry about was the German habit of leaving little surprises behind – in this case in the form of booby trapped windows – but these were dealt with without much harm to anyone.

Des would ensure that his pilots somehow always had hot water to wash in and a clean change of clothes when they returned, tired and dirty, from operations. This meant purloining every suitable pot and pan within sight and then spending the whole day heating gallons of water on primus stoves or whatever makeshift fire could be contrived. Washing the clothes with clumsy bars of soap, then getting them dry and ironed took up the whole day. But it was worth it. Derry and the other pilots appreciated these labours and several times John looked out for Des to thank him.

'You've no idea how much it means to us to be able to wash in hot water and change when we get back,' he told him.

Derry soon found his footing with the squadron. The Operations Record Book (ORB), kept daily, shows not only the facts of warfare – the missions flown and the damage inflicted and received – but also the spirit and morale of the men, which was very high during the last two months of 1944, despite the dreadful winter conditions that year. Derry flew his first sortie on 18 November, with seven other pilots, led by Squadron Leader Gray. The ORB shows that the weather was very bad, but the men flew to a small town and 'Liberated it in no uncertain manner', cutting railway lines and destroying buildings.

'This was Flight Lieutenant Derry's first operation with the squadron and he coped very well,' adds the note for that day. The next day was spent attacking enemy gun positions but then the weather became so bad that the pilots had to resign themselves to a film show and an evening spent celebrating the promotion of a flight lieutenant nicknamed 'Harbottle'. It is clear from the ORB that Derry took every opportunity to fly; when the weather was what is evocatively referred to as 'Clampers all day' and there could be no ops, he was the one who went out for a weather recce or took his Typhoon up for an air test. His first few weeks with the squadron saw the beginning of a big push into occupied territory and the pilots recorded much damage and destruction to locomotors, trucks, tanks, fuel depots and motor transport. They didn't escape unscathed and two of John's fellow pilots were killed at the end of November and his Tiffie was damaged by flak over enemy territory, but he managed to land safely. Early in December, 182 started to make long-range raids deep into the heart of the Reich where, according to the ORB: 'The squadron had a wonderful time, picking and choosing their targets.'

In the midst of the grim warfare there was quite a lot of light relief – such as that afforded by a Flying Officer Pattison, who, on 9 December, 'Endeavoured to qualify for the Royal Humane Society medal by rescuing his popsy from the icy water into which she unfortunately fell at the bewitching hour of midnight.'

Towards the end of December, the weather became so bad that Squadron Leader Gray insisted that all the pilots did half an hour's PT each day and by the 23rd the book laments: 'Everything is frozen stiff, including the pilots.' Despite this, the operations continued and John spent Christmas Day firing rocket projectiles and cannon fire at the enemy's motor convoys.

On Boxing Day the ORB shows that John took the chance for a little extra flying:

'During lunch Flight Lieutenant Derry jumped at the opportunity of accompanying Group Captain Green DSO, DFC, on weather recce.' Unfortunately, John came back alone, as the group captain's aircraft was hit whilst they were over enemy lines and he was forced to bale out.

The climax of the squadron's successes came on New Year's Eve when Derry and eight other pilots followed their CO into a raid over the St Vith area where, under pressure from heavy and intense flak, they pressed home their attack and destroyed a tank flamer, smokers, motor transport and a petrol dump. Sadly, two of the pilots failed to return and another, Flight Lieutenant Tommy Entwhistle, had to make a forced landing, but was seen to get away safely. The loss of the two men put a pall of gloom on the party in the mess that evening – but it was only a foretaste of what was to come.

Very early on New Year's Day, the German Operation *Bodenplatte* caught all the squadrons at Eindhoven by surprise. Twenty-three minutes of concentrated low level strafing from the Luftwaffe took a heavy toll on the aeroplanes, which were out on the field and also cost several lives. The RCAF squadrons, 438 and 439, both lost men and machines but 182 sustained only two human casualties, a corporal who was killed and an aircraftman whose foot was shot away. But when the Luftwaffe finally flew away, 182 had only one operational machine left on the ground.

The effect on the morale of the pilots was depressing and the Record Book shows the gloom of the occasion: 'A very quiet evening was spent in the Mess, most of us suffering from some degree of "twitch".'

Things were no better on the following day when the 'twitch' became widespread and an aircraft from 247 Squadron collided, in the air, with another from 168. The pilot of the latter was killed and, to make matters worse, the wreckage fell on the sleeping quarters of the pilots of 182, who found that many of their personal possessions had been destroyed. The only note of cheer in that gloomy beginning to the new year came on 3 January when Tommy Entwhistle (who had had to make the forced landing on New Year's Eve) arrived back at base, breathless and tired, having negotiated two minefields and a river to make it safely to the American sector before returning to Eindhoven.

John missed the excitement of Entwhistle's return and the demoralising cleaning up operations that were inevitable after the destruction wrought by the Luftwaffe on New Year's Day. On 1 January he became a flight commander with 181 Squadron, who were also at Eindhoven, and he flew back to England with most of the other pilots in 181, to re-equip with new Typhoons.

Flight Commander was the title given to the man who would lead a sortie or an operation and Derry, after only six weeks on active service, was to share the responsibility of leadership with his new squadron leader, Dave Crawford. However, before he could get back into action, there was nearly a month's respite in England – and John was anxious to see Eve.

While John was fighting in Europe, Eve had taken Carol up to her parents' home in Scotland and was staying there herself, having found work as a receptionist at the American Red Cross, with a part-time spell at the Overseas Club. Her duties included a stint at the bar each day at the Red Cross club and she found that her work seemed to consist of opening Coke bottle after Coke bottle and she soon became restless and bored. She was on the point of volunteering to go to Burma when Christmas came, but on New Year's Day she arrived home after another dreary stint at the bar to find a telegram awaiting her from John. He was coming home and would she meet him at Chichester?

Eve hardly waited to pack. She threw a few things in a case and caught the next train south to Chichester. John was not at the station when she got off the train, so she started walking up the road and, as she turned a corner saw a familiar tall, blond figure hurrying to meet her. They were so pleased to see each other that they could hardly speak at first. The leave was a short one while new plans were made for the squadron, but within a week Eve learnt that there was to be a longer rest period for all the pilots in 181 while their new Typhoons were prepared. She was summoned once again to join John, this time at Dorchester, where they were to stay at the Antelope Hotel, which wasn't too far away from nearby Warmwell, where John would have to report.

Eve packed once more and duly caught a train that pulled in to an almost deserted platform. No one else got off the train and there was no John there to meet her. She wasn't surprised. Although his reactions were split second sharp whilst flying or driving, he tended to be a little vague and forgetful once down on the ground and time didn't mean very much to him. So she sighed and was preparing to shoulder her case to the Antelope, when a good looking man in a tweed jacket walked up to her and said he'd come to meet her and would she like to go and have some tea with him at the Antelope Hotel? Eve thought that was a bit odd as she was staying there anyway, but she didn't argue as she was rather surprised that John had sent someone to meet her. Over tea in the hotel lounge she kept one eye on the door in case John should come in and she made small talk with her companion. After a pause in the conversation the man, who had been eyeing her elegant appearance, leant forward and said:

'I say, I've never met a Land Girl who looked quite like you before.'

The poor man, who was a local farmer, had gone up to the only woman getting off the train assuming that she was the Land

Army girl who was coming to help him with his cows and potatoes. He was covered in confusion when Eve explained his mistake.

John breezed in soon after the farmer had left to look for the real Land Girl – he had been out flying and had lost track of the time.

The stay at Dorchester was a fairly long one and important for John and Eve who had much to talk about and plans to make for the future.

John was determined that they should be married as soon as possible. It was over two years since they had first met and he was impatient for Eve to get the divorce, which her first husband was reluctant to allow. They had tried to make it easy by providing the necessary evidence in the form of hotel bills which they sent regularly to him, but this didn't seem to work. They both felt that there was only one thing left to do and that was to have a baby, a brother or sister for Carol. They knew that it would be born before they could be married and there was the possibility that John might not come back from his next posting abroad. Eve had to face the chance that she could be left on her own with two young children and, with the arrival of the next one, could be branded an unmarried mother. She could be as brave in her own way as John though, and she pushed all unpleasant thoughts of this nature away and decided to enjoy John's leave. Apart from getting stuck in an enormous snowdrift during an evening out with some friends and having to be rescued by a farm truck, they enjoyed themselves tremendously. But all too soon John went back to Europe and Eve faced the long lonely train journey back to Scotland.

By 4 February, 181 Squadron was settled in at Helmond with the other squadrons which had moved there during January, and Squadron Leader Dave Crawford and Derry led two 'shows' – long range armed recces over Germany.

'The second one led by Flight Lieutenant Derry was most successful,' says the ORB. 'Six locos destroyed, one damaged and a transformer station well pranged.' Unfortunately, the first show saw the loss of the CO, Dave Crawford – who, before leaving

Warmwell, had promised Eve that he would take good care of John. John, however, didn't seem to need anyone's care and plunged into his new role as flight commander with skill and relish, under his new CO, Squadron Leader Henry 'Poppa' Ambrose.

He was obviously a popular member of the squadron and soon the entries in the ORB start referring to him simply as 'J.D.' or 'our J.D.'. A few days after the sad loss of Dave Crawford, a bit of quick action from John and the Group Captain helped to save the life of another pilot: 'A type from 143 Wing pranged on the runway this afternoon. Flight Lieutenant J.D. Derry (J.D. to us) and the GC helped to pull him away from the blazing wreck.'

The following day the squadron had a field day over Germany:

'We had an excellent day against the Hun, destroying 15 of his locos and damaging five. Flight Lieutenant Boucher leading six got 8 and 5 and J.D. with the other five got the remainder. Unfortunately Flying Officer Keith Goddard was hit by flak but he did a wizard bale-out from 2/3,000ft (YES) and got away with it.'

The whole of 124 Wing of which 181 and 182 Squadrons were a part, received a message of congratulation for that day's work from the AOC.

The weather brightened up ('Wizard weather,' gloats the ORB, 'with the Bods sitting outside the Dispersal sunning themselves') and operations carried on deeper and deeper into the heart of the Reich until the Allies were ready to attempt to cross the Rhine. On 24 March John took part in this enormous operation, leading four pilots. The rocket firing Typhoons had the unenviable task of 'flak baiting' – weaving fast and low and attacking the ubiquitous flak posts, they drew enemy fire to themselves as a diversion to allow the heavy bombers to move in and do their work. Each Typhoon section flew low, attacking the gun posts for ten to fifteen minutes before gaining height while the section waiting 'upstairs' came down for their turn at this deadly game.

Inevitably pilot losses were high and many were injured including John who was hit by flak, his aircraft badly damaged and a large piece of shrapnel lodged in his thigh. However, he made it back to base and spent the next few days in hospital, to hear on his release, on 29 March, that he had been promoted to squadron leader and was to be the new CO of his old squadron, 182. He was up early the next morning with a large piece of padding bandaged to his bottom so that he would be able to fly: 'Squadron Leader Derry made a very fine gesture by joining the boys on runway readiness from 05.27,' says the Record Book.

But before the Rhine Crossing and his promotion John had an experience, which so sickened him that the memory of it stayed with him for the rest of his life. Squadron Leader Ambrose had been asked to take a small party to Belsen, now in the hands of the Allies, to make a report. He chose John and four other men to go with him. They returned, inarticulate with horror at the nightmare they had witnessed. Some of them had vomited uncontrollably, others felt inexpressible rage. One pilot was so angry that John and the others literally had to sit on him in the car on the way back to stop him shooting in his rage. When John returned home after the war, he never talked to Eve about the things he had seen at Belsen although he admitted he had had to have his revolver taken away at night afterwards until he felt less inclined to go out and shoot those responsible for the devastating cruelty.

After the Rhine Crossing all Derry's old friends were glad to see him back in 182 and his batman, Des Tyler, was no exception. The roles of the large group of men, living together in makeshift conditions, were different, but the shared dangers and deprivations brought them close in many ways. John and Des, roughly the same age, with very different backgrounds, had something in common – their girls back home. John would bring the post round when it arrived in batches and toss any letters for Des onto his bed and always ask if he had heard from his girlfriend. He would grumble good naturedly if there was no letter from Eve and would always spend a few minutes chatting to Des about his home and his plans for the future with Anita.

One day, shortly after John had been made CO of the squadron, the building was very quiet in the morning as the pilots had been flying late the day before and were having an extra hour or two in bed as the weather had closed in and there would be no operations. John had instructed Des and Bert to let everyone sleep on and to delay their morning cleaning up. So the two batmen brewed a pot of tea and were sitting having a chat, when a wing commander strolled in from another building. He didn't wait to ask any questions but started shouting at the two batmen to get the place cleaned up. Des, anxious that his pilots shouldn't be disturbed, found that this was more than he could take. His face went white and he lost his temper:

'You can't come in here shouting at us – my men are asleep and my instructions are not to disturb them,' he shouted at the outraged officer who promptly put him on a charge and told him to report for his punishment at a building on the opposite side of the airfield. By the time he had packed his things and had been told that his punishment would consist of cleaning out lavatories for a week, John was hearing the news from Bert who had managed to slip over and see his friend.

Des was just starting on his distasteful task when he was told to report to an office, where he found John waiting for him.

'What on earth have you been up to?' demanded his squadron leader, who then told him he could pack up and move back. As soon as he heard the news, John had asked every pilot to sign a piece of paper, which had a statement on it to the effect that the squadron felt that it could not operate properly without Des to look after the men. Des never found out exactly what passed between John and the wing commander, but he remained grateful to the young squadron leader who got him out of an unpleasant punishment. He even forgave John, who never cared much for 'spit and polish', his habit of ambling along on the weekly Airfield CO's parade looking rather casually turned out, despite Des's best efforts and on one occasion parading with rather a large hole in the seat of his trousers.

Des was not the only ground crew member who found that his CO took the time and trouble to treat him with courtesy and respect. Leading Aircraftman Les 'Kid' Tanner was a young airframe mechanic with 182 and he liked and trusted Derry whom he regarded with surprise as rather a humble person. One cold April night, Tanner was working with his fitter through the dark hours to get a Typhoon serviceable for an operation at first light. There was a sharp late frost and the two men, working by the feeble light of a torch, grew colder and colder as their fingers seemed to lose all feeling. Sometime after midnight a Jeep drew up alongside the Typhoon and Derry came over to see how they were getting on as he was anxious that there should be enough aircraft ready for the morning sortie. When he left, the two men sighed, thinking of their own nice warm beds. But about fifteen minutes later the same Jeep drew up again and they heard Derry calling to them to climb down from the innards of the aircraft.

'Have a drop of this – it should help to warm you up,' he said, holding out a bottle of rum and he poured them each a good tot. They didn't get to bed for another hour and a half, but the job was finished in a much better frame of mind.

Operations intensified in April and, on the 25th, Derry led no less than three major sorties on one day. He and his pilots attacked enemy gun positions, armoured convoys and an aerodrome which he joyously 'beat up'. They pressed home their attack despite heavy and intense flak and Derry's skilful leadership was recognised a few weeks later when he was awarded the DFC. The citation read:

'This officer has participated in a large number of sorties as air gunner and later as pilot. He has at all times displayed great determination and skill and his courage has been of the highest order. In April 1945 he led his squadron in an attack against enemy gun positions. Despite intense opposition the attack was pressed home with great accuracy. The success of this operation was due in no small measure to Squadron Leader Derry's gallant and skilful leadership. This officer has set a fine example to all.'

Des Tyler was sitting in his quarters sighing over a great heap of mending for the pilots when John poked his head round the door. Throwing a scrap of material at his batman he said:

'Tack that on the end, will you, Des?' and disappeared. Des was horrified at this casual treatment of the insignia which meant an honour for both the squadron and its CO and he decided that it would be properly sewn on in the right place. He also made sure that John's uniform suit was spruced up and thoroughly pressed before the precious piece of cloth was sewn carefully on, exactly where it should be according to regulations.

Later that night – or early the next morning, he was awakened by a terrific commotion in the passageway outside his room. In the middle of a crowd of cheering onlookers, who had clearly been celebrating their CO's decoration, were John and the Adjutant, circling round each other and making rather drunken 'ack-ack' noises whilst they tried to shoot each other down with soda syphons. The carefully cleaned and pressed suit was plastered – and so was its owner. Des sighed and went back to bed, forgiving John his understandable high spirits. But the next morning a contrite squadron leader came to find him especially to apologise for waking him up and for the mess he had made. Des told Bert afterwards that he would do anything for an officer like Derry.

By this time the squadron had made several moves forward into Europe – to Enschade, Rheine, Hanover and to Lüneberg. They were at Lüneberg on 2 May when Derry with another pilot, a Dutchman, Flight Lieutenant Van Zinnich 'Bergy' Bergmann, attacked an enemy airfield and John destroyed a Ju88 as it was about to take off, and flew rings round a He111, making it crash from about 50ft as it tried to avoid him. He detailed the attack in his official combat report:

'I was leading a section of two aircraft on armed recce in the Lübeck area. On Blankensee airfield I saw a Ju88 starting its take-off run. I attacked it and saw cannon strikes. After pulling up, I saw it was in flames and had stopped. An He111 coming in to land stalled in trying to avoid me and dropped from 50ft. I claim this as damaged.'

The following day the squadron attacked and damaged a vast amount of shipping and on the last operation of the day, Derry's

*John Derry at
Farnborough,
Thursday 4
September 1952.*
(Copyright Fox
Photos)

FROM THE DERRY FAMILY ALBUM

John and Aunt Connie, c.1927.

A day's outing in London.

Meadfield.

John (on right) camping in Canada, September 1939.

Eindhoven, 1944.

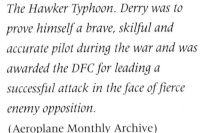

The Hawker Typhoon. Derry was to prove himself a brave, skilful and accurate pilot during the war and was awarded the DFC for leading a successful attack in the face of fierce enemy opposition.
(Aeroplane Monthly Archive)

In his time at Chilbolton Derry showed his outstanding ability as a demonstration pilot. The Seafire was a powerful machine well suited to his dramatic but safe displays. (Aeroplane Monthly Archive)

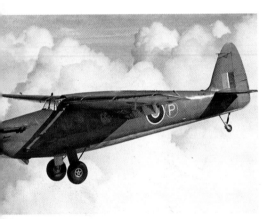

Derry flew some unusual types at Chilbolton, but perhaps the strangest was the Supermarine S/24/37, known as 'Dumbo'. It had a variable incidence wing and was notoriously tricky to land.
(Aeroplane Monthly Archive)

The Supermarine Sea Otter (G-AIDM) that Derry flew at Chilbolton and demonstrated at West Raynham in 1947.
(Aeroplane Monthly Archive)

Two-seat Spitfire TR8 (G-AIDN) taxies out in front of the prototype Supermarine Attacker at Chilbolton. (Aeroplane Monthly Archive)

A unique signed photograph of the Supermarine test pilots at Chilbolton in June 1947 with the prototype Attacker (TS413). Les Colquhoun (left), Mike Lithgow, Jeffrey Quill, Guy Morgan and John Derry. (Photo courtesy Peter Arnold)

It is easy from this picture to see why the 108 was known as the 'Swallow'.
(BAE SYSTEMS)

Moments before take-off for the 100km closed circuit record attempt. (BAE SYSTEMS)

Derry looks towards the camera as he lines up the DH108 for a beautiful picture. (BAE SYSTEMS)

John Derry at his desk in Hatfield studying the map of the 100km closed circuit course before his record-breaking flight in 1948. (Aeroplane Monthly Archive)

Climbing out of the DH108 after capturing the 100km closed circuit record. (BAE SYSTEMS)

Derry talks to the press at Hatfield and describes the flight. (BAE SYSTEMS)

Derry's scribbled notes on the back of a map of the 100km closed circuit course. He comments about being dazzled by the 'sun setting low' and the final note reads: 'Went like a bird – 635.' (Aeroplane Monthly Archive)

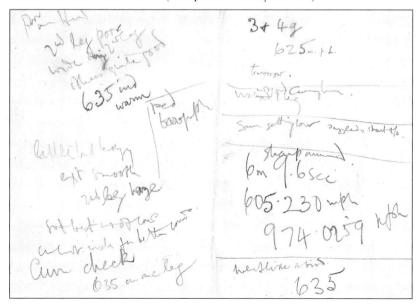

aircraft was hit by 40mm fire. He escaped unscathed, having leant forward at the moment the shell whistled through his cockpit, so that it literally passed him by inches. On 4th May the ground crews had just received instructions to fit long range tanks to the Typhoons, when things suddenly came to a halt.

'That's it. The war's over,' John told pilots and ground crews alike as the news filtered through to him.

Life took on a slightly unreal atmosphere after that. The squadron moved to Lübeck where, one evening, Derry disappeared with a few other pilots and came back an hour or so later with a plump pig. He didn't disclose where it came from but it was soon roasting over an enormous fire, which the men built by the lakeside. John slipped away again only to return with an old piano. He couldn't play himself – in fact he was a little tone deaf and didn't have much of an ear for music – but he knew that his batman was a dab hand when it came to entertaining. He marched Des up to the piano and gave him his orders:

'Play that thing!'

Des, in his element, hammered out all the popular songs of the time and sung his way through his repertoire of Al Jolson numbers. The men laughed and sang and drank and ate and when the fire was beginning to die down and Des was running out of steam, the flames were rekindled as the piano was slung bodily onto the glowing wood.

The days at Lübeck, at the lakeside, were spent happily by the pilots who went out on ops – on horseback and making rabbit shooting sorties, with a poor degree of success despite a battery of smoke canisters and 12-bores. Derry jumped at the chance of flying captured German aircraft, including the Fieseler Storch, the Me108 and the FW190, which surrendered at Lübeck, and he took every opportunity of going up in his own aircraft, his beloved Typhoon XM-F for practice flying. By the middle of June the pilots, indeed the whole airfield, were used to being woken up by the deafening roar of Derry's aircraft taking off at the crack of dawn as their CO treated them to a fine display of aerobatics nearly every morning. This went on until the middle of July when the squadron was delighted to be sent to Kastrup, Copenhagen, and Derry made them fly in a very pretty formation all the way.

In July Des suddenly became ill with a nasty bout of pneumonia and another man took over his duties. He came out of hospital, thinner and still rather weak, to find that many of the squadron were due for leave and one batman could have some time at home, too. John was in a dilemma over this. He wanted to offer the leave to Des who had been with them so long, but the other man was entitled to a chance, too. So he asked both of them down to the flight office and told them he was going to toss a coin, as he couldn't think of a fairer way. They watched breathlessly as the coin flashed in the air, spun and then rolled the whole length of the room on its side. But it came to rest with the tails side up – and that had been Des's call.

So he got his ten days at home and when he had to report back to John in England, he found that the squadron wasn't due to fly back for another few days. Hoping for a little more time with Anita, he asked John, who was back on duty, for an extra two or three days. John, who had spent his leave with Eve, who had given him the good news that she was expecting their baby, reminded Tyler that he had already had a long leave. Then he grinned and said:

'But if you'd like to clean my flying boots before you go, you can have three more days.' As an afterthought he called to the jubilant batman: 'Give my love to your girl!'

The squadron stayed together until 8 September and they were stationed at Schleswig when John called everyone together to say that they were now disbanded and to give them their new postings. Des Tyler and Albert Ward were the first two to be called out. John thanked them for looking after the whole squadron so well and gave them a fiver each from his own pocket. Then, with a broad grin on his face, he told them:

'I've arranged a good posting for you,' but refused to say what it was beyond the fact they were going to Detmold.

When the time came, they were waiting for a truck to pick them up and were rather taken aback when a large shiny car drew up. Des and Bert, two overawed aircraftmen, stepped in the back feeling sure that there was some mistake and that someone, most probably one of them, was going to be in trouble when the truth came out. The car pulled up outside a large, well kept building and the two dazed batmen were ushered into clean comfortable quarters where a bath was run for them and someone took their shoes away to be cleaned. They were then given the best meal they had had since the beginning of the war and they were starting to feel as if they had strayed into some kind of a fairy story.

It turned out that John had arranged for them to be in charge of the stores at the building, which was a Malcolm Club, and he had organised this reception for them as a way of saying 'thank you' for the way that the two of them had seen to the comforts of the squadron for so long.

Des never met John again after the war, although he followed his career in test flying with interest. When he learnt of the tragedy at Farnborough and heard that John was dead, he cried like a child.

'You can't let go of John,' he told Anita, now his wife. 'He was on the right side.'

Chapter 4

HIS WHOLE LIFE

*'I would not have him change his job for the world; it is his whole life
and must be mine, too.'*
Eve Derry, newspaper interview 1952

On a cold, windy mid-December day, with occasional darts of
thin, sharp sunlight making a dazzle on the glitter of the
Christmas decorations, which brightened the streets and shops,
John and Eve stood uncertainly outside Guildford Register office.

John had a special licence in his pocket and the Registrar was
waiting inside to marry them, but in their determination to slip
away and do things quietly and without any fuss, they had
forgotten to ask any witnesses to the ceremony. A road sweeper
shuffled past, dabbing unenthusiastically at the litter and the
leaves in the gutter. John rushed up to him, a note changed hands
and the three of them went up the steps into the office. It was all
over in a few minutes and at last, a few days before John was due
to start his new job as a civilian test pilot, they were husband and
wife. Neither felt any different once the legal seal was stamped.
The bonds of shared experience, of the hardships they had gone
through together, the fun they had had and the family they had
formed with their two daughters, had married them in the truest
sense. But a celebration was called for and they went off to the
nearest hotel to share a bottle of champagne.

The year before, when John came home from Europe, marriage
had seemed out of the question. Eve, due to have their baby in
October 1945, was living in lodgings in Worthing with an eccentric
landlady who took pleasure in harassing her tenants to the extent
of stealing their milk and going through their belongings. She

had discovered, whilst snooping, that the baby her pretty young lodger was expecting was not that of her legal husband and she made life unpleasant for Eve and Carol.

But John was home in time for Josephine's birth at a local nursing home and the new baby was registered in his name. The young father was delighted; he spent hours holding his tiny daughter and marvelling at the complexity and perfect functioning of babies, which he found much harder to understand than aircraft.

The four of them moved to Ferring soon after Jo's birth because of John's posting to Gatwick, and it was just after this move that the Worthing landlady flung her final dart of harassment at Eve, who found herself in court, accused of theft. The landlady, cowed into politeness by John's authoritative presence, had been pleasant enough when he came back from Europe to join Eve. But after they moved out she went to the police, accusing Eve of stealing some blankets. Eve knew perfectly well that she had replaced the blankets in the airing cupboard and she was determined to fight the charge all the way while John, furious at the accusation, insisted on standing in the witness box with her. The landlady was obviously well-known in the court and the magistrate seemed rather short with her. Peering at John and Eve, as they stood side by side in the witness box refuting the woman's claims, he dismissed the case saying: 'These two nice young people shouldn't be here at all.'

Things had started to go well for John and Eve at the end of 1945. After Jo's birth, Eve's first husband couldn't go on ignoring demands for a divorce and the papers were prepared, although they knew that proceedings would move slowly until the decree was absolute. There also seemed to be a gradual thawing-out of attitudes as far as their respective families were concerned as their relatives realised that this was not just another wartime fling but a serious commitment.

After a brief spell at Gatwick, John was posted to West Raynham in North Norfolk. They moved there early in 1946, finding a flat in a run down old rectory at Barsham. Their marriage was still in the future and although John, at twenty-four, had all the commitments and responsibilities of a married man, the RAF naturally didn't see matters in this light and he would not have been able to obtain married quarters. So they were still in the wartime position of having to look for somewhere to stay each time John was posted and although digs and lodgings were easier to find once the war was over, the places themselves were very little better.

The old rectory was a huge rambling draughty house, which possessed a fearsome stove of uncertain age and even more uncertain temper in the kitchen downstairs. Eve refused to get out of bed in the mornings until John had lit the thing – a terrifying process, which often resulted in flames shooting out in all directions.

They stayed at West Raynham for nearly a year, although luckily they were able to move out of the old rectory to a small cottage in a comparatively short time. But it was just before they left the uncomfortable flat that Rover joined the family. Eve's dog, Wendy, was a long-standing member of the household and as both John and Eve loved animals and found it natural to have dogs around the house, it wasn't surprising that they started to feed and look after the half-starved little puppy that was hanging around their flat. Rover became John's dog and would accompany his master whenever he had the chance, sometimes even into the air, in the days when John started work as a civilian test pilot.

In those early post war days the Central Fighter Establishment (CFE), which moved to West Raynham from Tangmere early in 1946, was a vital part of RAF planning. The Air Force needed to rebuild and re-equip and among the intensive courses at CFE was the Day Fighter Leader School (DFLS), which trained pilots for command positions. John was CO of the Tempest Squadron at the DFLS, a position that he took over from Squadron Leader Denis Sweeting. The other two squadrons in this unit were commanded by Bill 'Otto' Waterton, later chief test pilot at Gloster, responsible for the Javelin programme, and Squadron Leader J.S. 'Fifi' Fifield, who was to work with John at de Havilland, but on the production test side, and who later did much valuable work for Martin Baker, the company that makes the ejector seats that are fitted to most military aircraft.

The whole of this unit was under the command of another man who became one of John's firmest friends and who was also destined to be a fine civilian test pilot. Trevor 'Wimpy' Wade, chief test pilot at Hawker in the days of the prototypes that were to lead to the Hunter, was another man who lived for flying and whose natural exuberance sometimes expressed itself in a joyous burst of low level rolls or an earsplitting eruption of high-speed flight – upside down – over a startled airfield.

Young pilots coming to the Day Fighter Leader School were taught tactics, handling and the use of various armaments, and one popular exercise was a regular tactical 'bombing' of the bridge at the pretty village of Goring, in Berkshire. Perhaps the villagers became used to the sudden darting appearance of a bunch of assorted Spitfires, Hornets and Tempests converging in the air over their picturesque bridge or perhaps they found it exciting and reassuring that the RAF was keeping its hand in.

Besides the daily training, the tactical talks and raids, there was the constant business of planning for the future. British aviation and, of course, the RAF were just entering the jet age with the production and successful use of the Gloster Meteor, but the planners had to decide which of the older types of aeroplane to retain for Service use; to this end demonstrations of manoeuvrability and the other qualities of the aircraft were given to the 'brass' when they visited West Raynham. Civilian test pilots from the manufacturing companies brought up new machines to show their potential, but the RAF showed off their own aircraft.

Demonstration flying became John Derry's forte. At the end of the war, before his squadron was disbanded, he had spent much of his spare time taking his Typhoon, XM-F, through a series of aerobatics of his own devising, and he gave the whole concept of aerobatics as a means of demonstrating the qualities of an aircraft much thought. In 1946 his colleagues recognised his ability to give a polished performance which seemed to show the best the aeroplane had to offer, no matter what machine it was; by 1950, as a civilian test pilot, he was acknowledged to be among the top demonstration fliers in the world. His colleague at West Raynham, Squadron Leader 'Fifi' Fifield, himself a good pilot, especially when it came to showing what an aircraft could do, admired his friend's ability to pare his show down to the impressive essential manoeuvres and envied him his coolness and apparent lack of nerves. But Derry, too, felt the sickening pangs of 'stage fright' whilst waiting for his turn to fly. Fifi was very touched one day when they were discussing their own reactions to demonstrating an aircraft and John told him about the lurch in the pit of his stomach before he started the engine:

'It's the waiting around that gives me the butterflies,' he said. 'I have to press the starter button to make them disappear!'

John and Fifi both found themselves in mild trouble at West Raynham after the authorities discovered that some pilots were using the aircraft, quite legitimately, they had thought, as private transport. But they were told it was just not on to use a Tempest to get home or to go to some flying display in off duty hours in a RAF Hornet and, to make sure they kept on the straight and narrow, John Derry was made Station Duty Officer and Fifi, Orderly Officer, which involved paper work and regulations and wasn't appreciated much by either of them.

While Derry was discovering his talent for demonstration flying, he was also realising that his interest in things that flew went beyond aeroplanes. West Raynham, near the North Norfolk coast, is rich in bird life. The great flat marshy stretches of North Norfolk teem with river, estuary and sea birds. Frequent migrants rest there on their way north or south, according to the season, and John's boyhood interest in birds became a regular hobby. He started getting up early to watch the birds feeding on the mud flats and spent hours studying their flight patterns and habits.

One of John's commanding officers was wartime fighter ace Wing Commander Bob Stanford-Tuck who had many landowner friends in the county and sometimes, when he visited them, John would go up with him to note the geese and the waders and the sea birds coming down to feed as the sun came up on the reed beds.

For all his sociability, his reputation of being 'great fun', his love of speed and his urge to press on with whatever flying project was under way he, more than most people, had a great need to be alone and still. His love of wildlife fed this need and it became a habit with him to creep out of bed before sunrise, tucking the blankets firmly round Eve as he did so, to go out to listen to the dawn chorus or look for foxes and badgers, making sketches or simply sitting still for hours noting and questioning the things he saw.

He often told Eve that flying, being alone in a tiny cockpit, several miles above the earth, fulfilled the need for solitariness in him. He touched on this urge to get away from the small details of life and to be at one with his surroundings in his diary, which he kept during a holiday in the spring of 1952, in Scotland:

'I always like to get up on a bit of high ground so that I can see as much of the surrounding country as possible and also enjoy a climb thoroughly ... I am always deceived by Scottish hills. They look like smooth, unbroken slopes or cliffs until one is halfway up, when an unending series of ledges, colls and small valleys opens before the final climb to the peak. The time for a climb is always twice what I expect, but I never learn my lesson. The truth is that I am so attracted by these hills that subconsciously I banish the question of time . . .'

In the same diary his knowledge, by observation, of sea birds is evident:

'Saw two more mergansers or goosanders before sailing. Porpoises near the ship this morning when water was choppy. They porpoise exactly in formation. Noticed there were no guillemots or razorbills to be seen on way back across Minches. Although ocean birds, they seem to keep near land. Probably because of breeding. Fulmars disdain to take scraps from the boat and make gulls look like urchins scrambling with evil manners for bread. They do not seem to fish much for all their low flying. Saw sandpiper flying over loch this morning. Long pipe on wing then ripple after alighting. Phalarope!'

Eve knew and understood this lonely facet of John's personality, but it came as a surprise to many of his friends, some of whom were not even aware of it.

His was a complex character but it was fed by straightforward needs. His immense energy, both physical and mental, was directed straight into his job and flying was his life. But the stability of his family meant a great deal to him and although he and Eve made a great many friends and went to lots of parties, dances and shows where he enjoyed himself enormously, he liked best of all a simple home life, spending his time off playing with the children, gardening or going on family outings. To some measure he had inherited the directness and simplicity of his Plymouth Brethren forebears – the quality also possessed by Aunt Connie – which allowed him to go straight to the heart of a problem or a desire and to achieve the particular aim by the direct route, without allowing a clutter of confusing problems to creep in unnecessarily.

It might have been this quality that gave him the ease of manner and charisma that so many people remembered. He made friends easily and in those post war days many young people who had been forced to grow up quickly during the conflict were making up for the hardships by going out and enjoying themselves when they could. John and Eve were no exceptions, and John, with his ability to drive well and fast when no one else was in a fit state to do so, was much in demand as a chauffeur once the party was over. Fog was a constant hazard in Norfolk, but this didn't worry John who drove hard whatever the weather, with some uncanny sixth sense telling him when to slow down. The dash through a thick blanket of grey cotton wool must have seemed like a bad dream to many a morning-after partygoer waking up in a less euphoric state than that of the previous evening, but no one ever came to grief. He also put his split-second reactions to good use when driving home from the airfield – dawdling hares and pheasants that weren't quite sprightly enough to get out of the way were useful supplements to the pot in days of post war shortages.

By the middle of 1946, John was thinking about his future. There was a lot of flying, there was time for solitary reflection, and a happy family and good friends meant that there was a lot of fun. But John knew that he had to press on.

Aeroplanes had been the ruling force in his life since he was a boy. He wasn't and never would be content to fly within easy limits. As far as he was concerned he had reached those limits in the RAF. His friend, Fifi, recognised this urge in him and christened him a 'press on' type, driven to fly that little bit faster, to discover more about the mechanics of aircraft behaviour, to explore and push forward. So it was that he began to look for a job as a civilian test pilot. There was a vacancy at the Supermarine division of Vickers Armstrong and both he and Fifi, who also wanted a civilian job that involved flying, applied for it.

They flew down, separately, to Wiltshire for an interview with the chief test pilot, Jeffrey Quill, the man who had tested Supermarine's most famous product, the beloved Spitfire, from its prototype stages.

The airfield was then at High Post, near Salisbury, and from the moment that John walked into Jeffrey Quill's office, the experienced test pilot knew that this was the man he wanted. Quill wasn't quite sure what it was that made him feel this way, but he was looking for a man with fire in his belly and he knew from his own instinctive reaction based on a good deal of experience, having had many young test pilots through his hands, that here was a man who had it.

Supermarine, by then part of the Vickers group, was a company with an interesting history and the prospect of a bright future with its new jet aircraft developments. Its past was starred with the successes of its seaplanes, going back before the Schneider Trophy days, and, of course for its S5, S6 and S6B, all designed by the brilliant R.J. Mitchell and all winners of the Schneider Trophy itself.

At the time of the company's founding, at Woolston, near Southampton, in 1913, seaplanes, or hydro-aeroplanes as they were then called, were held as visions of future mass air transport. Noel Pemberton Billing, the company's founder, was a rather eccentric aviation enthusiast, whose main aim was to produce a flying lifeboat, which would successfully reach a wrecked vessel, land and then shed its wings, thus turning itself into a stable boat capable of sailing back to base. However, the idea never reached fruition and although Pemberton Billing did build and exhibit one example of his vision, it seems that it was never tested or flown. Supermarine was taken through the war by Hubert Scott-Paine, who bought out Pemberton Billing in 1916, and produced successful aircraft for the RNAS. Afterwards the company kept going by the simple expedient of buying these aircraft back and converting them to civilian use. By the time Scott-Paine sold his interest to Squadron Commander James Bird in 1923, Supermarine Aviation Works Ltd, with R.J. Mitchell established as chief designer, was set for rapid and successful expansion.

Mitchell's Schneider Trophy designs brought him acclaim, but so did the series of biplane flying boats, which became so popular between the wars, including such comfortable transports as the Southampton, the Scapa and the Stranraer. But it was well after the company had become part of the Vickers Group in 1928 that his most famous design, the beautiful Spitfire, appeared on his drawing board. Tragically Mitchell never lived to see the success of his concept as he died in 1937.

In the early years of World War Two, Supermarine's new purpose-built offices at Woolston were bombed and the company settled its design offices at Hursley Park, near Romsey, and production continued at South Marston near Swindon, Southampton and Trowbridge. But all flight testing and flying at High Post just after the war was due to move to Chilbolton in Hampshire, early in 1947, shortly after John Derry joined the firm.

John and Eve, with five-year-old Carol, baby Jo and the dogs, moved into their first real home – a lovely old cottage in the tiny hamlet of Fisherton de la Mere on the edge of Salisbury Plain.

John took up his new work as production and experimental test pilot with enthusiasm. Supermarine was a company with a reputation for good relationships with its employees and, perhaps because of this, the team that he joined was an exceptionally pleasant one. Headed by Jeffrey Quill, the pilots included Mike Lithgow, Les Colquhoun and Guy Morgan. Lithgow was a man with the same skill for analysis and detached observation as John himself was developing and he had joined the Supermarine team the year before. He tragically met his death nearly twenty years later whilst testing the effects of a full power stall in the BAC One-Eleven airliner. Les Colquhoun and his wife, Katie, became very good friends of the Derrys and there were many lighthearted moments at parties and dances in Salisbury and its villages. Les had good reason to remember John's generous nature when he and Katie had seen the house they wanted to buy but were being foiled by an unobliging bank manager in the small matter of a deposit. John had that morning received a substantial cheque from an uncle and when Les came in gloomily muttering all sorts of nasty things about bank managers in general, he handed him the cheque without hesitation.

In 1946 the Spitfire was still in full production, although the Mark 22s and 24s that were coming out of the factory were just beginning to give way to the new Seafires. Duties included production tests on each of these aircraft and there were also tests on the very fast Spiteful, a Spitfire variant with a 'laminar flow' wing. This aircraft was, however, officially cancelled and only a couple of dozen were ever made, although the aeroplane itself was interesting enough with its high speed characteristics.

The naval variant of the cancelled Spiteful was the Seafang which lost the contract to the Navy in favour of the more familiar Seafire 47, but was a useful test bed for the prototype E/10/44, Supermarine's first jet, which was later named the Attacker. The Seafang's wing was virtually the same as that of the new development, so much could be learnt in early tests.

The company's famous Walrus was still doing sterling work, and light relief at the airfield was provided by the rather peculiar S24/37 – better known to all the pilots as 'Dumbo', because of the variable incidence wing which may have reminded them of the ears of an elephant of the same name. Dumbo's undercarriage was a source of endless amusement to onlookers when the hapless pilot was landing the machine, because it was only if the man at the stick was extremely skilful – or incredibly lucky – that the aircraft could be put down without making a series of ever increasing bounces and bounds until it had slowed down to a speed where there was simply no more power left for another leap into the air. Derry has several 'circuits and bumps' entries in his log book for this aircraft and the 'bumps' part of it was probably very significant! But, despite Dumbo's faults, the machine was looked on affectionately and its wing design gave much help in the development of the Seagull amphibian.

John thought the most interesting production at Chilbolton was the E/10/44. Jeffrey Quill had done all the testing on the prototype and his number two, Mike Lithgow, was now doing the bulk of the work on the Attacker, as the aeroplane became known. As new boy, busy with other duties, John didn't fly the new jet for a considerable time. His log book entry for 'familiarisation' on Attacker TS413 is shown for 20 August 1947, when he took the aircraft up for just under half an hour.

In September he was testing its stalling characteristics and taking it on high Mach number runs. It wasn't his first jet, as at CFE he had tried out both the Gloster Meteor and the new de Havilland Vampire.

There is no doubt that Derry learnt his craft at Supermarine. A lot of the work, such as ferrying duties and routine production tests, may have seemed rather mundane to a man who wanted to press forward with the latest developments, but under Quill he learnt that method and care, meticulous observation and preparation and the patience for trying everything more than once were the foundations of a good test pilot's skill. Aviation writer Geoffrey Dorman particularly noticed the great care that Derry took with every aspect of his work both on the ground and in the air and in 1950 Dorman wrote in his book *British Test Pilots*: 'A genius has been said to be a person with an infinite capacity for taking pains. John Derry has that hallmark of genius.'

Day to day work at Supermarine brought a variety of tasks and a variety of aircraft to be flown. There was a lot of work on Spitfires and Seafires and Derry also learned to do waterlandings in the Walrus. He flew the familiar Dragon Rapide, an Auster and a couple of Spitefuls. One of these latter, RB518, was fitted with a Griffon engine with a special three-stage booster and it laid claim to being the fastest piston engine fighter in the world, having officially recorded a speed of 494mph. Although other fighters had made the same claim, there is no doubt that the Spiteful was a business-like machine, although this particular engine, strained by the tremendous boosting, had a nasty habit of packing up unexpectedly as it did when John flew it in June 1947 and he had to make a forced landing. He also tested and demonstrated the Seafang, the naval version of the Spiteful, but the aeroplane in which he had the most fun and gave convincing proof of his abilities as a demonstration pilot was Supermarine's new two-seat Spitfire trainer.

This was a converted Spitfire VIII that was flown, with or without a passenger, as a sales promotion demonstrator to potential buyers. Derry gave many displays through the summer and early autumn in that Spitfire (G-AIDN) to spectators at a variety of places, including the Battle of Britain show at Odiham, South Marston, Lympne, Eastleigh and Wisley, and immediately earned himself a reputation as an exciting and polished exhibition pilot.

However, the big show of the year has always been that organised by the Society of British Aircraft Constructors, later held at Farnborough, although when John flew for Supermarine it was given at its old home, Radlett in Hertfordshire. An old friend, Denis Sweeting, who was CO of the Tempest squadron at the Day Fighter Leader School just before John held that position, stayed with the Derrys at their Wiltshire cottage in the summer of 1947 and he went to Radlett to watch John. What he saw almost took his breath away, had the crowds gasping in admiration and established John as the star of the display. Flying a Seafire 47 (VP428), Derry treated his audience to ten minutes of unrivalled skill and excitement with a carefully devised programme of perfectly executed aerobatics and high-speed runs, culminating in a breathtaking outside loop – known as a bunt – which is an uncomfortable and difficult manoeuvre to carry out neatly, particularly in a fast and heavy fighter.

But there was still more excitement in store that week: the display linked up with the Royal Aeronautical Society Garden Party, which was held on the Sunday.

Still in VP428, John went through his programme as usual – but he was not aware of the mild sensation he caused during the final flypast, when all the aircraft dived steeply across the display field. He made a fast, clean, very steep dive and pulled up again very fast. The spectators, gazing after him, heard a gathering, rushing roaring noise coming towards them in his wake and as the sound reached them, the air rushed and eddied into miniature whirlwinds which swept coats, newspapers, and garden party hats up into the sky, to drop them a few yards away. The speed of the Seafire and the angle of the dive and climb had created wingtip vortices which, as they filled in with air, caused the noise and the turbulent eddies.

Production testing and ferrying duties were all part of Derry's work at Supermarine and during the first few months he carried out many of these routine tasks. But from the spring of 1947 his log book shows much more concentration on experimental test work. High-speed dives and stall tests on the Spiteful, straightforward testing on the Viking are shown throughout April and May, high-speed dives and drag measurements on both the Seafang and Spiteful during June and part of July, although much of the latter month was taken up with several demonstrations in the Spitfire trainer. August and September saw him start work on the problem that was to occupy him and absorb him until his death – the investigation of the 'critical' Mach number of an aeroplane. This is the speed at which an aeroplane, approaching the speed of sound, runs into 'compressibility', where the air in front has been pushed ahead so fast by the speeding craft that it is compressed and the aeroplane encounters many problems in flight behaviour and control as it goes through.

Nowadays these problems have been smoothed away by the designers and scientists, but only because of the work done in those post-war days by Derry and other test pilots who were nibbling away at the problem in the only possible way, by taking an aeroplane up into those unknown regions of speed, sitting it out and observing, noting and recording any relevant features of the aircraft's behaviour so that, little by little, enough knowledge could be stored and analysed for the day when truly supersonic aircraft could be contemplated. It was dangerous and uncomfortable work. Control surfaces often refused to respond, severe vibration set up and very often the aeroplane would dive wildly, totally out of control, until it reached the thicker air of the lower 15,000ft where the machine, reacting to the resistance of this thicker atmosphere, slowed up until full control could be resumed.

Derry began doing this sort of work on a Seafire 47 during the late summer and early autumn of his year at Supermarine, and although it was not until he joined de Havilland towards the end of that year that he started to press on relentlessly with his exploration of the sonic regions, his apprenticeship was well served.

For both John and Eve, 1947 was a happy and interesting year. But more than that, it was a year of consolidation, of development, for John. At twenty-five, the fearless young squadron leader had matured into a thoughtful and charming man whose general passion for aircraft was gradually being channelled into one direction – the desire to press forward in a single-minded investigation of flight in the sonic regions. His earlier, lighthearted impulsiveness had given way to a more methodical approach but he never lost the ability to take a childlike pleasure in a variety of ordinary activities, losing all sense of time in the absorbing nature of the moment, whether it was watching birds in country lanes or camping out in the garden with the children, when he would make sure that Eve joined in by lugging out a comfortable mattress for her.

The only smudge on the record of 1947 as a good year for the Derrys was the slightly sinister way that their beautiful rented cottage seemed not to like their presence. From the day they moved in, one or other of the children seemed to be ill, there were mysterious accidents in the house, the children fell down the stairs. Eve would always bear the scar caused by a shattering glass door which swung violently one evening and cut her very badly as she tried to stop it. When they left Fisherton de la Mere in November, the girl who lived in to help with the children and who had worked in the house before, moved with them. When they were safely away she told Eve that she had always felt that the house simply didn't like children. Eve and John, neither of whom had ever felt susceptible to any sort of supernatural experience before, had to agree that they both felt uneasy there at times, and that this explanation was as credible as any.

Despite these rather peculiar domestic problems, John was perfectly happy at Supermarine, looking forward to more high-speed work on the new jets when an offer that took some thinking over was made to him, out of the blue.

The de Havilland Aircraft company was one of the largest and most respected manufacturers in the country. Founded by Sir Geoffrey de Havilland early in the century, the company had produced some of the world's best loved and best known aeroplanes from the Moth series to the wooden Mosquito. Sir Geoffrey was still at his desk in 1947 and by this time de Havilland was renowned for its progressive designs and it was among the first companies after the war to press forward with a programme of jet fighter development, which included interesting research into the new idea of using swept wing aircraft for high-speed investigation in the sonic regions.

Their chief test pilot, Geoffrey de Havilland, son of the founder, had been killed in just such an aircraft and his number two, wartime hero John Cunningham, was now in charge of the development programme. Times were busy at Hatfield, de Havilland's base in Hertfordshire, as the new passenger jet airliner, the first of its kind in Britain, the sleek elegant Comet, was being planned and built. Cunningham had his work cut out and he needed a man who had the skill and courage to take over the high-speed research programme on the tailless swept wing DH108. He cast around and his eye alighted on Derry. After seeing John's display at Lympne in the Spitfire trainer at the end of August 1947, he felt that he had been watching a first class pilot who would match up to the exacting work demanded by the Experimental Flight Test department at Hatfield, and it wasn't long before he approached John with the offer of the job. Cunningham's old friend, Bob Stanford-Tuck, had spoken to him of Derry's prowess in the air and he was confident that he had chosen the right man.

John had to take the job. His ten months at Supermarine had pointed him in this very direction and although these months had been happy and worthwhile, he couldn't pass up the challenge of the job at de Havilland. He ruled a blue ink box in his log book at the end of the October entry and Jeffrey Quill put his signature to the 284 hours and 20 minutes of flying time that Derry had done with the company.

A week later, under the new heading 'de Havilland Aircraft Co Experimental Flight Test', he started work at Hatfield with flights in a Hornet, a Dove and a Vampire and, within a week, he was starting a programme which included a series of dives to measure Mach numbers achieved in both the Hornet and the twin boom jet, the Vampire.

Footnote: Spitfire G-AIDN, in which Derry gave such memorable displays during his time at Chilbolton, continued to be used as a demonstrator until 1952 and also took part in air races. After being in storage for a while it was sold to John Fairey, son of Richard Fairey, the founder of Fairey Aviation, and after several subsequent owners it went to America, where it was owned and operated in Oregon.

By the early 1990s it had amassed little more than 700 flying hours and did very few more before being sold to an undisclosed buyer in the UK in 2007.

Chapter 5

MORE OUT OF THE AIRCRAFT

'I knew I was going to get more out of the aircraft than before.'
John Derry, April 1948

O n a warm mellow evening, late in September 1946, Geoffrey
de Havilland junior died. He was flying the DH108, Britain's
first swept wing jet, faster than man had ever flown before, when
it broke up at nearly the speed of sound. Pieces of falling wreckage
were scattered in the thick mud and sand of Egypt Bay in the
Thames Estuary and de Havilland's body was later found at
Whitstable. He was just thirty-six years old and he died without
knowing what had gone wrong.

It was three months before anyone knew what had really
happened, and the investigation revealed dangers so appalling
that flying at the speed of sound began to seem to both pilots and
designers like a barrier that might never be crossed – yet if the
problems could not be resolved, then aircraft had reached their
limiting speed when the latest source of power, the jet engine,
had barely been developed.

Wartime experience, on piston-engine aircraft, had shown that
alarming things happened in high-speed dives. The usual sequence
was that the machine would suddenly feel nose-heavy, the pilot
would find it difficult to pull back on the control column and as
the aircraft went faster, the situation would worsen until he found
himself plunging earthwards in an uncontrollable dive. The
aircraft would also start to buffet and shake violently, hopelessly
beyond control, the victim of forces not fully understood. All the
pilot could do was sit tight, wrestle with the control column and
sweat with fear until the aircraft was slowed up by the denser air.

Then control could be regained, but there were more dangers, for if the elevator trim had been set in the 'up' position, then the pull out could be violent enough to break the aeroplane.

Wind tunnel tests did not give a realistic idea of what happened to the airflow at those high speeds, as shock waves tended to bounce off the tunnel walls and interfere with results. The only way to find out was for a pilot to try it himself, in the air. That was to be John Derry's main task, when he joined de Havilland – to take another 108 a fraction short of the Mach number that Geoffrey de Havilland had reached and make careful note of the aircraft's behaviour. It was the only way that progress could be made.

De Havilland were already well ahead in the new jet era; their very successful twin boom Vampire first flew in 1943, powered by the Goblin, which was designed and built by the firm's own engine company. Now, after the war, they were out to investigate the realms of transonic flight with the 108, an aircraft that marked the beginning of supersonic flight as we know it today.

With its swept wings the 108 looked startlingly futuristic and was every schoolboy's idea of a supersonic aircraft. It was originally built as a scaled down test bed for the Comet but the eventual airliner looked nothing like the little jet because a tailless swept wing layout proved to be hopelessly impractical and uneconomic for commercial use. So the 108 was switched to pure research work.

The concept of swept wings, which had been pioneered to some extent by the Germans during the war, looked impressive, but really there were a number of disadvantages, especially at low speed where a normal, straight wing was far more efficient. With swept wings the landing speed had to be much higher because of a tendency for the airflow to break down at the wing tips at low speeds, sometimes causing a tip-stall – disastrous as one wing could drop suddenly and violently and there would be no aileron response.

In every way, except near the speed of sound, the swept wing seemed to be inferior. Its one and only advantage – and this is why it was used – was that it would delay the onset of compressibility. At speeds approaching that of sound, which is about 760mph at sea level and 650mph at 35,000ft, shock waves begin to build up and the normally smooth airflow over the wings breaks down, causing the buffeting, shock-stalling and loss of control that beset the pioneers of transonic flight. On thick-winged aircraft these phenomena set in quite early, simply because the air was being accelerated locally to supersonic speeds, while the aeroplane itself was flying more slowly. Designers turned to thin wings and tried to eliminate anything that would cause drag. One obvious way of doing this was to forget about a tailplane and to let the longitudinal stability be taken care of by elevons, which are control surfaces on the outer part of the wings, which combine the functions of both ailerons and elevators.

Knowing all this, de Havilland designers began work on the 108. As well as producing a machine that was aerodynamically very advanced, they wanted to keep costs as low as possible and it was not designed from the outset as a supersonic aircraft. The Government had already refused to support such a project on the grounds that it was too dangerous – a misguided decision that Derry later publicly criticised in a lecture to the Royal Aeronautical Society. This timidity on the part of the Government led to the cancellation of the Miles M52, a straight-winged jet that was intended to be Britain's first piloted supersonic aircraft and work was carried out instead by pilotless models. But in those days of bulky transmitters, a model could not carry enough radio equipment to provide much useful information. So, from the start, Britain received a severe blow to progress with high-speed flight.

Meanwhile the de Havilland team worked at maximum speed, and the first 108, which was designed only for low speed experimental work, was rolled out at Hatfield for engine runs on 28 April 1946, only ten months after the first design calculations. It was a strange aircraft. Based on a standard Vampire fuselage, it was only 24ft long and its 43-degree swept wings spanned 39ft. It was taken by lorry to the RAF emergency airfield at Woodbridge in Suffolk for its first flight, as Hatfield was in the throes of having a new runway and perimeter track built. Woodbridge had a 3,000-yard runway and thick belts of trees, which would screen this revolutionary secret machine from inquisitive eyes.

On 11 May, Geoffrey de Havilland climbed into the 108, serial number TG283, and, to the characteristic whine of the 3,000lb thrust Goblin 2 engine, took the little machine down the runway for taxying trials. But almost at once the wheel brakes began to overheat and there was a frustrating hold up of four days before it finally flew on 15 May. The flight went so smoothly that it was almost an anti-climax. There had been dire warnings from the Royal Aircraft Establishment at Farnborough of poor low speed behaviour, including 'dutch rolling' (an unpleasant wallowing motion) and a tendency to stall early. In fact TG283, designed for a top speed of no more than 280mph, showed none of this, perhaps because de Havilland designers had guarded against stalling by fitting large fixed leading edge slats.

Meanwhile, work on the second prototype, TG306, was already well under way. This was designed to explore the other end of the speed range, but it was still not intended to be supersonic and it didn't look very different from TG283. The wings were slightly more swept at 45 degrees, it had automatic slats and the canopy was partly metal skinned for extra strength at high speeds. It was fitted with the more powerful Goblin 3 engine of 3,300lb thrust.

Neither prototype had an ejector seat. The Ministry of Aircraft Production wanted one fitted, but de Havilland felt that extensive redesign of the fuselage and cockpit would have taken too long.

The second 108, which first flew on 21 August again piloted by Geoffrey de Havilland, caused a good deal of public interest when it was demonstrated at the Society of British Aircraft Constructors' display, at Radlett, on Friday 13 September. In Geoffrey's hands it put up an exciting show for he was an extremely good demonstration pilot. He had been with his father's firm since 1928 and turned to test flying seven years later. Within a few months of becoming chief test pilot in 1938, he took the Flamingo airliner on its maiden flight, and from then on made the first flight of every de Havilland prototype up until 1945, including the famous Mosquito, Vampire and Hornet.

He loved flying and his ability was widely recognised, but as a person Geoffrey could sometimes be a little difficult and hot tempered. He reacted strongly, even rudely, to any criticism which he felt was unwarranted, and to those who didn't know him well he could appear offhand. But his friends thought him a warm and witty personality, who always referred to aeroplanes as 'boilers' and who often remarked that although he knew full well a 'boiler' might be the cause of his death, he wasn't going to let that prospect stop him flying.

There was one moment in his career that he would rather have forgotten. He was demonstrating a Vampire to a group of high ranking officials at West Raynham after the war and had put up his usual exciting performance and was taxying to a halt after landing. Suddenly the aircraft's wheels retracted and it flopped ungracefully onto its belly.

There was a pause and everyone watched with interest as the canopy slid back and out climbed the lanky but cumbersome frame of Geoffrey, who was virtually able to get out in one step as the aircraft was by now so low. He was purple with rage. 'Those idiots,' he roared. 'Those bloody idiots! I told them they'd put the undercarriage control in a stupid place and this just proves it!'

There was some truth in what he said, for the flap and undercarriage controls were next to each other, and in attempting to retract the flaps, Geoffrey had inadvertendy selected the undercarriage lever. It was an embarrassing moment but by the time he'd reached the bar and was drowning his sorrows, Geoffrey calmed down. 'I've made a bloody fool of myself,' he said ruefully.

After the SBAC show, the research programme with the second prototype 108 started in earnest, with the speed being gradually stepped up to higher Mach numbers. Although it was comparatively low powered, the 108 was a streamlined machine and its performance was so impressive – it soon exceeded in level flight the world's absolute speed record of 616mph held by a Gloster Meteor – that de Havilland decided to make an official attempt on this record over the course at Tangmere. Geoffrey had already touched 630mph in the 108 at 1,500ft, and he planned to make a final test run on 27 September before flying to Tangmere for the record attempt, the following day.

He was going to dive the aircraft from around 10,000ft to a Mach number of 0.87 (87 per cent of the speed of sound) to check on controllability, and then he would make a level run, at high speed over the sea to find out how the 108 behaved under record conditions. Good weather, the air free from bumps, was essential and Geoffrey had to wait all day for conditions to be just right.

By the evening it was warm and clear, with a slight haze forming, so Geoffrey took off from Hatfield, leaving his colleagues chatting on the airfield, eagerly awaiting the results of his flight.

He never returned. As the minutes ticked by excitement turned to anxiety and when it was obvious that the little aircraft's fuel must have run out, his friends thought he might have got into difficulties and landed at another aerodrome. But the telephone calls were fruitless, and then ominous messages began to arrive from air traffic control that an aeroplane had been seen breaking up over the Thames Estuary. Pieces of wreckage had been spotted falling near Egypt Bay, northeast of Gravesend, about twenty minutes after Geoffrey had taken off. Soon the worst fears were confirmed: it was TG306.

It was a terrible blow for a company in which the team spirit counted so much. It was an even more shocking blow for Sir Geoffrey de Havilland, whose first son had died in a mid-air collision in 1943 while testing a Mosquito. Now the chief test pilot, the leader of the 108 programme, was gone. But the show had to go on, and Sir Geoffrey knew it. The next month he announced that John Cunningham would take over his son's duties, and the Ministry allowed the firm to build a replacement 108.

In the meantime as much wreckage of TG306 as possible was being recovered and a thorough investigation of the cause of the crash was begun. But finding some of the badly damaged components was not easy, as many parts had fallen in the sea.

Wild stories appeared in the newspapers, which intimated that Geoffrey had opened the throttle wide and put the aircraft in a steep dive in a daring bid to be the first man in the world through the 'sound barrier', a subject that had already captured the public imagination.

The story was a popular one and some people still believe that Geoffrey exceeded the speed of sound just before the aircraft disintegrated. What he intended will never be known, but the 108 had not been designed to reach Mach One and although there were many mysteries about transonic flight in 1946, at least it was accepted that to attempt a supersonic flight at such low altitude would be certain to end in disaster as the airspeed would be so high.

There was no obvious reason for the crash and the investigation took eighty-eight days. The engine, found more or less intact in the mud, was cleared of blame. Other parts were examined in minute detail for stress marks or fractures that might yield a clue and it became fairly obvious that something had gone wrong at very high speed, but it was not easy to establish exactly what – and then came an extraordinary clue. After the accident de Havilland's mail consisted of the usual witness accounts of the crash, with a predictable sprinkling of offerings from cranks and mediums. But there was one letter from two women mediums that struck John Wimpenny, a senior aerodynamicist with the firm and later an executive with British Aerospace, as decidedly out of the ordinary and worth at least a second thought.

The message said simply: 'Trans-dunal trough – don't push it back.'

These words were meaningless at first but then the phrase 'trans-dunal trough' seemed to imply travelling across an undulating path – in this case it could be taken to mean an up and down pitching motion. There was a good deal of scepticism among the de Havilland staff, but in the end it was decided to follow it up and search for more substantial evidence. Renewed efforts were made to salvage the VG recorder that had fallen into the sea. This recorder was a simple and rather crude device for recording positive and negative g forces and consisted of a piece of smoked glass across which moved a trace, marking speed and g force.

Eventually the recorder, with its protective casing, was found and although it was severely damaged by the salt water, faint traces of massive positive and negative g were detected at the instrument's final moments of recording. This could only mean that the aircraft had developed a sudden and violent up and down pitching and it soon became clear that this had set in at a very high Mach number and was horrifically sudden. One second all was well, with the 108 diving at high speed and under perfect control. Then, at a fractionally higher Mach number and with no warning at all, a violent pitching began, with a frequency of about three cycles a second – much too rapid to be corrected. Half a second later this oscillation reached disastrous accelerations and the wings failed.

It can never be known whether this message, which the mediums had said was Geoffrey's final thought, was geniune or merely coincidence; but there is no doubt that this pitching motion – this 'trans-dunal trough' – caused the wings to break. Although Geoffrey could have done nothing about this, he was not entirely blameless. On that fatal evening he had allowed his enthusiasm for a crack at the world speed record to take over, with the result that he had gone too fast at too low an altitude in the areas of uncharted speed. It was a cruel price to pay, but from then on courage and an adventurous spirit on their own were not enough to explore transonic speeds; dead heroes were of little use to designers and aerodynamicists who needed men not only brave enough to face the dangers time after time, but who could fly carefully, methodically and with the necessary restraint to bring back meaningful results.

The tests had to go on and it was with this unnerving yet challenging knowledge that John Derry took over the 108 programme.

John arrived at Hatfield a few weeks before Christmas 1947, and with his infectious smile and pleasant manner soon made friends with everyone including the ground crews and maintenance staff who were quick to criticise anyone whose behaviour didn't justify his position. On Christmas Eve, after a period of flying Vampires and Hornets, John put his head round the door of the experimental flight shed and asked the men what arrangements had been made for them for a Christmas celebration. Nothing at all, he was told. Within an hour or so they were celebrating in grand style after John had sent out for enough Christmas cheer to get everyone in a festive mood. He loved Christmas and the following year donned a red and white gown, glued on an impossible beard and pulled on Wellington boots before climbing into a Mosquito and roaring off to visit some of his old RAF airfields and to distribute presents to the children. He arrived back in time to be the Father Christmas at his own village party where he put on such a good show that his own children didn't recognise him.

He and Eve and the children had moved into a large bungalow at Rabley Heath, a little village about nine miles from Hatfield. Greensleeves had plenty of space, a large garden and orchard and room to keep chickens. It also had a mortgage on it, as John and Eve decided that it was high time that they bought a place of their own.

After Christmas, settled in nicely and thoroughly familiar with the aircraft at Hatfield, John started work in earnest on the 108 programme. Cunningham had already flown the third prototype, VW120, and had taken it at high altitude to about Mach 0.88. It was basically the same design as its fated predecessor, although the whole structure was much stronger and it had a redesigned cockpit and a longer, more pointed nose. The pilot's seat had been lowered and an ejector seat was at last fitted – although chances of escape at above 400mph were remote.

VW120 also had a more powerful engine. The Goblin 4 gave

3,750lb thrust and, early in the flight test programme, power boosters were fitted to the elevon controls in a bid to help the pilot overcome the high forces generated at transonic speed. Apart from these boosters, the control system was unremarkable and was operated by the usual cable system.

Geoffrey de Havilland's accident showed there was a definite hazard in flying tailless aircraft above a certain Mach number, and this was backed up by the results of wind tunnel tests at RAE Farnborough. The pilot could expect a sudden nose down pitching, severe and fluctuating loss of stability, and even, under certain conditions, control reversal caused by flexing of the wings. All or any of these could lead to complete loss of control and the margin between disaster and safety was shockingly narrow; without any warning an increase in Mach number as small as 0.005 – too small for the pilot to anticipate or correct – could instantly plunge the aircraft into a potentially catastrophic situation. At low altitude it could be even worse, as it was found that at Mach 0.87 a moderate breeze of 15mph could raise the Mach number to 0.89 and generate forces of minus 7g in about half a second, and that could break the wings.

So when John began the serious high-speed test-programme in February, there was no early attempt to take it to these kinds of speeds. He began a series of carefully controlled tests taking aerodynamic load recordings across the wings. This was done by pressure plotting, a process that needed specialised instruments to measure the loading at various speeds and Mach number at a series of points across the chord. It needed patient and painstaking flying in which everything had to be tried more than once – a point later touched on by John in his Royal Aeronautical Society lecture 'High-speed Flying'.

Throughout the second half of February, John did ten of these pressure-plotting flights in VW120, gradually building up speed in shallow dives, until high Mach numbers were being reached. These flights were done at heights of 35,000 to 40,000ft. In the following months his experimental dives built up a picture of the height/speed combination at which the pitching instability occurred and his flight test reports, sent to RAE Farnborough who were following the work with interest, were studied minutely and de Havilland were congratulated on the extremely valuable work programme. There was no doubt that, up to these critical high speeds, the 108 was a pleasant and manoeuvrable aeroplane with very good handling and performance and de Havilland decided to take time off from the relentless testing to enter it, piloted by John, for the 100-kilometre closed circuit speed record.

This was a very hotly contested event for an international record administered by the Fédération Aéronautique Internationale (FAI) and was usually held over a three, four or five-sided course chosen by the contender. At the time the record was held by Mike Lithgow in an Attacker at 564.881mph, over a four-sided course from Chilbolton. Lithgow had broken the three-week old record made by Bill 'Otto' Waterton (542.94mph) in a Gloster Meteor IV. The previous holder was Derry's colleague John Cunningham who had averaged 496.88mph in a Vampire at Lympne. In the space of seven months the record had been pushed up by 68mph. Could Derry better this in an aircraft designed purely for research as opposed to the manoeuvrability necessary for the military requirements of the previous record holders?

Selecting a suitable course was not easy and the de Havilland team spent six weeks studying a number of possibilities and rejecting them one by one after flying around them. It was essential to search for prominent turning points, for the record was not only to be made at very high speed but also at very low level and there was no question of anything like a computer to eliminate error; it was a question of man and machine working at the limits for something over six minutes. In the end a five-sided course was chosen with moderate turns of 92, 56, 64 and 66 degrees with a straight run in and out. This layout would not only give the least theoretical loss of speed on the turns, but four of the turning points would always be visible from the previous one under good conditions. The course, in Hertfordshire, was also chosen because it avoided, as far as possible, built up areas and it measured 100.15km. It ran from the BBC station at Brookmans Park, north of Hamels Park, Puckeridge, on to the brickworks near the Three Counties Station in Letchworth, past the cement works at Upper Sundon, followed by a turn south west of Beechwood House, Markyate, and finally back to the BBC station.

The attempt was fixed for Monday 12 April, and it was planned to make the run in the early evening to avoid any bumpy air which would not only make things uncomfortable for John, but would limit the speed. However, first he wanted to be thoroughly familiar with the course and check out the turning points. His log book shows that he made two practice runs in the 108 on the ninth of the month and another one the following day. All went well and he found that he was able to take a tight, fast line through the turns. From his point of view there was now little to be done until the big day which, barring mechanical trouble could only be jeopardised by the weather.

The day dawned fine and clear and early in the morning reporters and cameramen, already used to the procedure, for it was the third attempt on the 100km record within eight weeks, arrived at Hatfield to set up their equipment. The 108, which they colourfully described in their reports as a 'peculiar little bat-shaped plane with a shark-like stabilising fin', aroused a lot of interest, being so different from the previous record holders.

At midday, with the weather still fine, John took off in VW120 to make a final check for any snags and put in one last run round. Trouble struck almost immediately after take-off; a fuel leak caused the cockpit to fill with a cloud of dense white vapour and, although John was wearing goggles, he was unable to see to land as the mist was so thick. But after several minutes it cleared a little and he touched down safely, frustrated and disappointed, though outwardly calm, at the thought of a long repair job and the possibility of postponing the attempt. The ground crew worked like men possessed and by tea time it was clear that they were going to have the aircraft ready in time. Meanwhile Jack Arthur, the test pilots' secretary, drove off to Rabley Heath to collect Eve, while John waited for the 108 to be ready. When she arrived he was his usual collected self, neither worried nor excited. It could have been just another day of routine flying – if any high speed flying in those days could be so described – instead of an attack on a world speed record.

At 5pm, the fuel leak repaired, John took off for what he hoped was the final check run in conditions that seemed from the ground to be ideal. But the air was still rough, causing accelerations of up to 3g so that he had to throttle back from 625mph. However, the chances were still good and the FAI team went ahead with their final preparations on the aircraft and the Press, sensing that the time was near, closed in with their newsreel cameras mounted on car roof tops.

In their excitement, which was all focussed on John and the 108, they had not noticed Sir Geoffrey de Havilland on the outskirts of the crowd, nor had they seen Eve – but as usual, she kept well in the background. The sun sank lower as John Cunningham took off in a Vampire to see if the air was still bumpy and, after flying the course, reported that at last everything was still and calm.

With the evening haze forming on the horizon, John walked over to the 108. He looked casual, in pinstripe slacks, open-necked shirt and light zip-up jacket; air friction at high speed over the aircraft's surface would soon make him very hot and he wanted to be as comfortable as possible. He climbed in, went through the usual cockpit checks and then closed the canopy. The Goblin whistled into life and the little aircraft taxied out onto the runway. Seconds later it was disappearing into the sunset and was soon out of sight, leaving behind it a tense atmosphere on the airfield. Shortly afterwards it came in low and very fast from the London direction on the first leg of the course and then disappeared in the haze to the north. The minutes ticked by as the crowds waited in silence. Eve was standing next to Sir Geoffrey who became restless and began looking at his watch. 'He should be here by now,' he muttered.

Eve picked up his anxiety and began to feel uneasy, wondering if the fear that was always close at hand had become reality.

She need not have worried; John was flying flat out, the countryside ribboning away beneath him, his face distorting under the high g turns, the little 108 going like a bird. He later described the flight in the *de Havilland Gazette*:

'Climbing to 1,500ft, I turned towards Elstree Reservoir, accelerating all the time. As I turned over Harrow I could not see Potter's Bar or the starting point at Brookman's Park, but here my practice came in useful and, lining up on the Barnet bypass, I began to lose height.

'The rules state that the aircraft must be level 300 metres before the start and that the finish must not be made lower than the start. In fact I was flying level for about five miles before the start and still accelerating. I crossed the line as near as I dared go to the aerial masts and about 300ft above the ground; my speed was about 620mph, and as I settled down to the first leg I knew I was going to get more out of the aircraft than before owing to the remarkable smoothness of the air. Every bump seemed to have disappeared and we hummed at 500ft past Hertford and up towards the Puckeridge aerial.

'I started to apply bank about 1½ miles before reaching the turning point in order to be able to pull the aircraft round at the right moment. The best turn is made by starting wide, passing the turning point in the centre of the arc of the turn and then finishing wide. I used 4g instead of 3½g as on previous runs, and owing to haze on this leg I was unable to see the next landmark.

'When I passed the church at the halfway point on this stretch I knew that the tighter turn had led me off on a slightly wrong line. I corrected course, regretting the lost seconds, and rounded the brickworks corner. I was out of the haze and on the next leg and the ASI showed 635mph as I approached the Sundon Cement works – still at 500ft. Now I could see my landmarks and was able to straighten up for this turn heading for the plume of white smoke which indicated the last turn.

'I pulled round this bend at 4 to 4½g and about 628mph, and concentrated on flying a straight course over the north of St Albans past the end of the Hatfield runway, and on towards the BBC masts at Brookman's Park, where I made a slight turn to cut the finishing line as soon as possible. The indicated speed was 635mph.'

When John circled round to line up for a landing at Hatfield the result was already known. Public relations man Martin Sharp was standing on a car running board excitedly waving a piece of paper on which was written the speed and the time. John had clocked an amazing 605.23mph, which was over 40mph more than the previous record. Cheering and clapping broke out as this was announced and the crowd milled towards the 108 as it taxied in. Eve hung back, but for that day at least, her fears were over.

John pushed back the canopy as the whistling of the engine died away. Looking very hot, but happy, he began to climb out and the result was thrust in his hand. Sir Geoffrey was the first to congratulate him and then, as the crowds jostled closer, someone shouted out to make way for Eve. There was just time for a smile, a kiss and to light a much needed cigarette for John before the microphones were thrust at him. He whispered a few words, being careful to point out that the record had not, at that stage, been made official, and he said simply that the aircraft had behaved beautifully. He often appeared diffident, even offhand, to the Press but he was only anxious that he should not be misquoted.

Moments later, after he had signed some autographs, John slipped quietly away with Eve and drove home.

He had taken the 108 to its limits and that was his definition of high-speed flying: to fly at, or near, an aircraft's limiting speed. He had taken himself to the limits, too, and this was recognised when he was awarded the Segrave Trophy for 1947, for the greatest performance that year on land, sea or in the air.

Chapter 6

THE BIGGEST BARRIER

*'It has, in truth, been the biggest barrier we are likely to
experience in flight progress for many years hence.'*
John Derry, *The Times Survey of British Aviation*, September 1952

New limits were waiting to be reached and conquered; the sound barrier was just a tantalising few hundredths of a Mach number away from the 108.

The Americans had already cracked it, although their approach was totally different from the British effort and involved a purpose built aircraft that bore no resemblance to a conventional jet. Called the XS-1, it was built by the Bell Aircraft Corporation and was a rocket-powered machine with straight unswept wings – but, because of its fuel supply, which was limited to a fast burn on the rockets, it could not take off under its own power. Instead it was dropped at 25,000 to 35,000ft from the belly of a B-29 Super Fortress bomber, the motor was ignited and it accelerated away for a short but very fast flight, finally gliding back to earth as the fuel was exhausted.

On 14 October 1947, piloted by Major Charles 'Chuck' Yeager, it was dropped on its historic flight. A quick blast on its rocket motor took it to Mach 1.06 in level flight, which was so much safer than the perilous dives of the 108.

It was a magnificent effort, but somehow summed up the American policy of 'do it big, do it quick – and damn the expense'. Britain, on the other hand, plodded on in a less spectacular way in terms of fast results, although had the Miles M52 project not been cancelled, there is a chance, albeit a small one, that she would have got there first.

Meanwhile John Derry carried on with the series of high Mach number dives in the 108, plunging towards the earth as he nudged it nearer the speed of sound, each time bringing back a little more information on the pitching and oscillating, so that the aerodynamicists could assess just what was happening. Derry's lucid and accurate reports, often obtained under the most alarming conditions as the aircraft neared the limits of controlled flight, were very useful when studied in conjunction with the pressure plotting results and VG recordings.

The dangers were never very far away. On one flight, under the most carefully controlled conditions, he came within an ace of Geoffrey de Havilland's fatal crash. The pitching, as usual, came on suddenly and after the flight the VG recorder showed that in less than one and a half seconds VW120 had been subjected to positive and negative accelerations of $3\frac{1}{2}$g. In another second the wings would almost certainly have failed as the g forces escalated. It was only Derry's immediate reaction to throttle back that saved himself and the aircraft. Geoffrey, of course, had not been forearmed with any knowledge of the pitching, or of its dangers.

But the 108 was by now becoming known to the British public after the 100km record success, for which John received a welcome cash bonus from de Havilland. John, too, was in the public eye in the many newspaper reports about the record under such headings as 'British Jet Smashes Air Speed Record' to the more riveting 'Bat Jet Flies at 605mph'. He bore the accolades gracefully if not easily.

De Havilland were riding high with his achievement, for only three weeks earlier they had gained another world record when John Cunningham took a Ghost-engined Vampire (TG278) to an altitude of 59,492ft, thus beating the record established in 1938 by Italian Lieutenant-Colonel Mario Pezzi who flew his Caproni biplane to 56,049ft.

Derry had done the altitude check on Cunningham's Vampire on 27 February 1948 with a flight in it to 58,000ft. Today there would be no hazards in such a flight, but in those days it was a very different matter, for although the Vampire's cockpit was pressurised there were no complete pressure suits. Should the canopy have cracked, which was by no means impossible, the only emergency measure was a battery of oxygen bottles which could be triggered to release what the designers hoped was enough pressure to enable the pilot to dive to a lower and safe altitude, provided he did it quickly enough. Loss of pressure at those high altitudes would mean death within seconds and Cunningham's Vampire was fitted with a partly metal skinned canopy, similar to that of the second 108 prototype, to minimise the chance of failure. The other hazard that was always present, even at more moderate heights, was oxygen starvation. The pilot always had to be careful about regulating the oxygen he breathed under pressure through his face mask, and the usual procedure was to select the correct supply for a few thousand feet higher than he intended to go, for a mistake could, and often did, lead to death. The symptoms of oxygen starvation are treacherous simply because they are so pleasant, not unlike the early stages of intoxication, with a feeling of over confidence and light-headedness. Loss of consciousness and death follow rapidly.

Squadron Leader Denis Sweeting, Derry's old friend from CFE, West Raynham, had had an almost miraculous escape from a Spitfire during the war when his oxygen was not switched on. All seemed to be well on a routine patrol over Scotland until he suddenly found himself waking up in a screaming dive in thick cloud, the previous moments a complete blank. There was no time to think but he reacted by instantly pulling back on the stick – hard. Then he blacked out again. When he came to, he was still falling earthwards at speed – but this time without the Spitfire. His shoulders ached horribly, he was still in thick cloud and he had no idea of his height or whether he was over land or sea.

Panic almost took over but then his basic survival training paid off and he instinctively walked his fingers round his waist as he had been taught to do, until he came to the ripcord. He pulled it and promptly passed out for the third time.

When he regained consciousness he was relieved to find that he was on dry land. The two crofters bending over his inert body seemed to be convinced that he was dead, and by all the normal chances he should have been, for when he pulled the Spitfire out of its dive after he had blacked out through oxygen starvation, the wings broke off at the roots. The aircraft promptly went into a bunt so violent that Sweeting was rocketed upwards, his seat straps torn off and his unconscious body smashed headlong through the canopy, before he regained consciousness in time to pull the ripcord.

Although the dangers facing John and other experimental test pilots were new ones associated with high speed flying, the old ones were still there, the unforgiving and inevitable consequences of a moment's inattention. Throughout the summer of 1948 John pressed on with the 108 programme, gathering more and more information in the long dives, edging the Mach number up each time, repeating flights again and again to check the sequence of events. It was all too easy, he knew, for a test pilot to think he had given an accurate report of a certain sequence, when subsequent flights would often prove him wrong. One mistake in the build-up to supersonic flight could be disastrous.

The 108 programme was the most important and dangerous work that John was doing during 1948, but he was also involved continually with testing many other de Havilland aircraft. Some flights, which look innocuous enough on the bland pages of a log book, were in fact anything but routine.

'Tuft dives', for example, is the bald description of many flights in the log book's 'duty' column. One of the ways of determining airflow behaviour was to attach a series of wool tufts over specific parts of the aircraft and either carry an observer to watch their behaviour or photograph the results with a cine camera mounted on the airframe. This sounds a crude measure, but was in practice effective. It also shows that the scientists weren't always stuck behind their desks. On 11 March that year, de Havilland senior aerodynamicist John Wimpenny climbed into the cramped bubble canopy of a Hornet (TT202) and crouched there, observing the tufts, while John took it to its ceiling of about 45,000ft and then put it in a full power dive. When a Hornet reached high Mach numbers it made its feelings known rather differently from most aircraft; instead of going nose down, it went uncontrollably up which was almost as unpleasant.

That flight was in fact one of seven that Derry made that day in a total of four different aircraft: four in the 108, two in different Vampires and the Hornet tuft test. This would seem strange to a modern test pilot who is lucky if he becomes involved in the development of more than one particular type. The variety of flying that was done by test pilots in the early days of transonic flight is shown by an entry on a typical page of Derry's log book of 1948:

Aug 18	Vampire	VV219	Preston-Hatfield
Aug 18	108	VV120	Oscillations
Aug 18	Mosquito	VT652	Delivery
Aug 18	Vampire	VT818	Spinning
Aug 19	108	VW120	High MN Dives
Aug 19	Dove	G-ALBM	Climbs
Aug 19	Hornet	TT202	Dives
Aug 20	Vampire	VF345	Demonstration
Aug 20	108	VW120	High MN Dives
Aug 23	Vampire	VF345	Demonstration
Aug 23	Hornet	TT202	Rad flap check
Aug 23	Vampire	VT818	Spinning
Aug 24	Dove	G-ALBM	Photography
Aug 24	Vampire	VV190	From A&AEE
Aug 24	Vampire	VT818	SBAC practice
Aug 24	Consul	J2	Hatfield-Boscombe
Aug 25	Leopard	G-ACMA	Trim check
Aug 25	108	VW120	Oscillations
Aug 25	Vampire	VV217	Asymmetric fuel in drop tank
Aug 26	Dove	G-ALBM	CAA clearance
Aug 26	Vampire	VV190	Demonstration
Aug 26	108	VW120	High MN Dives
Aug 27	Vampire	VV217	To Lympne

John made two more flights on the 27th, one doing high Mach number dives in the 108 and, in complete contrast, spinning in a Chipmunk. The Vampire that he had flown to Lympne that day was to be entered for the high speed handicap races, an event that attracted a good crowd and that year promised to be a pretty noisy affair with a mixture of jets and piston-engine aircraft.

The handicap arrangements, however, proved to be rather unsatisfactory, with the organisers going to extremes to give the propeller types a chance against the jets. The result was that John's old friend and colleague from Supermarine, Les Colquhoun, flying another old friend, the Spitfire trainer G-AIDN, had little trouble in finishing well ahead of the opposition. Derry could only manage fourth place in his handicapped Vampire while ahead of him were John Cunningham (Vampire) and J.O. Matthews in a Fairey Firefly FR Mk IV, while behind John was Lettice Curtis in her blue Spitfire PR Mk XI. Guy Morgan from Supermarine in another Spitfire and Trevor 'Wimpy' Wade, chief test pilot of Hawker, in a Fury were also flying but were again heavily handicapped.

It was all very good fun, exciting for the spectators but also very dangerous for the competitors with the aircraft going flat out at low level and overtaking where they could, with no right-of-way rules laid down. With the dawning of the jet era the days of such races were numbered as it seemed as if they might develop into some form of disorganised suicide.

Within his first nine months at Hatfield John had gained himself quite a reputation in aviation circles and among the general public. But although his colleagues found him eager and willing to talk about aeroplanes anywhere and at any time, he was more reluctant to talk about himself and his job to newspapers or even friends at home. Regulars at his local, The Robin Hood in Rabley Heath, found he was diffident when asked about his work and contemporary newspaper reports about his achievements invariably give him the tag 'modest and unassuming' – which was how he must have appeared to reporters after his momentous flight on Monday 6 September 1948.

The morning dawned cloudless and warm and started in an innocuous enough way with Derry making a ten-minute check flight in a Ghost Vampire. Shortly afterwards he took off in another Vampire which he delivered to Farnborough for his demonstration at the SBAC display which was to start the following day – the first year it was held there.

At about ten o'clock that morning, the weather still fine and clear, he climbed into the cockpit of VW120, preparing for another high Mach number flight. Wearing a pressure waistcoat and oxygen mask, he took off and climbed into the deepening blue sky to 45,000ft. He was planning to take pressure plotting records with the trim flaps up and down at various Mach numbers, but first he intended to try to obtain further camera records at Mach 0.96 to match up with those of a previous flight.

Levelling off at 45,000ft, John opened the throttle and the Goblin's revolutions rose to 10,450 a minute. When he reached Mach 0.85 he pushed the stick forward and put the aeroplane into a 30-degree dive to gain speed. He was over the Windsor–Farnborough area and in the crystal clear weather could see the ground perfectly. The speed built up and at a Mach reading of 0.91 the nose heaviness set in, easing off at Mach 0.93 to be replaced by a wallowing motion. At 0.94 the 108 began a slight up and down pitching that was hard for him to handle, but nothing that he worried about. He watched the meter reach 0.95 and felt the nose heaviness return so he increased the engine speed from 10,600rpm to full throttle at 10,750 and found that the aircraft's speed did not increase. He also noted a feeling of high drag, so knowing that the only way to increase speed was to dive more steeply, he pushed the stick forward a little further, very cautiously, and saw that the speed built up to Mach 0.96. Very suddenly there was a strong nose down movement and a feeling of instability – but he carried on.

The dive steepened, the nose down pitching became more violent and more unstable with accelerations of up to minus 2g. He knew he could still pull out, so he decided to go a step further and he pushed the nose down even more.

The 108 took over. At 38,000ft the dive went beyond the vertical, pulling minus 3g as it did so and Derry felt that his eyeballs were bursting from his head. He was now hurtling earthwards at almost the speed of sound in an aircraft that was nearly out of control, the airflow a mass of shocks and forces against which the elevons were useless. Pulling hard on the stick, John managed to recover the 108 until the dive moderated at between 60 and 80 degrees, but the speed was still building up and at Mach 0.98 he was unable to hold it and again the aircraft went over the vertical, diving at well over a mile every six seconds and now quite beyond control. At these speeds the ground was less than a minute away and the aeroplane was going faster and faster.

Derry pulled back on the stick using all his strength with both hands – it was no use. He couldn't move it. At that moment he saw the Mach meter pass the magic Mach 1.0.

He was now flying faster than any British pilot had ever flown and his normal coolness had given way to some excitement; but he retained his ability to think and act rationally. As the needle edged round to the zero stop – approximately Mach 1.04 – Derry immediately shut off the throttle. It made no difference, the 108 still dived vertically at the speed of sound and the control column was still solid. So John turned to the last resort, the trim flaps, which he pulled up to their maximum. The aircraft responded almost immediately – either through the use of the flaps or because it had reached the lower, denser air – and began to pull out, but with little loss of speed.

Gradually, as the needle dropped to Mach 0.98, Derry found he could move the stick and at 23,500ft the 108 was flying straight and level at Mach 0.94. All seemed to be well but just as John thought that the drama was over, the un-damped pitching set up. He immediately put the trim flaps to zero and the movement stopped.

He then slowed down, climbed steadily back to 29,000ft and cruised back to Hatfield, wondering if the Machmeter had been accurate, if he really was the first British pilot to break the sound barrier. There was no way of telling for certain until the instrument was checked and any corrections made. Derry felt elated knowing that he had been working up to this moment and knowing that even if he had been able to check the wild dive, he would have gone on until he passed the speed of sound. The 'press on' spirit had taken over to achieve what was described at the time as the most significant step in aviation since the Wright brothers flew.

The whole flight had taken three quarters of an hour, the dive itself only about a minute. After landing, he taxied the 108 towards the hangar and left it in the hands of the waiting ground crew, saying nothing to them of his dive. Their immediate concern was with the state of the aircraft and John wanted to wait until the result was official.

When the instrument was corrected it was found that the true reading was Mach 1.02. Britain had a supersonic aircraft.

Derry's report to the design team was received with a good deal of enthusiasm. John Cunningham felt that maybe slightly too big a step had been taken too soon; Derry was lucky to have got the 108 down in one piece. John on the other hand, felt he was lucky to have got himself down in one piece. Later he drew a sketch, tracing the path of the 108 in its erratic dive and adding his comments on the situation at each stage.

The sketch ends with a drawing of a pale 108, beads of sweat dripping from it, as it finally flies straight and level after its alarming gyrations. If John was feeling like that himself, as he probably was, he never told anyone, least of all the Press. The day after he became the fastest man in Britain, John gave a brilliant performance in the Vampire, which he had taken to Farnborough just before his dramatic flight. His high-speed runs, loops and hesitation rolls had the crowds on their toes, although at this stage they did not know that this was Britain's first supersonic pilot.

Later that week the Ministry of Supply, satisfied that Derry had flown faster than sound, called a Press conference in London to announce the fact to the world. John wasn't a lover of that kind of meeting and when he appeared before the battery of reporters and photographers he became nervous and immediately lit up a cigarette.

He spoke quietly and briefly about the flight. Newspaper reports varied, but John undoubtedly played the whole thing down, making the flight seem less dramatic than it was. He didn't go beyond saying that he had a queer feeling in his stomach as the aeroplane approached Mach One and that the controls were very heavy. He described the flight as a 'routine job to get more records'.

The Press made much of it: 'The Bat Man Did it by Accident' was one heading, 'Bat' referring to the shape of the 108; 'I Heard Radio as I Beat Sound' headed an article by Basil Cardew of the *Daily Express* and referred to the fact that John had heard the conversations of other pilots during his dive, although he had not spoken himself.

'Visibility was very good when I flattened out,' he told Cardew, 'and the aircraft was going like a whizz-bang ... I found I was somewhere between Farnborough and Windsor and all I had to do then was pedal back to Hatfield.'

This epic flight did not, however, disturb the carefully controlled programme of pressure plotting and oscillation tests on the 108 and by mid-September Derry was again investigating the problems. At one stage he agreed to take part in an experiment, which, had it failed, would have led to disaster. Hydraulically operated friction dampers were fitted to lock the elevon control pulleys temporarily to see if the pitching was reduced. To some extent they were successful, but had they failed to unlock, all control would have been lost. The high Mach number dives went on and gradually facts emerged which threw new light on the impossibly high forces needed to move the control column – forces so high that on one occasion John bent the stick by exerting a desperate pull of at least 280lb. He thought this was because the power boosters, known as Servodynes, could not overcome the air pressure and shock waves at those speeds, but after a series of similar dives, he found that in fact the aircraft was diving vertically with the elevons fully up.

'This ineffectiveness of controls was not fully appreciated before,' he wrote in a flight report.

'Neither was the fact that the elevons can be pulled onto the stops at Mach 0.97. Originally it was thought that the prohibitive pull force at Mach 0.97 to Mach 1.04 was due to reaching the maximum power of the Servodyne to overcome the hinge moment. It is now obvious that during the dive to Mach 1.04, the elevons were in fact on the stops, so that the large stick force obtained is hardly surprising.'

He gave a lengthy written report of these dives, adding:

'A history of these runs is included to give a clear picture and in order to emphasise the true characteristics as opposed to those which were thought to be present from earlier work. This is interesting in that it lends power to the argument that first impressions are unreliable, particularly when compressed into a very short space of time, and therefore repetition of each characteristic, several times, is essential.'

Derry's first supersonic flight was not a freak occurrence: towards the end of February 1949 he had been making a further series of high Mach number dives and on 1 March had already made three such flights up to Mach 0.97 when he climbed the 108 over 40,000ft to make a fourth. As before, he set the trim flap to two degrees down and the dive progressed normally up to Mach 0.97. But then there was a sequence of sudden changes; the dive was a little steeper than the others and, as the stick was pulled back almost onto the stops, the Mach number increased to 0.98 and the nose down pitch set in. So, at Mach 0.99 John decided to pull out by using the trim flaps, but, just before he applied them, the dive steepened. He quickly set the flaps to the full 'up' position but nothing happened. He shut the throttle but the 108 carried on diving steeper and faster. There was now nothing he could do and for no apparent reason the aircraft began a slight roll to port. This steepened the dive so John, holding back hard on the column with both hands, put on full opposite aileron, which checked the roll a little. For a moment he thought that recovery from the 60-degree dive was near but suddenly the aeroplane rolled uncontrollably the other way, until after 90 degrees of roll and considerable negative g, he found himself in a vertical dive.

'There was absolutely no control at this point,' he reported afterwards 'and all the lateral control, which had been effective after all else, had now disappeared. What now happened is hard to believe – and indeed was so at the time – but every evolution of the aircraft was quite slow and could be followed and remembered clearly.'

The 108 dived beyond the vertical, pulling more and more negative g and the spiralling almost stopped. At this point with the throttle fully closed, it exceeded the speed of sound. Derry was still wrestling with the stick when the aeroplane completed the latter half of the bunt and then slowly rolled out until it was flying level in a much shallower dive.

The controls became effective again with such suddenness that Derry described it as a 'bump', and, as the aircraft began to climb with a speed still as high as Mach 0.98, the elevons and trim flaps began to respond. As on the first supersonic flight the pitch oscillation set up, this time at Mach 0.95, but it was slight and faded out as John reduced the trim flap.

'The remarkable dive was in many ways similar to that of 6 September 1948,' wrote Derry, 'but went a stage further, probably because the nose down pitch at Mach 0.98 occurred at a higher altitude.'

John saw the Machmeter go right off the calibrated scale but admitted, 'There was little time for watching instruments!'

Towards the end of his flight programme in the 108, Derry deduced that its comfortable limit was Mach 0.97, which could be reached in a 20 to 25-degree dive and if the dive angle was kept constant, then that speed would not be exceeded. 'If any further acceleration is allowed after the nose down pitch at Mach 0.99, the trim flaps become ineffective and a continuous increase in nose down pitch occurs as M increases without any method of control.'

Derry's deductions were remarkable at the time, for not only were the cockpit instruments very basic by today's sophisticated computer technology standards, but he was often noting and analysing a series of frightening events with the knowledge that his own safety was in jeopardy in an aircraft that, because of the limited understanding of transonic design, was woefully inadequate for the tasks it had to perform.

The test programme on the 108 came to a close in the summer of 1949 when de Havilland felt that they had learnt all that the revolutionary aeroplane had to show them. John shared the workload in the last few months with his number two, test pilot John Wilson, who had joined the firm in 1948. At the beginning of August the little craft was scheduled for what should have been its final moment of glory in Derry's hands.

It was entered for the SBAC Challenge Cup in the National Air Races at Elmdon Airport, Birmingham. Held over the Bank Holiday weekend, this was an enormously popular event and one of the most exciting races was for the Kemsley Trophy, for aircraft capable of more than 300mph. Neville Duke in the Hawker P1040 just managed to scorch ahead of Cunningham's Vampire 3 within the length of the aerodrome, both having left the piston-engined types way behind.

John was to take part in the Challenge Cup for jet aircraft and, as scratch man, looked a certain winner against 'Wimpy' Wade in the P1040 and Cunningham in the Vampire. But it was not to be; in the humid atmosphere the 108 looked impressive with vapour mists shimmering over the wings, but it was suffering from an unscheduled handicap – one of the undercarriage doors failed to retract and acted as an effective airbrake. It cost Derry, who came in last, the race, as the 108 undoubtedly had the best performance.

This was the last of the jet air races. The crowds loved them, but the pilots and organisers began to feel that they were a form of aerial madness.

On 19 August Derry made his final flight in VW120, a sedate ten-minute delivery run to Farnborough where, like the slow speed model TG283, it was handed over for further research work. But the days of both aircraft were numbered. Six months later VW120, working on a programme of longitudinal stability crashed, killing its pilot Squadron Leader Stewart Muller-Rowland DSO, DFC. The aircraft disintegrated at high speed and low level and although a lengthy investigation was carried out no fault was found. It appears that shortly before the flight Muller-Rowland had an argument with an officer and took off in anything but a calm frame of mind, climbing to high altitude. It seems that he had omitted to switch on the correct oxygen for that height and the aircraft broke up when it was out of control after he lost consciousness.

The following May, TG283 was destroyed, also killing its pilot, Squadron Leader Eric 'Jumbo' Genders AFC, DFM, who was carrying out a programme of stalling tests. He was flying at 8,500ft over Hartley Wintney in Hampshire when the aircraft apparently got into an inverted spin. He recovered from this, but a spin in the other direction started and although he deployed the anti-spin chutes, there was a problem in that one of them either did not deploy or failed to jettison. Genders decided to leave the aircraft, which was by now descending rapidly. But he could not push himself clear and was seen clinging to the outside of the cockpit as TG283 crashed into a field. Genders died instantly. A small cross in memory of Genders was nailed to a tree at the crash site. It is still there today.

No more 108s were built. A lot had been learnt from both prototypes and in particular from Derry's high-speed flying. The tailless jet had an incredible performance considering its low thrust, but by now opinion was hardening against tailless aircraft whose drag-saving assets were outweighed by the difficulties they encountered in the transonic regions.

Derry received a surprise award in 1948 when Prince Bernhardt of the Netherlands came to London to invest him with the Bronze Lion of the Netherlands for his part in the liberation of that country during the war; the following year he received one of the highest accolades the aviation world has to offer when he was rewarded for his work with the 108 by the Gold Medal of the Royal Aero Club. This coveted award, made for outstanding achievement in the air was presented because of his supersonic flight, but this must be seen as the culmination of the whole programme of dangerous and exacting work carried out in the DH108.

Chapter 7

LIKE A DREAM

'Paris to Cannes in 45 minutes! Three quarters of an hour!
It's like a dream.'
Nice Matin, April 1949

In 1947 a startling challenge was thrown open to aircraft companies and pilots worldwide – and it was the inspiration of a charming Frenchman who had a lifelong interest in aviators and aeroplanes.

Eddie Dissat, who had spent part of the war as Liaison Officer to the 101 Army Field Company, Royal Monmouths, and had been awarded the OBE for his work, was also the owner of a smart hotel in Cannes – the Montana. After the Allied landings in the South-East of France, most of the big hotels were used solely as rest centres for American military personnel. But Monsieur Dissat, an Anglophile and a man who was passionate about the pioneering role of flying, resolved that his hotel should be reserved for the sole use of British and Commonwealth pilots and crews. And so it was that from 1945 to early 1947 the Montana became the RAF rest centre.

As soon as the war was over, the aircraft companies' priorities switched from mass production to new development, especially as far as increased speeds were concerned. Air Marshal Sir John Boothman, concerned with boosting the speed of RAF aircraft, organised an attempt on the absolute world speed record by the new Gloster Meteor jet. The Meteor was to be piloted by Group Captain Teddy Donaldson, who was promised that if he broke the speed record he and his wife would be invited to spend a fortnight at the RAF rest centre in Cannes.

Eddie Dissat was thrilled at the idea, and although the Montana was no longer reserved for the RAF by the time the record was smashed by Donaldson, he invited him and his wife to stay as his guests for the two weeks. They became very friendly and spent many evenings discussing aircraft and high-speed flying, and when Donaldson was asked to fly the Meteor to Paris to demonstrate it at the Salon de l'Aéronautique during his stay, the germ of an idea came to M. Dissat.

'If you can fly that Meteor from Paris back here to Cannes in under one hour,' he told Teddy, 'I will donate a special prize.'

Gloster's man in Paris, a Mr Greenwood, heard of the challenge and suggested that the competition became official. So the Aéro Club de France and the Fédération Aéronautique Internationale became involved and a list of regulations was drawn up for the Coupe Montana, which was thrown open to the world in 1947. Donaldson never attempted the record in the end, as Cannes-Mandelieu airfield was reckoned to be too short for a jet to land. A lot of excitement was generated by the challenge, which seemed to hold a special attraction in that it wasn't a deadly serious world record attempt which could make or break an aeroplane, but it was officially recognised by the FAI, the body responsible for overseeing all world air records; the glamour of the film star city Cannes gave it an extra fillip and, while the promise of a good holiday at the Montana for the winning pilot plus a big cash prize offered by the town was a lure in itself, the worldwide publicity which the winning aircraft would attract was tempting for any forward-looking aircraft company.

But always there was the problem of Cannes-Mandelieu airfield, which was too short for a jet to land in safely. Yet no aircraft other than a jet could possibly fly the 432 miles from Paris in under an hour …

Months went past and the deadline for the end of the competition, Easter Sunday, 17 April 1949, drew near.

Around this time, de Havilland had just completed an agreement to the manufacture, under licence, of their Vampire Mk V and they were anxious to prove to the French public the wisdom of equipping the Armée de l'Air with the little jet in preference to several likely looking prototypes beginning to emerge from the French manufacturers. So, almost at the eleventh hour as far as the Montana challenge was concerned, they entered a standard Vampire Mk V (VV217) and asked Derry if he would pilot it.

Through much of March and the beginning of April, John had continued with the exhausting and concentrated 108 programme, often on the knife edge of safety, so the chance of a dash to sunny Cannes with the prospect of a free holiday in the South of France was tempting, and he jumped at the opportunity.

John thought things through carefully and plotted his flight meticulously. He knew that his navigation would have to be spot on because fuel margins would be low for the flight. His machine was loaned officially by the Ministry of Supply who, with the manufacturers, were the joint entrants in the challenge. The whole trip was organised and carried out in a sort of holiday spirit – a mood apart from the serious and important everyday business of test flying and aircraft manufacture.

The little Vampire left Manston on 7 April en route for Paris, and it was there long before John Cunningham arrived with Eve in the company's hack Dragon Rapide G-AHKA. With the following party went Frank Lloyd, de Havilland's sales representative, and Frank Reynolds, who was one of the firm's senior engineers. While they were in the air, the British Air Attaché in Paris, Air Vice-Marshal 'Bobby' George, was flying his Devon down to Cannes to greet Derry when he arrived.

Before the Rapide left, the weather closed in over the Channel and the North of France – and suddenly the flight decision was in Eve's hands:

'All the French airports are closing, Eve,' said Cunningham. 'It's up to you whether we take off.'

She could hardly back down:

'We go on,' she said.

After a rough and lurching flight through wind and rain they eventually arrived safely in Paris and headed for an evening out. Eve, whose French was very good, nudged her husband crossly when he kept asking for 'coffee with lait' – but then she reflected that perhaps his mind was on other things.

The holiday mood wore off somewhat for John the next day when he was faced with a frustrating wait at Le Bourget. Although the Vampire was a great attraction as far as sightseers and tourists at the busy airport were concerned, his take-off rated low in priority when there was so much civilian traffic to get off the ground. However, he was finally cleared for departure at 2.48pm and, levelling out at 25,000ft, he kept the Goblin turning at 10,000rpm.

Luck was with him in that the foul weather of the previous day had turned into a brisk tail wind and he soon found that he was passing landmarks on the route well ahead of the planned time, so he increased the revs to the maximum of 10,200 with little appreciable increase in the fuel consumption.

Eve and John Cunningham were still on the ground at Lyons when John flashed overhead, and from the clear skies over the Alps he was able to spot les Iles des Lerins, the twin islands off the coast of Cannes, eighty miles ahead. So he began his shallow descent and encountered the only bumpy air on the whole trip – the Vampire was shaken about so badly that he had to throttle back. But after a perfect landing, using only half the runway that was believed to be too short for jets, he stepped out to hear his time of 44 minutes 51 seconds – an average of 580mph.

'Le Blond' English pilot was already something of a hero in France. His needle-sharp aerobatic displays at air shows had found a following among the aviation enthusiasts who were doubly impressed by his tall good looks and easy manner. The French used the phrase 'le Derry turn' for the impressive low level reverse turn which he introduced and which few pilots could copy neatly. His tight low level turn followed by a roll underneath and an equally tight turn in the opposite direction excited admiration at any air display. So there was quite a crowd of admirers gathered on the small Cannes airfield to watch John step out of the cockpit.

'Poor Jules Verne . . . where are you now? . . . all that you foresaw has been more than fulfilled – even those things which seemed the most unlikely and far-fetched. Paris to Cannes in 45 minutes! Three-quarters of an hour! It's like a dream,' enthused the French Press.

John, climbing out of his flying overalls, posed for photographs in front of the Vampire, looking cheerful and unruffled in a lounge suit – for all the world as if he'd just enjoyed a leisurely drive to Cannes in a comfortable car rather than a near-600mph dash in a cramped cockpit. Grouped around him were the Mayor of Cannes looking both roguish and Gallic in an enormous beret and a flamboyant white beard, Colonel Duperier, vice-president of the Aéro Club de France, Air Vice-Marshal 'Bobby' George, who had also taken advantage of the brisk following wind to reach Cannes before schedule in his Devon, Eddie Dissat and his wife, and Frank Lloyd, who by now had arrived with Eve and John Cunningham in the trusty Rapide.

In fact John disliked having his photograph taken; many hastily snapped shots show him caught with his eyes closed as he blinked at the wrong moment, and with his hands clasped uneasily as if he were willing the photographer to hurry up and finish. So it was probably with some relief that he joined the party heading for the airfield bar where a local personality, Monsieur Leopold, offered him celebratory champagne. And that champagne set the scene for the next ten days when John and Eve were feted and feasted along the Riviera coast.

John Cunningham took a break from his own arduous testing programme as he relaxed in Cannes with the Derrys before he flew the Vampire back to Hatfield, leaving the Rapide for John and Eve to come back in at the end of their stay. But before the record-breaking aircraft was taken home to England, John Derry enthralled spectators up and down the coast as he demonstrated its aerobatic qualities. These demonstrations obviously made a deep impression; one of the startled onlookers sent home this report to the *de Havilland Gazette*:

'A party was arranged at midday on the terrace of the Carlton Hotel. Derry flew inland and then turned in the direction of the sea and dived between the two towers on the corners on the front parade of the Carlton. He thus arrived absolutely without warning, making waiters drop glasses, and a poor old sleepy horse drawing a cab along the Croisette, looking as though he hadn't been able to get out of a slow ambling walk for the past twenty years, disappeared in the direction of Palm Beach at a cracking gallop.'

When John wasn't entertaining the guests at the dozens of parties that were organised in his honour, by his breathtaking aerobatic displays, he was always the unconscious centre of attention at the party itself. His height and his blond hair made him stand out in any crowd – but there was something more to it. Film star Ann Todd, who was to know him when he did much of the flying and gave technical advice on the set of *The Sound Barrier*, the award-winning film in which she starred, was intrigued by the unusual quality he possessed which drew people to him.

'I saw it as a gold light around him,' she would say. 'He always had that; a sort of inner strength. He was such fun, but without being obtrusive or loud in any way. He "lifted" people when he came in a room with them.'

Another friend of John's, one of de Havilland's top men in Canada, Russ Bannock, also admired this quality in John: 'His personality was effervescent but gentle – he literally stood out in a room of people soon after he had anything to say. It was always a delight to be in his company.'

Most of Cannes clearly felt the same way.

John and Eve, staying at the Montana, found themselves gazing longingly at the beautiful sandy beach, only a stone's throw away, but so many parties and outings were organised for them that they didn't get the chance to slip away and sun themselves.

Monsieur Antoni, the Mayor of Cannes, gave an official reception where John was handed a cheque for 100,000 francs, which was the prize money from the City. This money in fact melted away back into Cannes in just a few hours when John and Eve decided to spend it on a cocktail party for everyone who had entertained them so royally. They were also asked to sign the Register giving them the Freedom of Cannes. John signed perfectly, but Eve managed to drop an enormous blot on the hitherto unsullied pages of the impressive-looking book.

'You've certainly made your mark here,' observed John, grinning at her.

The enormous trophy, a large swooping bird with long, thin albatross-like wings and a divided swallow tail, diving over the foaming crest of a wave, was officially presented to John at an evening Gala in the Salle des Ambassadeurs. Eve had been rushed away that afternoon, first to the hairdresser and then to the salon of top dress designer Maggy Rouff, where a variety of evening gowns were paraded in front of her and she was told that she could have whichever one she wanted. Luckily she was tall and slim like the models in the salon, and so no alterations had to be made to the dress she chose.

At the presentation John met inventor Robert Esnault-Pelterie and Monsieur Pescara, who produced autogyros in Cannes. Monsieur Esnault-Pelterie invited John to visit his works, and the enormous factory, filled with rows of the weird spidery-looking machines, silent in the dim light, was an eerie sight.

Another local celebrity who was pleased to meet John and to watch his thrilling aerobatic display was the widow of pioneer aviator Louis Blériot. Madame Blériot was a sprightly, stately old lady who described her husband's epic flight across the Channel in 1909 and talked with interest and authority on modern aviation.

Some of the entertaining was on a very grand scale indeed. One party at a cliff-side mansion was memorable for the gold plates off which everyone ate, and the sumptuous food and wine. Everything was very gracious, but John began to feel restless when Eve went to look for the cloakroom – and didn't come back.

He was beginning to worry when she finally turned up, looking a little flustered.

She explained that the enormous room had been opulently decorated and panelled in sparkling glass. The trouble was that once inside with the door shut, she had been unable to work out how to get out – all the walls looked the same and there was no apparent door handle. She spent a long time finding a catch to slide the right panel back.

Before John Cunningham took the Vampire back to Hatfield, he and John were asked if they would like to try some aqualung diving from the Ile St Honorat. This island is the home of a very ancient abbey, which was the starting point for the journey fifteen centuries ago of Saint Patrick as he travelled to convert the uncivilised Saxons in the British Isles. The two visiting Saxons jumped at the chance of enjoying the warm Riviera waters and, with borrowed gear and a host of eager instructors, they managed extremely well. The water was crystal clear and, as they swam and dived, they encountered hundreds of interesting small fish and other sea creatures. Both Cunningham and Derry were so enthusiastic about this sport that was new to both of them that they resolved to start it up in England when they returned. But the colder, murkier waters around the British Isles put paid to their idea of forming a sub-aqua club!

The ten days flew by all too quickly, and on 22 April Derry's log book shows that 'Mrs Derry' was his passenger in the Dragon Rapide back to Hatfield from Cannes. The flight took nearly six hours and when they landed in England to clear Customs, they were dismayed to find the Excise men, after practically taking the aeroplane apart, demanding a large sum of money as duty payable on all the gifts and presents which had been showered on them in Cannes and which they had brought back. At least, Eve was dismayed – John, normally slow to anger, was furious:

'All right, you can keep the lot!' he told nonplussed officials as he strode away from the Rapide. But suddenly it was decided that the Derrys could, after all, keep the French presents – many of them gifts for Carol and Jo – and Eve and John flew on to Hatfield after an otherwise uneventful trip.

Once back at de Havilland, work carried on with the programme of high Mach number dives in the 108 and similar tests on Vampires. Despite the importance of all the aircraft and the urgency of the programme in view of fierce competition from other manufacturers, there was still time to give members of the ground staff the occasional 'joy ride'. Eddie Short, who had spent most of his working life at de Havilland (now BAE Systems) was then a member of the Flight Shed personnel and one of the many young men working on the ground who regarded Derry, with his friendly manner and infectious smile, with a great deal of admiration and respect. Like most of the young men at Hatfield, Eddie was passionately interested in the machines on which he worked and was always eager for a flight if the opportunity arose.

Derry had an ease of manner and the type of frank nature that made all of the men at Hatfield feel that there was no difficulty in communicating with him. They appreciated the little courtesies which John, unlike a lot of test pilots, was careful to observe, such as letting them know when he would be ready for the aeroplane so that they weren't kept hanging around in the cold for hours waiting for him. And a flight with him, which he never refused them if at all possible, was always memorable.

One day, Eddie Short went up in a two-seater Venom with Derry at the controls, and during the flight Eddie remarked that it didn't seem an easy aeroplane to leave in a hurry. John looked very serious as he told Eddie:

'If anything looks like going wrong, you'll be the first to leave. I'll see to that with no difficulty.'

These joy rides were a departure from the usual work, which, though never routine, followed a careful pattern and programme. Obviously the biggest part by far of a test pilot's job was to find out as much as possible about the machines that his company was producing and to iron out any problems before they went into service. But a large part of the selling of those aeroplanes also fell to Derry. Buyers such as military chiefs or heads of state looking for replacements for their armed forces would often be treated to private displays or invited as special guests to the big public shows. At Hatfield, John was nearly always the man who showed off the capabilities of de Havilland's military aircraft.

There were several demonstrations each month, including, of course, the climax of the year as far as displays went at the prestigious Society of British Aircraft Constructors' show at Farnborough.

John's log books for 1949 show that he displayed various Vampires during the year, including the by now well known VV217, and there was a scorching show given to RAF personnel at West Raynham in one of their own machines. He also demonstrated the high-speed 108 to the King of Siam in August, gave shows in the Chipmunk, which was still sought after as far as buyers were concerned, and in September at Farnborough he delighted the crowds with his tightly controlled displays in the prototype Venom, VV612, which had made its first flight only a few days before.

By now he was acknowledged to be one of the country's top demonstration pilots, and over the next year or so the number one position in that field was indubitably his. But showing off an aeroplane wasn't a task that he undertook lightly.

His own serious approach to demonstration flying echoes the deeply held views of one of his mentors, his former boss, Jeffrey Quill, at the time in charge of the programme at the Supermarine Experimental Flight Test. Quill, who had had many young pilots through his hands, had realised with a touch of delight as he watched John's flying in the early days that here was a first-rate natural aerobatic and demonstration pilot. He knew that few people had this ability naturally, even though they might be skilful, meticulous and reliable in the normal course of their duties as test pilots.

Quill felt strongly that a good demonstration pilot will show off the aeroplane rather than himself.

'Aeroplanes need to be demonstrated in such a way that it

becomes apparent to the watchers that the aeroplane is likely to be excellent at the job for which it was designed, but at the same time the demonstration must present a pleasant, interesting and preferably elegant spectacle for the assembled company.

'Obviously the task differs greatly between demonstrating a very large and heavy transport aeroplane and a high performance fighter. There is nothing more sadly ridiculous than pilots trying to throw large transport or bomber aircraft around the sky as if they were overgrown fighters. It is somewhat analogous to a twenty stone ballerina trying to dance "Giselle".'

Quill, who insisted that a demonstration pilot must above all be a professional in his approach to this type of flying, pointed out that showing off fighters was a quite different matter:

'And obviously easier to demonstrate provided you really know how to fly it. You must demonstrate its great speed, its great rate of climb, manoeuvrability and general agility. The demonstration must be exciting but not dangerous. If it is practical, the aeroplane should at some point pass in front of the crowd at the maximum absolute airspeed at which it can safely be flown near the ground; at some point it should rocket skywards to underline its climb potential; its low speed handling should be demonstrated. It is not possible in public to demonstrate its fire power, nor range, nor certain other military factors, so they can be left to the commentator to deal with, but its agility and control can be demonstrated by a carefully planned programme of aerobatics which, if accurately and prettily executed, will delight any crowd.'

As Jeffrey Quill was probably the man who first recognised John's excellence at this type of flying, it is not surprising that the two of them had similar views on the way a demonstration pilot should approach his work. Both men felt that 'cowboy' type flying was to be deplored and could do nothing but harm the industry.

Quill had some tart thought about pilots who tried to show off:

'What is unforgivable, and was at one time all too prevalent, is if pilots use public or semi-public occasions and highly important aeroplanes to try to demonstrate their own daring. I saw too many people roll or loop themselves into the ground, and still more very nearly do it, and I became bitterly hostile towards the slightest lack of professionalism in demonstration flying.'

But he recognised in John Derry a pilot who became a real professional in this matter:

'Always exciting, always elegant and very often highly original in devising his programme, he performed the classic manoeuvres accurately and smoothly and above all safely, and so was a pleasure to watch. His aim was to leave the audience saying, "Phew, what an aeroplane". He wasn't trying to make a public reputation for himself, only for his aircraft, and so was doing one important aspect of his work superbly well.'

Derry summed up his entire approach to this part of his work in an article that he wrote for *Aeronautics* in 1952. He and Quill, not surprisingly in view of their earlier working relationship, shared the same beliefs about a good pilot's approach to entertaining and informing his audience, and Derry felt that the proportions – that is of entertainment and information – should vary as the pilot considered the type of audience.

He knew that he was flying for a variety of types:

'There are the people who go to judge the show with a critical and experienced eye,' he wrote. 'There are those who, though not connected with aircraft, get genuine enjoyment and excitement from the sight of polished formation aerobatics or the erupting passage of a high speed prototype.'

He wrote with some regret of 'those who go because they consider these as circus acts with no safety net'.

Derry was wise enough to realise the folly of arrogance on the pilot's part: '… the Bohemian attitude of "if they don't like it, it's because they don't understand it" will result in failure as far as display value goes.'

In his article, 'Analysing the Art of the Demonstration Pilot', Derry told his readers what to look for when judging a display. He concentrated on what he felt was the most popular item (and the one, of course, which he was most used to displaying) – the high-speed fighter, and he discussed first of all the value of the pure high-speed fly-past and then the importance of aerobatic manoeuvres:

'In a show lasting five or six minutes, the pilot cannot waste any time and if he wishes to include some aerobatics it may profit him to make his fast run as part of this sequence. The way this is done can give a very good idea of the aircraft's acceleration. On the other hand, if the pilot considers it of sufficient importance to get the absolute maximum speed of his aircraft, he may deem it worth giving away one or two minutes to achieving an accurate run-in . . .

'Consider, therefore, whether the pilot has made the best use of his acceleration (and deceleration) or, if neglecting it, he has gained in other directions.'

Derry acknowledged the value of the high-speed fly-past as pure spectacle and he knew how the experienced pilot should make his arrival as effective as possible:

'. . . the attitude of the aircraft, the direction of the run, use of a following wind (this is surprisingly effective), unexpected arrival, and use of trees and buildings as a backcloth to give the maximum relative motion, are all points which are within the pilot's control and can contribute towards making his run the most impressive, even though the competition in speed may be close.'

Aerobatics were in some part a measure of a fighter's powers of manoeuvrability, Derry wrote, and he pointed out that the sequence should be carried out smoothly:

'Too often each run over the crowd is punctuated by a pause and rush, rather like a short-winded bowler who takes a very long run.

'In a good display the aircraft is not performing a series of separate manoeuvres but one continual action, which holds the attention from beginning to end.'

Towards the end of his article he has a word of admonishment for those who want to see a perilous-looking display:

'Perhaps the most difficult decision a pilot has to make is how to carry out his various antics. There may be some who prefer a dangerous looking show, but the best advice to these people is to stick to the fairground. Air displays, or at any rate demonstrations of different types of aircraft, are not intended to appear hazardous. An individual item which looks unsafe is usually badly executed and is often less safe than one at a lower height but skilfully directed.'

Like Quill, Derry felt that while people who went to see air displays should be entertained and informed, the main point of each individual demonstration was to show off the character and the virtues of each particular aircraft being shown. You must ask yourself, he said:

'Has the pilot given you the best demonstration, under the circumstances, of the aircraft's character? That is: speed and crispness in a fighter; smooth, effortless and, if possible, silent flight in a transport; docile obedience in a trainer.'

The only possible answer to that question in the case of John's 1949 SBAC display at Farnborough with the new Venom was 'yes'. Piloted by Derry, VV612 had only gone on its maiden flight four days before the show's opening and in the short time available he made no less than nine flights – de Havilland were not going to miss the chance of showing off their new machine, which was a development of the Vampire, and they wanted it to put in enough flying hours to be allowed to give a full display.

And it did. From the moment John took off from the Farnborough runway, the crowds were riveted by its performance. Most pilots would take off and accelerate away towards Laffan's Plain before coming round to give their display. But not John: as soon as the Venom left the ground, in a remarkably short length of runway, he kept the throttle wide open and pulled the aircraft straight up into a loop, rolling off the top right in front of the spectators. It was as unexpected as it was spectacular, and his display carried on with the same verve, the huge crowds gasping at his aerobatics – especially his inverted reverse turns. This manoeuvre, which had become known as The Derry Turn, was now a hallmark of his displays – and again it was the surprise element that made it so effective, coupled with John's absolute precision and timing.

But equally spectacular, and still talked about today, was his slow roll, executed over the length of the runway in front of the spectators. To those who knew anything about aircraft, this was the high spot of his display, for it is a most difficult manoeuvre and one which few pilots can carry out without letting the nose drop at some point. As John wrote in his article:

'A very high rate of roll masks any inaccuracies; little or no co-ordination is required. The original slow roll is still one of the most difficult aerobatics. Success is due in some part to the aircraft's qualities, but more to the pilot. Remember, a slow roll is carried out from first to last in level flight, requiring co-ordination of all three control surfaces.'

But an example of what could go wrong, even in the surest and most experienced hands, was given by Neville Duke – unintentionally, of course – in the Hawker P1040, prototype of the elegant Sea Hawk naval jet fighter, an aircraft which Duke always found a delightful machine to fly. He was making a spectacular low-level inverted flight in front of the crowd, but in concentrating on keeping the nose well up made what he admitted was an error, and he suddenly became aware that the test pilots' tent was getting uncomfortably close. The test pilots and their wives became aware of a similar feeling about Neville, and it was only by a spot of quick thinking that he slammed the stick forward to bring the nose up, kicked over on opposite rudder and rolled out, leaving a gaggle of pallid faces in his vortices. It was the closest view they had ever had of the top of an aircraft while it was flying.

One of John's display specialities was the vertical roll, which he performed in the Venom. He was the leading exponent of this manoeuvre in jet fighters, and possibly the instigator, for it is a far more difficult sequence than spectators may realise:

'For a modern jet aircraft it is almost certainly true that the control co-ordination is less exacting than in a low-powered biplane, but it is equally true that the line and accuracy of any aerobatic is much harder to achieve when sitting in the very front of the aircraft with no reference point except a short sloping nose cowling, which is sometimes liable to be more misleading than helpful. For this reason there is a greater difference than meets the eye between an upward roll in a 45-degree climb and the seldom witnessed vertical roll, which deprives the pilot of any reference point and requires a much finer sense of timing.'

John also demonstrated the slow speed qualities of the Venom as well as its acceleration, high speed and manoeuvrability. Looking rather like an aggressive insect darting about the sky, it was admirably suited to his crisp and polished flying.

Obviously no test pilot could claim that demonstration work was the most important part of his job, but it did give the general public and more importantly, the big military buyers, a good idea of the machines – and, incidentally, a vivid interest in the men who flew them.

In those post-war years there was a generally rapid development in the aircraft industry, hastened by the wartime work on the jet engine, and the men who risked their lives (more than thirty test pilots lost their lives in their machines in the first six years after the war) became famous through the developments that were part of their work. Derry, Duke, Lithgow, Cunningham, Wade and Waterton often made the headlines as speed records were pushed forward and machines designed to nibble away at the sound barrier were produced. Derry was aware of this as a responsibility but could not understand that his exploits should be recognised as anything particularly brilliant. He often told Eve that he felt his job was something that many people could be capable of doing and he seemed genuinely surprised when he was congratulated for something that was, for him, simply part of his work.

Aeroplanes and everything to do with them came first with him – or perhaps it would be fairer to say that they came first jointly with his family. Eve and the girls were just as important as they had been in the very early days and he took the responsibilities of

The record is set, the sun is sinking: John and Eve Derry leave Hatfield for their home at Rabley Heath after John captures the 100km closed circuit record.
(BAE SYSTEMS)

Ground crew at work on VW120. (Aeroplane Monthly Archive)

Year		AIRCRAFT		Pilot, or	2nd Pilot, Pupil	DUTY
1948		Type	No.	1st Pilot	or Passenger	(Including Results and Remarks)
Month	Date					
—	—	—	—	—	—	——— Totals Brought Forward
	6	108	VW120	*Self*		First flight M = 1·0
	7	Vampire	VV219	"		SBAC Show

John Derry's log book.

Mach meter calibration after Derry's first supersonic flight.

form 23	○	MEMO	○ File		
From.......*J.d.dy*...... To..*aerodynamics*.... Date *14·9·48*					
Copy to..*aero flight test*					

CALIBRATION

MACH METER IN C/P DH 108 VW120.
FOR FLIGHT ON 6/1/68 ONLY.

True "M." No	INST READING	CORRECTION	HEIGHT
1·020	1·04	— ·020	30,000 FT

K.Rudle.

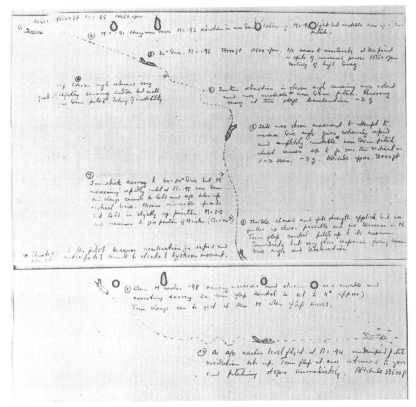

Notes from the sketch made by John Derry after his first supersonic flight in the DH108, 6 September 1948

1. *Level, 45,000ft, M=.85, 10,450rpm.*
2. *M=.91, strong nose down. M=.93, reduction in nose down. Wallowing. M=.94, slight but unstable nose up and down pitch.*
3. *30 degree dive. M=.95, 39,000ft, 10,600rpm. A/C ceases to accelerate at this point in spite of increased power. 10,750rpm. Feeling of high drag.*
4. *Up elevon angle reduced very gradually causing sudden but small nose down pitch. Feeling of instability.*
5. *Further reduction in elevon angle causing more violent and more unstable* nose down pitch. Recovery easy at this stage. Acceleration -2g.*
6. *Still more elevon movement to attempt to increase dive angle gives extremely rapid and completely unstable* nose down pitch which causes a/c to go over the vertical in 1-2 secs. -3g. Altitude approximately 38,000ft.*
7. *Immediate recovery to 60-80 degree dive but M increasing rapidly until at M=.98 nose down trim change cannot be held and a/c takes up vertical dive. Elevons immovable upwards but held in slightly up position. M=1.0 and increases to zero position of Machmeter (M=1.04?)*
8. *Throttle closed and full strength applied but no further up elevon possible and no decrease in M. Trim flap control pulled up to its maximum. Immediate but very slow response giving decreasing dive angle and deceleration.*
9. *When M reaches .98 recovery increases and elevons now movable and assisting recovery so trim flap control is set to 4 degrees (approx). Trim change can be felt at this M when flap moves.*
10. *As a/c reaches level flight at M=.94 undamped pitch oscillation sets up. Trim flap at once returned to zero and pitching stops immediately. Altitude 23,500ft.*

* Unstable to the pilot because acceleration is rapid and even when anticipated cannot be checked by elevon movement.

Left: Derry enthralls spectators with a demonstration of the Vampire, an aircraft in which he displayed his mastery of his own 'Derry Turn', a dramatic manoeuvre still widely used in air shows today. (Aeroplane Monthly Archive)

OPPOSITE:
Top:Derry climbs into the cockpit of the prototype Venom (VV612) for its maiden flight in September 1949. Watching him is Sid Parsons, Experimental Department foreman. (BAE SYSTEMS)

Centre left: A fine study of Derry in the Vampire. (BAE SYSTEMS)

Centre right: It wasn't always serious: John in festive role on Christmas Eve, 1948, when he loaded a Mosquito with presents and distributed them to various airfields. (BAE SYSTEMS)

Bottom: The glamorous side of it: John chats with film star Joan Fontaine in Cannes after winning the Montana Cup in Vampire VV217. (BAE SYSTEMS)

Above: Derry brings the prototype
Venom (VV612) in low for a dramatic
flypast. (BAE SYSTEMS)

Left: An atmospheric view of the
Venom. (Aeroplane Monthly Archive)

Bottom left: Derry brings Vampire FB5
(VV217) in for a close-up.
(Aeroplane Monthly Archive)

Opposite top: Construction of the
prototype DH110 (WG236) well
under way at Hatfield in 1951.
(BAE SYSTEMS)

Opposite bottom: The cockpit of the
first 110 prototype as the aircraft nears
completion in the Hatfield factory.
(BAE SYSTEMS)

The first 110 prototype after roll-out at Hatfield. (BAE SYSTEMS)

Two Rolls-Royce Avon RA3 engines at close quarters were deafening. Derry (left) plugs his ears as the prototype WG236 has its first engine run. (BAE SYSTEMS)

fatherhood seriously, thoroughly enjoying his games with the children and taking them, especially Carol who was old enough to appreciate a good outing, riding, swimming – and even flying.

Other breaks from the day-to-day testing programme came when aircraft had to be delivered abroad. The Vampire was one of de Havilland's biggest successes, especially as far as the export market was concerned, and this aircraft in its various roles of ground attack, interceptor, night fighter and carrier-based naval fighter was widely used not only by the RAF and Royal Navy, but also by the air forces of many other countries, including Italy, France, South Africa, Australia, Norway, Egypt, Switzerland, Canada, Sweden, India and Venezuela. In 1949 John wrote to his brother Hugh, who was then at Plymouth, and mentions a delivery trip:

'I often look down on Plymouth from 30 or 40,000ft, but that is about as close as I get!

'We are in the process of delivering a batch of Vampires to Switzerland, so every month or so I get a day or two around Lucerne. The last trip was magnificent, snow having fallen recently on the high ground. We drove into the mountains during our one-day stay and had some really magnificent views. Sometimes when approaching the Alps at 30,000ft or so we can see the whole range from France to Austria. It is a worthwhile sight.'

What he didn't say to Hugh was that although the trips to Switzerland were fun and looked forward to by all the pilots (who brought back as many Swiss goodies as possible to England which was still in the throes of post-war shortages) the navigation had to be perfectly accurate as the mountain ranges could make flying hazardous, and on the approach descent the canopy would often mist up completely and then ice up to such an extent that the pilot had to scrape the ice off with his fingers before he could see anything. There wasn't a lot of fuel left after landing, either – often only thirty or forty gallons, which was barely enough to cover the bottom of the tanks.

However, the British pilots made the most of their day's leave in the Alps and some of the younger ones would head for the bright lights as soon as they checked in at their hotels. This worried John Cunningham, who felt himself responsible for his colleagues, and on one occasion 'Fifi' Fifield, by then a production test pilot with de Havilland, and others, including Chris Beaumont and Geoffrey 'Iser' Pike (nicknamed thus because of his habit of invariably beginning a sentence with the words 'I suggest') were on the point of heading for town when they were checked by a gently frowning Cunningham who chided:

'Now, chaps – no beastliness!'

In another letter to Hugh, John tells of his enthusiasm for his work and the variety that it afforded him:

'We are very busy here and look like continuing that way through the year. It is a fascinating job, which, by its ever-changing nature, never permits one to be bored or to have too much to do.'

That was written in 1952 after John and some other test pilots, including his old friend Les Colquhoun, his colleague John Wilson, and Mike Lithgow and Dave Morgan from Supermarine, had all experienced a taste of a very different sort of life – that of the film world.

The news of John's first supersonic flight in 1948 wasn't announced dramatically to an awaiting world. In a way, the newspaper stories echoed the achievement itself: the breakthrough had come as a result of months of patient and dangerous work, not as a sudden perfect act. Gradually, supersonic flight was developed and the public heard about aeroplanes such as Hawker's Hunter, the Javelin from Gloster, the Supermarine Swift and, of course, de Havilland's 110, all of which could fly faster than sound in a shallow dive.

Writers and film makers sensed the behind-the-scenes dramas that would surely have box office appeal to a public eager to be told about the struggles behind the facts of supersonic flight, and in 1951 Alexander Korda directed the award-winning film *The Sound Barrier* which was produced by David Lean and had an all-star cast which included Ann Todd, Ralph Richardson, Dinah Sheridan, Nigel Patrick and John Justin.

David Lean, not unnaturally, turned to de Havilland to ask for technical advice, so that the scenes showing the struggle to go through the 'barrier' would not put across a totally false image in the minds of a public ready to believe the embroidery of a writer's imagination rather than the hard facts. And de Havilland, again not unnaturally, sent him to see John Derry who was, after all, the first man in this country to have encountered the problems successfully.

Alexander Korda and David Lean were determined that the film should be made properly. All the flying was done by de Havilland and Supermarine pilots – Derry and Wilson from de Havilland flew a two-seater Vampire and Mike Lithgow, Les Colquhoun and Dave Morgan flew the 535 Swift (VV119) called, more dramatically, the 'Prometheus' in the film, of which it was really the star. It was a development from the original 510, which was a swept wing Attacker, but this later version had a longer nose and a tricycle undercarriage.

Looking back, the film featured superb air-to-air photography under the direction of Jack Hildyard, and without any of the tricks that are so often used now. None of the sequences employed model aircraft and the flying from five of the country's top test pilots gave it a rare authenticity. Although most of the sequences were shot at around 5,000ft, the use of infrared film made the aircraft appear like a piece of quicksilver against an inky black sky, giving the illusion of much greater height. Supermarine test pilot, the late Dave Morgan, who did some of the flying for the film, later described the effect as 'absolutely electric' and said this was just how things appeared at 40,000ft.

The technical problems were not so easily dealt with, though. Studio shots showing the buffeting experienced by pilots in some aircraft at transonic speeds were not easy to make realistically, and John spent many hours at the studios at Denham going over and over the sequence with actors trying to make the motion authentic.

Terence Rattigan wrote the script and, while John's technical advice was followed as far as the behaviour of the aircraft was concerned, he obviously had no influence on the actions and reactions of the characters in the story. He often doubted very much whether he or other test pilots and their wives would react as the film demanded and would take his copy of the script home as bedtime reading and lie there shaking with laughter.

There was a point in the film where the breakthrough, the defeat of 'the sound barrier', had to come. John knew, as all test pilots knew, that there was no simple solution, no one action that could suddenly and magically push a buffeting aircraft smoothly through Mach One. But the film makers sacrificed authenticity to achieve dramatic effect at this point and they made their hero suddenly pull his out of control aeroplane out of its supersonic dive by desperately reversing the controls – in other words, pushing the stick forwards instead of pulling it back.

This was discussed and debated beforehand and dismissed scornfully afterwards by some people involved in the aircraft industry. But looking back at the whole film as a reflection of the spirit of the time as far as the pioneering soul of the aeroplane business was concerned, and of the awareness of the dangers faced by those test pilots, it must be counted a success.

But, despite the more dramatic aspects of the story, John and the other test pilots enjoyed their foray into the make-believe world of the film industry.

And, for their part, the actresses and actors relished the experience of working with people whose day-to-day life bore a tinge of the drama akin to their own world, but with a reality that was difficult to approach.

Ann Todd found the excitement of working at Chilbolton and Hatfield aerodromes, where experimental projects meant that there was a certain amount of necessary secrecy and security, heightened the general atmosphere of the film. And, like all the people who came into contact with John, she thoroughly enjoyed his company and respected his experience. When the filming was over, John, typically generous, went to a London jeweller and had a little gold Vampire, with a tiny ruby representing its starboard light, made. He gave it to Ann Todd for her charm bracelet.

There was much celebration as the London première of *The Sound Barrier* drew near and a big party was given after the first showing. The test pilots and their wives all went. Jane Wilson, the talented young wife of John's colleague John Wilson, danced with David Lean and gently took him to task over the way the test pilots were portrayed in the film.

'We don't really live like that,' she told him. 'Come to dinner and we'll show you.'

To her great surprise, he eagerly accepted the invitation and he and Ann Todd, who was then married to him, duly turned up to dinner. John was there, but Eve had to miss the party as she was ill. Halfway through the meal, made hilarious by David Lean's light-hearted banter and John's high spirits, there was a desperate banging on the door. John Wilson went to open it and there stood a young woman, dripping blood and crying, saying that she had been attacked in the lane. The police were called and the girl tended – but David Lean, who very much enjoyed the evening, could never be quite persuaded that the whole affair hadn't been cleverly stage-managed for his benefit.

Footnote: Vampire VV217, in which Derry won the Coupe Montana Trophy, has been preserved and is stored at the North East Aircraft Museum in Sunderland.

Chapter 8

NEW TERRITORIES OF SPEED

'It is through the hard school of research and development and,
later, operational flying, that the new territories of speed
can be made safe and comfortable for all.'
John Derry, *Times Survey of British Aviation*, September 1952.

'**D**ear Hugh,' John wrote to his brother in January 1950, 'Many thanks for the delightful book on John Constable. The reproductions have impressed me so much that I am going to mount and frame two or three of them for the home.'

All the Derrys shared a strong interest in art or literature and, although John was never a great reader, he had always enjoyed drawing and sketching. Wildlife was his favourite subject and when he took up scraperboard sketching he found it not only a relaxing pastime but also a rewarding one. One of his first efforts was of an inquisitive badger in the woods at Meadfield and he sent a print of it, together with some other scenes, as a Christmas card to Hugh:

'I'm glad you liked the Christmas card. It was a change to make one's own, and rather fun. I did these as four different pictures all printed from scraperboard drawings, which I have been playing with in my spare time recently. It is particularly suited to bird sketches, which I am keen to master in time.'

As with the sketches that followed, John had paid particular attention to detail, capturing the delicacy of the ferns and bracken, and he later made many bird scenes in which he tried, with a fair measure of success, to give an accurate portrayal of their individual flight characteristics.

The solitary hours in the woods and fields and the relaxation of transferring the scenes to his scraperboards was a pleasant contrast to the stresses of test flying and he would carry on with his hobby at home, endlessly sketching the dogs, Chips, Daxy and Rover, whenever they would sit still long enough. On 22 May, Eve's birthday, there was a new addition to the animal faction for him to sketch. John had risen early for a morning walk with the dogs in Knebworth Park, leaving Eve tucked up in bed and for once sparing her the usual birthday 'treat' of being woken up to hear the dawn chorus. He and the dogs were enjoying the warm early morning air when suddenly Rover's attention was drawn to one of the oak trees. Chips and Daxy joined in, so John went over to investigate the frantic barking and tail wagging. There, cowering pitifully on a lower branch was a mere scrap of a kitten, not more than a few weeks old. She had obviously been abandoned and left to die, and would have done so, had the dogs not found her. Tenderly John lifted her down and walked back home with the kitten tucked snugly in his jacket pocket.

When he arrived with his new friend, Eve was just beginning to stir and could dimly hear a voice: 'Darling, look I've got something here – but you don't have to have it. It really doesn't matter if you don't want it, I can find somewhere for it. ...'

Eve surfaced sleepily from the bedclothes wondering what on earth John was talking about, until he took the tiny animal from his pocket, still saying that she didn't have to keep it if she didn't want it. But as John hopefully showed the tiny creature to Eve she was overcome with amazement and delight: 'John, of course I want it,' she said, 'of course I do.' And so Scruffy, the surprise birthday present, joined the family and grew up happily with the dogs who accepted her, and later her offspring, without any jealousy.

During the summer John would often walk the several miles to work across the fields and take Rover with him. The dog was quite content to spend the day under his master's desk in the little office at Hatfield, although he sometimes found himself in a more exciting situation when he was treated to a flight in one of the firm's runabout passenger aircraft. One day John was flying a high ranking naval officer down to Portsmouth in the company's Rapide and during the trip the man dozed, lulled by the hum of the engines, unaware that there was another sleeping passenger, under the seat. The officer's peaceful dreams came to an end as he awoke with a start to find his face receiving the attentions of Rover's long, friendly and very wet tongue. This was one of the many lighter moments in John's career and he related the story with glee to Eve.

Incidents like this lightened the more serious business of testing and, after the 108 programme had come to an end, John found himself occupied with the new Venom. Most of the work on the two prototypes, VV612 and VV613 fell to his lot, although at the 1950 Farnborough SBAC show he demonstrated the night fighter version with its redesigned front fuselage to accommodate radar gear and a two-seat cockpit, similar to that of the Mosquito.

The Venom's performance was impressive; with a top speed of 640mph – 100mph more than the Vampire – it was the fastest operational type fighter in the country at the time. The Vampire had proved itself a thoroughly sound design with good handling characteristics up to its critical Mach number. So the designers had thought it logical to develop it, to make it more powerful, give it a thinner wing and with other modifications there seemed to be no reason why it could not be made even better.

So the Venom was developed, and it became a successful machine – but it did have its problems. Its cleaner aerodynamics and a de Havilland Ghost 103 engine of 4,850lb thrust, a big improvement on the Goblin's 3,500lb, merely put it within quicker and easier reach of the dreaded compressibility problems, although it was a potent machine up to that point. At anything above Mach 0.84, the Venom became an unwelcome handful, dropping a wing violently in a high-speed dive, sometimes to the point where it was impossible to correct. As the dive progressed, control would be lost and the aeroplane would plummet to a low altitude before recovery was possible.

John soon found that it was an unpleasant machine at high

speed in turbulent air: 'The worst aircraft in my experience in bumps,' he wrote in a flight report.

The Venom was also prone to aileron flutter at high speed and this proved to be a problem. Flutter was a phenomenon that gave designers and aerodynamicists concerned with high-speed flight many headaches in the late forties and early fifties. Control surfaces – ailerons, elevators or rudder and in extreme cases the whole wing, could suddenly start fluttering at speed, with varying degrees of violence. In some cases it would be no more than a worrying vibration, while in a bad form the whole component could disintegrate in a matter of seconds and a number of test pilots lost their lives when an aeroplane suffered in this way.

The ailerons were the trouble spot with the Venom; at certain speeds they began to flutter seriously and John Derry and John Wilson both made many flights with cameras mounted on the wing, photographing wool tufts so that the aerodynamicists could determine the cause of the flutter. In the end the trailing edge of the ailerons was redesigned and this helped to a large degree. But the problem went deeper than that and John was one of the first test pilots to talk publicly about the need for irreversible power controls on machines that were to cope with high-speed forces.

It was becoming obvious with machines such as the Venom that aircraft speeds had outstripped the poor technology of control surface operation. The cable-operated controls with which the Venom was fitted were in common use, and these were prone to stretch, so that at high speed the ailerons, for example, would not go to their full travel. Power operation was in its infancy and the fully irreversible power controls that were later to become standard for high-speed aircraft were still in the future.

Despite the problems which beset all aircraft manufacturers, de Havilland kept well to the fore in design and production and their designs were looked upon with a great deal of interest by other companies. Although they were first in England with a swept wing aircraft, the DH108, other companies were not slow to catch up. Hawker had already produced a swept wing experimental version of the P1040 and it became known as the P1052. It retained its predecessor's straight tailplane and the peculiar bifurcated twin jet outlets behind the wing roots. Its performance was very good and Hawker's chief test pilot, 'Wimpy' Wade, and his number two, Neville Duke, were able to exceed Mach 0.9 at high altitude and well over 600mph at sea level. Later the tailplane was modified and the jet outlet was moved to the rear of the fuselage and this new design, known as the 1081, began to take on the now familiar shape of the Hawker Hunter.

With these two aircraft, Wimpy and Neville began to use a new and invaluable aid to test pilots. The wire recorder, obtained from the musical instrument people Boosey and Hawkes, was an early kind of tape recorder, which consisted of a wire running between two spools. Hawker had the brilliant idea of wiring up one of these machines in the cockpit so that Wimpy or Neville could give a running commentary of the flight. The test pilots' secretary would then play it back and type out a transcript so that every scrap of information from engine temperature to control characteristics would be noted at the time and as the flight progressed, and a lot of tedious jotting on the knee pad was done away with.

John Derry and John Cunningham were very interested when Wimpy and Neville talked about their wire recorder. 'Any chance we could come over and hear a play-back?' asked Derry. The two Hawker test pilots said that they would be delighted and, when they were alone, decided that they'd lay on something a bit special. . .

They recorded a gripping commentary from a very dramatic flight – but Wimpy never turned a hair, for he did all the 'flying' from his office desk. Neville produced the sound effects by switching on a vacuum cleaner in the next office. It all sounded very convincing, the hum of the cleaner in the background giving a good imitation of the noise of a jet engine from the cockpit.

'John, that wire recording you wanted to hear,' said Wimpy in a matter of fact voice, over the telephone. 'We've got one here – come over when you like.' The four of them met in Wimpy's office and the recorder was switched on. The value of the instrument was quite clear and John Derry and John Cunningham were obviously impressed – but then their expressions took on a change, which they tried hard to disguise as the recording progressed.

'Diving now . . . Mach point eight ... point eight five . . . nine . . . point nine five . . . Mach point nine seven . . . nine eight. . . Mach point nine nine.'

Were Hawker really this far ahead, they wondered?

Wimpy and Neville were practically beside themselves with suppressed laughter, for the P1052 had never reached anything like this Mach number and, a few moments later, catching them exchanging amused glances, the two Johns from de Havilland began to realise that perhaps the instrument hadn't recorded such a momentous flight after all. There was much laughter and drinks all round, but the de Havilland pilots had heard enough to convince them that the recorder really could be useful in test flying.

The idea was taken up by de Havilland and by the time John started his test programme on what was to be the company's final military project, wire recorders were an invaluable part of the cockpit equipment. This new aircraft, which occupied all John's attention when he had finished the Venom programme, was the big, powerful DH110. It was a large, swept wing, twin jet, high-speed, interceptor. It was the heaviest, fastest, most advanced and costliest fighter they had conceived.

Even before John had joined the company at the end of 1947, there were tentative drawings being produced at Hatfield, which closely resembled the eventual 110. But lessons learnt from John's work on the 108 provided useful information for the designers, and the finished machine, rolled out in the summer of 1951, was one of the strangest looking British aircraft ever built. Yet with its complex and sweeping fuselage contours, sharply swept wings, raked fins and a tailplane mounted high over its twin booms, it possessed a beauty of line that was all its own.

It was built, as was the Gloster Javelin, to Ministry specification F4/48. The Ministry would put in an order to two companies for prototypes so that there was a guarantee that one of the finished aeroplanes would be suitable. From the point of order, Gloster and de Havilland were in fierce competition.

When work began at Hatfield on the new aircraft, de Havilland used the same method of wing construction that had been perfectly successful on both the Vampire and the Venom. This method was unusual when compared to the practices of other manufacturers who would put vertical shear webbing from the wing root to the tip, fixed to the front of the upper and lower parts of the main spar. This is an effective way of absorbing bending and twisting loads.

De Havilland had a different method for catering for the heavy stresses on the wing. There was no webbing for the ribs on the outer half of each wing and instead they used a thick gauge wrap-around leading edge skin, which did the same job and was lighter, thus giving better manoeuvrability to the finished airframe. It was well proven de Havilland practice and calculations had shown that it would be satisfactory on the big, heavy DH110.

Outwardly the aeroplane differed little from those very early drawings, except that the tailplane was straight instead of swept and there was a single streamlined, bubble-type canopy with a curved screen. This was offset so that the observer could sit beside the pilot, but in the fuselage. The observer's position was not as claustrophobic as it might sound as there was a large window in the upward opening hatch and another to the side.

Still, however, the old system of cable control was used on the 110. John, at the time the most experienced pilot in Britain in the realms of high-speed flight, knew that the only satisfactory answer was a fully powered irreversible control system and he said as much when he was asked to give a lecture on High Speed Flying to the Royal Aeronautical Society at the end of November 1950.

'Power boost controls require new techniques of flying and testing, particularly when irreversible,' he said. 'Their use appears to be doubly important in view of flutter experience.' He did warn that such a system could bring a new danger in that it would override the old problem of stick immovability as Mach number built up, which was in itself a built-in safety factor, so that a pilot using power controls might break the aeroplane – 'But in the interests of trim changes and ineffectiveness, such considerations must not be allowed to cloud the issue . . . the future should provide a more straightforward approach to the speeds which are now obtained under the most disagreeable circumstances.'

When he gave his lecture, a suitable system of fully powered control over a supersonic aircraft simply had not been developed, so the 110 was fitted with the old fashioned cable arrangement, but, from the lessons learnt on the 108, it had power boosters at the ailerons and elevator.

The big silver 110, serial number WG236, was rolled out at Hatfield during the summer of 1951 for engine runs, taxying trials and short hops. Chief test pilot John Cunningham was at the controls and on 26 September the powerful machine thundered off down the runway for its first flight. It was an impressive and exciting moment for the de Havilland staff who had gathered to watch and an exhilarating experience for Cunningham for, compared to the relatively low power of the Vampires and Venoms, the twin Rolls-Royce Avon RA3 engines promised a shattering performance.

That was to come later at the hands of John Derry who, earlier that year had received a sad reminder of the dangers facing test pilots.

'John, what is it?' asked Eve, who had seen him one evening wandering aimlessly around the garden ever since he returned from work. 'Wimpy's dead,' said John. 'He was killed today.'

No one ever discovered what had happened. Wimpy Wade had been flying the P1081 from Langley to Farnborough when something catastrophic went wrong. Wimpy ejected, but never released himself from his seat – which did not have automatic release – and he was found dead, still strapped to the seat, in the woods at Ringmer in Sussex. The aircraft was completely wrecked and the cause of the crash remained a mystery.

John was never able to shake off the death of a colleague very easily and losing Wimpy affected him deeply, as it upset everyone who knew him. He had been an unforgettable character, full of exuberant good spirits, and his place as chief test pilot of Hawker was taken by Neville Duke, whose name will forever be linked with that of the Hawker Hunter.

The Venom test programme finished at the beginning of 1952 and on Tuesday 22 January, John first flew WG236. From then on he was responsible for the 110's flight test programme, a gruelling and exacting commitment that at times was to sap his mental and physical energies, although from the start he was enthusiastic about this high-powered machine.

Until the end of February he flew alone, with no flight test observer, and he concentrated on general handling checks. The aeroplane had not yet flown supersonic. On Saturday 1 March, he was accompanied by Anthony Max Richards who was to be his observer on nearly every subsequent flight. Tony Richards, who had tasted life inside the fuselage of the 110 when he went up with John Cunningham earlier, was a very different sort of person from John Derry. An only child, he was quiet and rather reserved but with a pleasant manner that made him popular with his colleagues. He'd come to de Havilland from the Paddington Technical Institute in 1944 when he was seventeen and had studied at the company's Aeronautical Technical school until he was apprenticed. Here he had worked quickly and steadily for his HNC in Aeronautics and later qualified as a Graduate of the Royal Aeronautical Society by which time he was working for the de Havilland flight test section. The years of training were paying off, and at last he was able to apply his work to the practical side of test flying.

John was pleased to find that he and Tony worked well together and within two weeks of team work they gave a special demonstration at Hatfield, and one that they looked back on with pride. The Duke of Edinburgh made an informal visit (in so far as any royal visit can be called informal) to de Havilland on Thursday

13 March. It was a cold and chilly day, but the weather did nothing to cool the enthusiasm of the directors and staff and the Duke, always an avid aircraft enthusiast, received a very warm welcome.

The Comet jet airliner had aroused a great deal of interest all around the world and de Havilland were envied by other manufacturers for being the first in the field with an aeroplane of this sort, so it was an exciting moment when the Duke climbed aboard G-ALYP to be given a flight by John Cunningham, who had done all the development work and had set up an impressive clutch of speed and distance records in the Comet, and his co-pilot, Peter Bugge, who had worked closely with him throughout the programme. Later the Prince was taken to the de Havilland engine company's combustion research laboratory, where he saw the Sprite rocket motor in action. This was designed to give aircraft a short and rapid take-off boost and was to be demonstrated at Farnborough in September.

But what really interested the Duke was the 110. He inspected the aircraft and asked John many questions about it and was intensely interested when John and Tony taxied out onto the runway to give a demonstration flight. As WG236 roared off under the overcast skies, the Duke, Sir Geoffrey de Havilland, the Duke's equerry, Lieutenant-Commander Michael Parker and Air Commodore E.H. 'Mouse' Fielden (Captain of the Queen's Flight) all settled down to watch. They were not disappointed as John gave what was later described in the *de Havilland Gazette* as 'a thrilling aerobatic display' and in fifteen minutes did low level high-speed runs, reverse turns, loops and rolls, watched avidly by Prince Philip. Afterwards he thanked John and told him how impressed he had been. It was a proud day for de Havilland, but the next day it was back to routine test flying.

As the DH110 programme progressed, householders in and around Hatfield found that a shattering double boom occasionally disturbed the peace. It was, of course, John with Tony diving WG236 faster than sound. Until then no one had heard a sonic bang and the noise resulted in a great deal of excitement and sometimes annoyance. Small boys were invariably thrilled as were many adults, but there were some gardeners for example, who did not find anything very exciting about having the windows of their greenhouses rattled or even, in extreme cases, shattered. It was a phenomenon that created a tremendous amount of public interest, although there was much speculation on the cause, but it was soon accepted that the deep boom was the result of the shock wave hitting the ground.

John and Tony first took the 110 through what had become known as the 'Sound Barrier' on Wednesday 9 April 1952, and in doing so made a little bit more history for de Havilland: the aeroplane became the first operational type aircraft to exceed the speed of sound and the first two seat and twin-engined one to do so; Tony was the first British flight test observer through the barrier and, at twenty-four, was certainly the youngest man in the country to reach such speeds.

John's sister Helen and her husband Michael were living in Surrey at the time and John would sometimes feel mischievous enough to take WG236 low over their house, and Helen, dreading the disapproval of the neighbours as the powerful machine shattered the peace, would dash out into the garden and ruefully shake her fist at him as he disappeared. But lighthearted moments like this were rare as John concentrated carefully on the work in hand. As with the 108, John had stepped up the Mach number carefully, recording the results on each flight, but it proved to be a much smoother business in the new aeroplane.

The lack of a tailplane on the 108 and, to some extent, the flexing of the wings, had caused the dire pitching oscillations which made high speed flying so unpleasant; compared to that the 110 was almost viceless, with none of the heart-stopping nose down plunge, cinema-style wrestling with the stick or the complete loss of control at the speed of sound. But it wasn't all easy going. By the end of April John had made over forty high-speed flights in WG236, many of them well over an hour in duration. He found that it suffered from an annoying wing drop and a slight nose down pitch at high Mach numbers but, more seriously, there was a worrying amount of 'snaking' at high speed. This was easily traced to flexibility (known as aeroelasticity) in the twin booms.

On the advice of John Cunningham, an incredibly crude but very effective step was taken as a stopgap measure. Four massive steel reinforcing strips were machined and riveted onto the exterior surfaces of the booms. The fitters and ground crews found it possible to shuffle along them as they were so thick and soon everyone was referring to them as 'railway lines'. At the same time, fin extensions were faired onto the line of the rudder trailing edge, curving under the rear section of the booms to give added stability.

The 'railway lines' proved effective and the new prototype, nearing completion, should suffer from none of the 'snaking' troubles as its booms were being made from thicker gauge aluminium alloy.

In the middle of the summer John found that WG236 was suffering from cable stretch problems in the controls.

'Under most operating conditions the port aileron is only moving up to one third to one half of the total travel with full stick movement,' he reported at the end of June. 'The starboard aileron is better, but is itself not reaching anything like full movement under high Mach condition ... it is quite clear that we are losing an enormous rolling potential due to cable stretch alone.'

There were also problems with the elevator: 'The same story seems to apply,' wrote John in his report. 'High speeds at low altitudes using a minimum tailplane angle and relying on the elevator have produced large stick movements with relatively little effect.' The indications were that the cable stretching was worsening, but at least the 110 did not appear to suffer from the transonic bugbear of flutter and its performance at high speed and in rough air was outstanding. 'It is most interesting, 'wrote John, 'that bumps are not a serious deterrent to high indicated airspeed on this aircraft. The difference between this machine and the Venom on the same day is most marked.'

Nearly all of John and Tony's flights were conducted at high altitude and most supersonic dives began at around 40,000ft. The method of entering a steep dive was rather dramatic, often done by executing a half roll and then pulling the stick back until the aircraft was in a vertical dive. In one such dive in WG236 on 26 August, something most unusual happened.

'We'll go right down,' said John after he had switched the wire recorder on. 'Are you set for that? We shall be steepening up a bit too, with airbrakes out. . . coming down now.' The speed built up: Mach 0.95, 0.96, 0.97, 0.98, 0.99 . . . Mach One. They were flying faster than sound but then, as the 110 began to slow down in its dive, it gave a peculiar little shudder.

'Oh my God!' exclaimed John, 'do you know what that was? That was the bang going past us ... there's the other one! Did you feel it?'

'Certainly felt a pitch there,' admitted Tony.

John was getting very excited. 'I've felt it before – that's what it is. Staggering isn't it?'

'Certainly peculiar,' agreed Tony. 'I would have thought that it was way ahead of us.'

'No,' said John, 'because we went up to quite a high true Mach number, you see? It's absolutely fantastic. Two, one after the other. I've heard them before, but I didn't want to say too much, because I wasn't too sure about it... nothing else to cause it at that high Mach number. I've had it about four times. I'd better climb up again, I think. There must have been about seven seconds between them.'

John's musings about the phenomenon are interrupted by a few points he has to attend to on the aircraft: 'Switching off starboard [fuel tank] turning onto cross feed. Switching off starboard tank pumps.' He carries on explaining about the bangs to Tony: 'If we stay in front of it, supposing we go a hundred feet a second faster than the bang – to simplify it, say in six or seven seconds we are seven hundred feet in front of it. Then we come down to about 25,000ft and it's only catching us up at five per cent – ie thirty feet per second – and it's already 700ft behind us so it takes quite a few seconds to catch up – about twenty to thirty seconds. I worked it out that we can very nearly get down with it. If you went to Mach one point two and maintained it at 30,000ft and kept at least one down to twenty [20,000ft] you could be down in front of it.'

This flight occurred during a general working up for that year's SBAC display at Farnborough, although de Havilland's were going to enter the now completed second prototype 110 for its public debut, and John began to wonder if it would be possible not only to treat the spectators to the excitement of sonic booms for the first time, but also to create an unbelievably spectacular effect by doing a low level high speed run past the crowds at the same moment as those bangs arrived.

Inevitably, after a while, this concentrated testing of the 110 took its toll on Derry, both mentally and physically.

'It shags you out, this business,' he later remarked to Richards during a high-speed flight, and after several months he began to sleep badly and to suffer from nightmares. Photographs taken of him during 1952 show lines around his mouth and he suddenly looked older than his thirty years. Eve, too, had noticed a change in him and was determined that they should have a relaxing holiday on their own – but she knew they could not afford anything expensive.

Unexpectedly, her father came up with the solution when he asked her what she would like for her birthday, which was towards the end of May. Mr Moffat, her father, was the director of a small shipping line in Scotland, and one of the company's boats, the SS *Hebrides*, spent its working life plying between the beautiful Western Isles, carrying cargoes of cattle and grain. Eve asked her father if she and John could spend some days on this boat as passengers, living with the crew.

It was arranged, and John took leave from de Havilland from

15 May until Saturday 24 May, when he was due back at Hatfield to resume work on the 110. Carol was away at school and Jo went to stay with her grandparents in Scotland, while John and Eve boarded the SS *Hebrides* in the unsalubrious atmosphere of Glasgow docks.

John, pleased to be without the responsibility of his exacting work, was delighted with everything, from the beauty of the Isles to the intricacies of manoeuvring the boat, the varied and intensely interesting bird life and the personalities of the officers and crew.

He kept a personal diary* over these few days, recording in pencilled notes in a red school exercise book everything that interested him and observing with a sharp eye the whole picture of a way of life in a beautiful part of the world.

This diary reflects in everyday life his professional capacity for detailed observation and analysis, and what the holiday meant to him is summed up in these words that he wrote at the time: 'The peace of these islands and this ship cutting between them surely cannot be equalled. I can feel fatigue and worry soaking out of me.'

* See Appendix III.

John Derry's sketch dated 23 May 1952 showing dawn over Applecross Forest.

Chapter 9

LET'S DO ONE MORE

'Let's do one more if you can bear it.'
John Derry, August 1952

In the final months of his life John made a decision that, had he not felt a strong sense of loyalty to his employers, would have saved him from the tragedy that was to come. He made up his mind to leave de Havilland. But he also decided to postpone any move until after Farnborough Week in September.

His resolve to leave the firm after almost five years of test flying a vast number of DH products, including more than 140 flights in the high-speed version of the 108, was the result of a mounting frustration. John had been the king pin of the high-speed experimental tests, but overall responsibility for the programme rested with Chief Test Pilot John Cunningham. Derry knew that he had reached the top as far as his own prospects at de Havilland were concerned. John Cunningham had long been established as the head man and there was no sign that he had any plans to move – nor was there any reason why he should. Derry had confidence in his own ability to be in command of a complete flight test programme, yet he knew that he was never likely to achieve his aim to be chief test pilot at de Havilland. He also knew it was unlikely that the company would design another military aircraft, as their future seemed geared more to civil development, and this worried him: as long as he was engaged in experimental flying he wanted this to be, as it had always been, with military machines.

There was yet another cause of discontent, but John was not alone in feeling dissatisfied with his salary. Test pilots' pay had improved in the early fifties but was still a source of anger and discontent to him and to many of his colleagues. Was it right, they asked, that test pilots, who risked their lives every day in untried experimental aircraft, should be paid less than airline pilots who were flying thoroughly tested and theoretically safe machines?

John had no wish to become what he termed a 'bus driver', but he would have been better off financially, and safer.

Over thirty test pilots had been killed since the war, so in a life that had a likelihood of ending suddenly and soon, the last thing the Derrys wanted to do was to worry about money. Consequently Eve and John ate well, entertained, sent the children to good schools, ran a fast car – and always seemed to be at the limit of their financial resources. It was something that John Cunningham had noticed and vaguely disapproved; he often spoke to John about it, told him he ought to be a little more careful with money. It didn't make much difference – John just laughed it off.

Most test pilots felt that a salary of around £2,500 did not compensate sufficiently for a job that carried an appalling risk factor. But the employers, however, did not see it quite like that. In the eyes of the public, test pilots were heroes as the speeds and the dangers increased; they were seen as an elite band, leading brave and glamorous lives, men to be revered, men whose names were on the lips of every schoolboy. To the employers the test pilot was important, certainly, but was no more than the one who tested the theory and was merely part of the team. Designers, aerodynamicists and stressmen, who all had high academic qualifications, but whose lives were rarely at risk, received better salaries. Many embittered pilots felt that the attitude of some aircraft companies seemed to be that it was a privilege for anyone to be allowed to test their creations and the salary was a bonus on top of that.

John and Eve lived for the moment – the future was something uncertain, especially as many test pilots, including John, were not insured against an accident whilst working, either by their employers or by themselves. Their occupation was not viewed too kindly by the insurance companies and the premiums were too high for private policies.

But the mainstream of John's frustration in the late summer of 1952 was directed at the knowledge that he could go no further at de Havilland. Fuelled also by an uncomfortable feeling that the company was expanding so vastly that the personal touch and intimate atmosphere of the team spirit were slipping away, he began to cast around for more agreeable prospects.

Ironically he found them at Gloster who, with their GA5, later named the Javelin, were in fierce competition for the same Ministry contract as the DH110. John went for an interview and on the journey found he was delighted with the Gloucestershire countryside, preferring the rolling, wooded hills to the flatter and more densely populated Hertfordshire. Negotiations went well and the tentative arrangement was that John would take over as chief test pilot after working for a while as Bill Waterton's number two.

Nothing was down on paper at this stage. 'I'll see de Havilland through Farnborough before I settle anything,' he told Eve. 'It's only fair that I do – and I'll sell that plane for them, even if it kills me.' In any case, he was unwilling to abandon work on the 110 at such a stage in the programme and he was looking forward to testing the second prototype, now nearing completion at the Hatfield works.

Before it flew, in late July, they took the children on holiday to Cornwall. They had planned to go to Brittany but funds would not run to it so they settled for their usual haunt at Praa Sands near Helston. By this time the hotel was fully booked, but the owners, with whom they had become friends, said they were very welcome to park a caravan in a field belonging to the hotel.

The night before they set out to collect the caravan was not an unqualified success. Six-year-old Jo was in a difficult mood and wanted Eve to put her to bed. John said no, as Eve was busy packing, he would do it. The result was a lengthy battle of wills that was as fraying for John and Jo as it was hilarious for Eve. In the end John won, but later, as a way of a peace offering, he took his stubborn daughter a hot drink and apologised. Jo responded with equal warmth by throwing it over him . . .

The feud continued the next day during the journey until Jo saw a pheasant dash in front of the car: 'Oh, mind, Daddy!' she cried, instantly regretting being the one to have spoken first. But it broke the ice and from then on all was well. John had the holiday worked out: 'You're going to have a complete rest,' he told Eve, 'I'm going to do all the cooking.'

Eve was delighted, although she knew that John could be a trifle ponderous and irritating in the kitchen. The trouble was he always wanted everything he did to be just right; it was a matter of great concern when he discovered a rotten tomato in the picnic hamper he had prepared. They were nicely settled on the beach by then, but John didn't let that worry him. He leapt into the car, drove the seven miles to Helston and complained bitterly, returning in a happier frame of mind with just one tomato given to him by an apologetic shopkeeper. As he unwound, John enjoyed himself on the beach and in the sea as much as the children; it sometimes felt to Eve that she was on holiday with three children. But the holiday mood wore off on the long journey home when they were delayed, caravan in tow, at Exeter and finally arrived back at Rabley Heath utterly exhausted.

Within a few moments of their arrival, the telephone rang. It was Hatfield: would John report to the airfield as soon as possible to start test work on the second 110 prototype as it was important that the aircraft put in enough flying hours for it to be allowed to give a full display at Farnborough.

Eve was furious and John was far from happy, as he was so tired, but the holiday was over and Wednesday 23 July found Derry and Richards in WG240 ready for its first flight. However, after a short test hop a fire broke out on the starboard wheel brake and the flight was postponed for two days. But from then on the test programme got underway.

'Just going to do a loop here. I don't think we can get round really and I don't feel like going into cloud at low speed . . . just going to do a slow roll. Rudder is airy, using a surprising amount of elevator there. Going to do one the other way.' The date was

Sunday 24 August. John and Tony had been testing the new prototype for over a month and on that day were giving a demonstration at Panshanger aerodrome, then the Herts HQ of the Air Training Corps, just a few miles from Hatfield. The weather was poor with a lot of low cloud, hence John's reluctance to do a loop, and the visibility was bad, with a hint of drizzle. But it was really the kind of weather in which the 110 had been designed to operate and a few days earlier the machine, which started life silver, like WG236, had been sprayed satin black, befitting its role as an all-weather night fighter. It looked sleek and evil.

Conditions were certainly far from ideal for demonstration flying on that day, but John put on a show that was memorable for the masterly and breath-taking way he showed off the 110, even adjusting his carefully worked out schedule to climb spectacularly into a patch of blue that suddenly broke through the overcast skies. But first he lined up for a searing, low-level fly-past:

'Seven hundred miles an hour, I have to jig around a good deal because I want to avoid built-up areas on account of the noise. Coming back here in a moment. You may be able to see me on the skyline as I corner. Visibility very bad and I am shaking off the airfield again as I come round . . . banking steeply to the left ... I am going to put on the airbrakes now, and when I come past you I will be going quite slowly – ie, about 250 miles an hour.'

'Did you see what this temperature thing went up to?' asked Tony, feeling uncomfortably hot. 'About 45 degrees,' replied John 'It's warm.' Like WG236, the second prototype suffered from cockpit temperature problems and the pilot had to make constant adjustments to the heating control. It also suffered from the same annoying misting up of the canopy on a fast descent from height.

The display carried on: 'I'm coming round and down to 270 knots and when I've turned round, I shall be doing little more than 200 miles an hour. Now doing a steep turn at about 200 knots – quite manoeuvrable, and I am going to change direction and come over the airfield like this. Coming back now and I'm going to do a vertical reverse and changing direction by going through inverted.' (This is his spectacular 'Derry Turn'). 'Change of direction, first one way . . . like that, and then the other way . . . like that. Cloud has cleared a little and presently I will do another high-speed fly-past and a climb. First of all, a slow roll.

'Accelerating now up to high speed again and will climb away from you so that you can see me disappear through the breaks in the cloud. Worth trying, in spite of the cloud. Patch of blue to north-north-east of aerodrome. I will climb to north-north-east. Starting now ... up we go. That's all; I want to carry this on to see where we get to for this SBAC effort.'

Just as he completed his display, the rain started: 'Drizzle. Maximum oil about 82 degrees during all that high speed running. Difficult, needs one or two practices at Farnborough. Time 15.43. My watch has gone haywire – must be the "g", I think. Started runs about 15.29. We were about ten minutes. Getting low in fuel. Oxygen connector has just come off, there's no cord on it for some reason – bouncing about during high speed runs . . . try a loop, not a complete one.'

Once down, John wandered off to find Eve and the children who had been watching and they all went into the bar to have a drink. Chatting with friends, they suddenly realised that Jo wasn't playing nearby as she had been a few minutes before and John started searching for his daughter. She was nowhere in sight but then someone told John that a little girl looking like Jo had wandered out to the airfield. John rushed out just in time to see an Anson, busily engaged in giving joy rides, take off. He waited until it had landed and then, to his relief, saw the small plump figure of his younger daughter climb out and start to run towards him. She'd attached herself to a party of people going up and had an enjoyable little adventure.

Back at Hatfield there were flight reports to be made and, as the test programme on WG240 progressed, John realised that this second prototype was a fantastic machine to fly. It was lighter than its predecessor and fitted with more powerful Rolls-Royce Avon RA7 engines. 'Acceleration is out of this world,' John had enthused during a flight in August, and he had commented in the appropriate report: 'The performance of the aircraft is absolutely outstanding compared with 236.'

But, as with 236, there were drawbacks. Its cable control system stretched and the servodyne power boosters tended to stall at speed. John stressed that this must be improved before the aeroplane went to the Aircraft and Armament Experimental Establishment at Boscombe Down for trials. The all-moving electrically operated tailplane with cable actuated elevator had its problems too, and this had stuck during the Panshanger demonstration while John was making his low level high speed run.

John found the most serious problem on this aircraft was caused by the starboard engine, which had an annoying tendency to run hot. Owing to some tightness in the bearings, the engine had had this weakness even on the test bed, before it was fitted to WG240.

During flight testing it often overheated and John would have to throttle back. A replacement engine would have been the logical answer, but getting one from Rolls-Royce would have meant a long delay and consequent hold-up on the flight programme, so the company decided to carry on with what they had. A couple of days before the Panshanger demonstration John and Tony found the engine was overheating:

'Nowhere near full revs on that level run over the airfield,' said John as they were in the middle of a general handling check at Hatfield. '79 on starboard' (7,900rpm).

'I didn't realise you were clear to 79 now,' remarked Tony.

Then the temperature started to rise. 'Temperature on the starboard engine is considerably over the top,' said John. 'I've got to throttle back to keep down to 660 – down to 7,750 to keep down to 660 degrees C.'

Flight testing on any aircraft in those days was a long and arduous business, for although John had first flown faster than sound four years earlier, the ideal design for supersonic flight, allied to existing technology, was still a long way off. Nor was there the luxury of advanced computers and foolproof wind tunnels to give more or less ready-made answers, so that the test pilot's lot was still to 'fly it and see'. The 110 was the most advanced military machine in the country at the time and each flight for John and Tony was a long and draining period of intense concentration. 'Until the perfecting of a telemetering system is complete, the responsibility for missing nothing rests with the pilot,' John had told the audience in his lecture on High Speed Flight.

There were some alarming moments with WG240, as there are in all test flying. On one occasion John attempted an outside loop in her when he was suddenly thrown forward in his straps as both engines flamed out, starved of fuel during the manoeuvre. He was quick enough to catch the starboard one just in time but the port engine went right out and refused to relight.

Much of this particular period of testing involved a general build-up and practice for the SBAC show at Farnborough at the beginning of September, for de Havilland were understandably keen to see off the Javelin, their delta rival from Glosters, by now labelled unkindly 'The Trug'.

Less than a week before the display, John and Tony took off from Hatfield on the morning of 26 August:

'Thirty thousand feet over Crawley – very rough up here this morning. . . 41,500, Mach 0.89, turning towards Hastings. Starboard wing drop again.' John opened the throttles and the 110 dived towards the sea between Hastings and Newhaven: 'We'll do one more high speed run. I want to try and get a bit more speed – we didn't get any misting there anyway, because we didn't have it on cold. That's the position at which we'll have it – stops at that little rivet mark.'

Moments later the 110 screamed along the coastline at nearly 700mph. It created a lot of excitement and John was aware of this with some satisfaction – 'That gave them a run for their money,' he remarked as they pulled up into a climb. 'I don't suppose they've seen anything that fast here before. It was about 617 knots, about as much as we can get, I think – about 620. A little bit dicey over the sea – you can't quite tell where you are.

'Newhaven – going onto cold for a minute, I'm getting warm. I'll need to have early sleep at Farnborough – it shags you out, this business.'

It was on days like this that the pressure began to build up on John. He was starting to feel the strain once more and Eve noticed how tired and drawn he was looking. She was also aware of an irritability that was new; a tendency to snap, to take innocent remarks the wrong way. At times she was careful what she said to him.

There were two more flights in the 110 on that day. One was in 236 – and this was the dive on which they felt the supersonic bangs go past them. The other was a further handling check on the newer 240 and was made during the afternoon. From about 40,000ft, John opened the throttles and put the nose down. The speed built up:

'Very late wing drop there – port wing drop after the starboard at about Mach 1.02. Fairly steep dive with quite a lot of lag. Getting big wing drop today.' Later in the flight John levelled out to do a high speed run.

Then, without any warning, and to Tony's alarm, the aircraft suddenly pitched violently downwards.

'Well, my giddy aunt,' said John. 'Tailplane's run away. I must have pushed it, I suppose – what a prize ape.'

'Cor blimey,' said Tony, 'I wondered what on earth was happening.'

'I must have pushed it as I went over,' said John.

'Just held it on?'

'What?'

'Just held it on, you mean?'

'Yes.'

'I heard some horrible crack as we started over – I wondered what it was.'

'Let's try it again. I think I must have pushed it – yes, I must have done; it's as still as a rock now. Let's do one more if you can bear it. OK?'

'Yes, OK. The first one presumably was your pushing the tailplane that caused that great lurch?'

'Yes. The elevator seemed to be over-balancing. . . One more – cameras holding out, that's something, anyway. Yes, by George, that was a bloody silly thing to do. I got hold of it with two hands. I do sometimes for aerobatics – a bit more accurate, it's steadier, a slower progressive application. I always use two hands for shooting, you know.'

'Oh, yes?'

'Sighting and shooting – like that very much more, somehow. It's partly psychological, I think, because it has the result. We found we got much better results when we used two hands.'

'I often wonder,' said Tony, 'how do you steer this thing upside down? It must be bloody awkward.'

'Yes, well I haven't done very much of that really, what with stopping the bloody engine last time.' (John is referring to the outside loop a few days earlier when the engines were starved of fuel.) 'To get the nose up is the big thing. Yes, I'll do one more roll over the field. Yes, I'm quite sure one of these days we are going to unearth a pair of pliers or something . . . gear going down, flaps twenty degrees. I bet that other thing will appear quite slow after this.'

'The Gloster?'

'236.'

'Oh, 236!'

Before Farnborough John and Tony had a couple of days' break from the 110. They needed it. Their final routine test in 236 was on Thursday 27 August, and involved wing drop tests and nose up pitch with double wing fences. The standard metal ones had been removed and temporary wooden ones fitted.

The long tiring flights in both prototypes coupled with the pressure of giving a crucial demonstration at Farnborough in de Havilland's most important military aircraft was enough to play on John's nerves. Although he managed, as he always had done, to keep these pressures isolated from his flying, they showed at home. He was sleeping badly, his restless nights often filled with lurid dreams. In one he tossed and turned so violently that Eve was flung out of bed. John woke up:

'What on earth are you doing down there?' he muttered.

Ruefully Eve told him.

'My God,' he said. 'My God – I dreamt I was in a burning aeroplane.'

It was every pilot's nightmare.

Chapter 10

WE LOST JOHN THIS AFTERNOON
(Eve Derry)

Farnborough was two days away. It was time to deliver WG240 to the Hampshire airfield. The second prototype had been picked for the display, partly because its performance was considerably the better of the two, but also because in its new black finish it looked smarter, sleeker and somehow deadlier than WG236, which was still fitted with the ungainly boom stiffeners, crudely obscuring the RAF roundels, and was looking generally rather down at heel, its silver finish well worn after nearly a year of concentrated test flying in which it had flown faster than sound more than 100 times.

But WG240 was still dogged by its old enemy the starboard engine, which continued to run hot, surge and annoy everyone who had anything to do with it.

On Saturday 30 August, John and Tony took off from Hatfield for Farnborough in a twenty-minute flight on which they continued the test programme by a further investigation into behaviour at both ends of the speed range – from supersonic to the stall.

John switched on the wire. The troublesome engine was already beginning to misbehave.

'Starboard engine hot at 7,750. Now 10,000ft. The aileron trimmer doesn't quite trim down without help ... cloud ... engines get a lot cooler between 35 and 40.' (35 to 40,000ft)

'Amazing how that starboard engine pops up like that, isn't it?' remarked Tony.

'It was a hot engine on the bed,' said John. 'Pity, really, because we're losing thrust on it for that reason.'

The 110 levelled off at well over 40,000ft and John opened the throttles, building up the speed and pushing it into a supersonic dive. All was well, and then they headed towards Farnborough – but during the descent the canopy misted up, which was one of the aircraft's minor irritating characteristics, and for some reason it was much worse on WG240 than on the first prototype. When it cleared, John prepared for a high-speed low level run over the airfield, but the starboard engine had other ideas:

'Blast! I've got starboard coming on,' said an exasperated John. 'It's taken us a minute to do that turn . . . puff from the port engine.'

'This thing really butts you in the back,' said Tony.

'We're getting a little bit of jerk from these things,' said John. 'We're only getting about Mach .93 going over the airfield, 610 knots . . . Mach .94 ... 6,600ft, 79 on port, 77 on starboard – starboard down, throttle back owing to high temperatures.'

Tony asked John if they could do a stall check before they landed, and then they touched down at Farnborough after a twenty-minute flight. Tony had a feeling all had not been well with the tailplane at one point.

'In that last run, did we have a case of tailplane sticking, John?' he said.

'Yes we did ... air off ... switching off everything.'

It was now just a question of waiting until Monday 1 September, the opening day of the show.

The early fifties were the heyday of the SBAC displays and they have never been repeated, for those post-war years were the most exciting ever seen in the aircraft industry – especially 1952, with the promise of sonic booms for the first time. If the media had tended to romanticise and fictionalise some of the dangers of transonic flight, then at least the public were well aware that the new and extraordinary shapes which appeared in the sky each year were flying into new regions of speed and the men who flew them were risking their lives. There was a tremendous national pride in the country's aeronautical achievements, and it was an era when test pilots were heroes, when no one minded too much if a supersonic bang broke a window or two, when the noise and speed were all part of the excitement.

Every September the crowds came to Farnborough in their hundreds of thousands and the approach roads would be jammed with cars filtering into the main enclosures, everyone excited and expectant, eager to see their heroes in action.

One of those heroes was Neville Duke, Hawker's chief test pilot. Before the end of that Farnborough Week, Duke was to show what living up to that so easily bestowed tag really meant.

His supersonic booms and high-speed fly-pasts had the crowds on their toes in 1952, gasping at the speed, the noise, the sheer spectacle. And no one could whip the spectators into a frenzy of excitement better than commentator Oliver Stewart who, never at a loss for words and reluctant to use the comparative when the superlative would do, managed to make Duke's approach sound more like the closing moments to a photo finish at the races.

Farnborough Air Display has always been a masterpiece of good timing. Duke would take off, exactly on cue, and during the climb-out to 40,000ft the interval would be filled by one or two aircraft that were a complete contrast – perhaps a Percival Provost, or a Viscount airliner – but when a supersonic aircraft took off the crowds were left in no doubt that they were in for some excitement.

'He's starting his dive now,' came Stewart's voice over the public address system, which, because of the various banks of loudspeakers, resulted in a triple echo effect for many spectators. 'Neville Duke has started his dive from 40,000ft in the Hawker Hunter. In a few moments he will be flying faster than sound.'

Then Stewart would urge everyone to silence, as more than 100,000 pairs of eyes searched the sky, squinting against the brightness for a sign of the rapidly descending aircraft. On a clear day it was sometimes possible to see the vapour trail, which would bend sharply as the aeroplane began its dive. But very often nothing could be seen – not even a glint in the sunshine.

Suddenly a double thunderclap rolled across Farnborough, the booms sounding like an anti-aircraft gun. The marquees shook, there were gasps from the crowd, an excited murmur, sporadic clapping. Then Stewart took up the commentary again:

'That was it, ladies and gentlemen, that was Neville Duke breaking the sound barrier in the magnificent Hawker Hunter. In a few moments he will be with us. He is approaching fast from the Laffan's Plain end of the runway . . . yes, he's started his run-in for the fly-past – I can see him! Yes, I can see him now!'

Necks craned, all eyes to the left, excitement mounting as Stewart's commentary built up. At first just a far off speck, the duck egg green Hunter (WB195) was coming in very fast and in almost uncanny silence. Stewart was practically beside himself:

'Here he comes, he's really coming in fast, he's doing well over 700 miles an hour, it's Neville Duke in the Hawker Hunter – he's . . .' the rest of Stewart's ecstatic torrent was lost in the shattering roar that shook the ground and was felt in every stomach as the Hunter streaked past, vapour shimmering over the wings, vortices streaming from the tips as it banked away, the noise a shocking contrast to the silent approach.

But this kind of spectacle was only one of the reasons for the Society of British Aircraft Constructors' annual display. Another, and more important, was to demonstrate the industry's latest products to potential overseas buyers. Farnborough was quickly established as the best shop window for the British aircraft industry, the Monday, Tuesday, Wednesday and Thursday being the all-important trade days.

The guest list was invariably impressive: heads of state, government ministers, eminent aircraft designers and thousands of representatives all came to see what Britain had to offer.

Lavish trade exhibitions were organised in the static park, marquees and tents housing the latest electronic and navigational aids together with armaments, jet engines, propellers, landing gear and other ancillary equipment, all glitteringly displayed. But visitors would also be able to take a look at many of the types of aircraft that would be flown, and as the actual display did not start until 3pm, this was always a big attraction.

So Farnborough was, and still is, a vast meeting ground for the buyers and sellers, and this in turn led to aircraft companies adopting the most aggressive sales techniques as competition was, perhaps at that time more than any other, very intense. In each company the pressure was inevitably passed down the line until it stopped at one man – the test pilot. He was the one who would demonstrate the machine to potential customers, and if his display was not up to the mark of his rivals, then no amount of brochures, talk and figures would be likely to save the day. In his outspoken book, *The Quick And The Dead*, Bill Waterton attacked Farnborough in those days as being akin to 'a Roman holiday' and maintained that relatively untried aircraft were pushed, often beyond their recommended limitations, as pilots were urged by their employers to outdo rival companies, and he claimed that in many cases some of the aircraft had done almost no previous flying before being put through a series of spectacular manoeuvres.

He felt that in the eyes of the public the pilot, rather than the aircraft, received the glory. This may well be true, for at the time Derry, Duke, Lithgow and Waterton were household names and were all part of the attraction. The glory was an inevitable consequence of their job. However, Waterton, although an excellent pilot, was not beyond giving the occasional hair-raising demonstration himself.

John's approach to demonstration flying was made very clear in his paper 'Analysing the Art of the Demonstration Pilot'. He believed that for a show to be successful there should be a very distinct difference between flying for the public and for those in the trade:

'A demonstration of a certain advantage in a particular aircraft, while being impressive to those who understand it, may leave many people cold and completely unaware of anything unusual. Conversely, members of the aviation world may be bored and blasé about a manoeuvre which brings the general public to their feet in excitement... it is fairly obvious that any show must be both entertaining and informative, though the proportions may vary.'

John was always careful to stress the difference between a demonstration that was exciting and one that was frightening, and he advised those who looked on displays as 'circus acts with no safety net' to 'stick to the fairground'. It was his safe but exciting approach that made him such an outstanding exhibition pilot.

His appearances at Farnborough had, until 1952, been in Vampires or Venoms. His reputation as the first British pilot to fly faster than sound always guaranteed a lot of interest, and he had an immense public following: yet no one had seen him give a public display in an aircraft that was anything like supersonic.

Farnborough 1952 was to change all that, with the debut of the 110. Monday 1 September was the start of an important week for de Havilland, the company more anxious than ever to give a good showing against the rival Javelin. On the face of it, things looked quite good for de Havilland but rather less so for Gloster. The 110, in flying faster than sound on 9 April that year, became the first twin jet aircraft in the world to go supersonic – and the fact that Derry was to fly it at the display was an added attraction.

The Javelin, on the other hand, had crashed at Boscombe Down on 2 June after Waterton had lost the elevators, which were torn off in a severe bout of flutter. He landed the aircraft, but the undercarriage legs ruptured the fuel tanks during the high-speed touchdown and it burst into flames as it skewed off the runway and slithered to a halt. Waterton, who only just managed to get out as flames engulfed the cockpit, was awarded the George Medal for getting the machine down and saving valuable flight data when it would have been a lot safer for him to eject. He, however, felt that the medal merely focussed attention away from the defects of the Javelin. He could sometimes be a difficult man to please!

In spite of the Javelin's misfortune it eventually won the contract, for – at least on paper – it seemed to offer advantages in performance. But there is no doubt that, aerodynamically, the 110 was a much better design. The Javelin had a ridiculously thick wing, which was handy for carrying a lot of fuel but not so good for transonic flight, and the tailplane, mounted on top of the fin over the wing, could result in a disastrous flat stall. The machine would just sink horizontally out of the sky, the airflow over the elevators blanketed by the huge wing. One Javelin was to crash in just this way, killing Peter Lawrence, a young Gloster test pilot.

This was the extraordinary design with which John Derry was planning to become involved – but the immediate commitment was to see de Havilland through Farnborough, to put up the best possible display in the 110, and then think about the future. So on Sunday 31 August, John and Eve arrived at the Frensham Pond Hotel on the outskirts of Farnham, not far from Farnborough airfield. This is a large hotel overlooking the picturesque Frensham Pond and had become the customary annual meeting place for the display pilots from de Havilland and their wives. During the week they would invariably ask other test pilots and their wives, often in less salubrious accommodation, over for an evening meal. Farnborough Week was always a memorable social occasion for them all.

John particularly liked Frensham Pond because he enjoyed an early morning row on the lake, and he took the opportunity of making a scraperboard sketch of the hotel seen from across the water. It was the last sketch he ever made.

The children were still on holiday from school and were spending the week with Eve's parents in Scotland. Jo, only six, had never been too keen on air displays, spending most of the time with her hands over her ears, while Carol, who was eleven, would have liked to have gone but was also keen to spend the time with her grandparents – especially as there was a big exhibition on in Scotland that she very much wanted to see.

Although Eve often went to displays where John was flying, and always to Farnborough, she could never watch without feeling frightened for him. It was the lot of all test pilots' wives who, drawn together by a common understanding, formed themselves into an exclusive and warm circle of friendship. John tried to comfort Eve: 'You mustn't worry,' he told her. 'Farnborough is the safest of all the flying I do – it really is.' However, like the other wives, she was always glad when the display was over.

Farnborough 1952 marked the gathering of the greatest number of revolutionary aircraft this country has ever seen in one year. It was a week of indifferent weather, but the enthusiasm of the spectators was at a pitch that has probably never been reached since. There were cheers and clapping at the majestic arrival of the mighty ten-engined Saunders Roe Princess flying boat – a sight that sent the effervescent Oliver Stewart into a gust of superlatives.

There were gasps of amazement as Roly Falk turned across the airfield in the Avro 698, prototype of the Vulcan bomber, the vast moth-like planform of the gleaming white delta flanked on either side by the colourful little Avro research deltas, the 707A and 707B. Although the 698 had done only a few hours flying, Falk threw it around the sky in a most impressive way, pulling it up into a climbing turn to a near vertical bank.

The shatteringly loud high-speed runs of the Supermarine Swift had many spectators wincing and covering their ears, and by the time they had gathered their wits the aircraft had disappeared into the clouds in a rocket-like climb, later followed by a series of sweeping turns and lightning fast rolls. Not many would have believed they were looking at a design that was to be a hopeless failure as a fighting machine, for its display in the hands of Dave Morgan and Les Colquhoun was outstanding. Les had recently been awarded the George Medal for successfully landing an Attacker at Chilbolton after the starboard wing tip had folded up in flight, jamming the ailerons and making control almost impossible. He refused to leave the stricken machine, and managed to bring it down on rudder and elevators, screeching to a halt with only yards to spare at the end of the runway.

Another high spot at Farnborough was Vickers' chief test pilot

'Jock' Bryce's display in the Viscount airliner, which he flew past the crowds on only one of its four engines.

But soon it was Derry's turn. The sight of the black 110 taking off was another startling contrast to the shapes that had gone before and, in his virgin white pressure suit, John stood out sharply against the satin black of the aircraft, and as he and Richards roared off into the distance towards Laffan's Plain, the crowd's excitement was almost at fever pitch.

This was on the Tuesday, a day of much better weather than the overcast skies and drizzle of the opening day, and Derry had taken off ahead of his turn to give himself time to climb to 40,000ft in an attempt to aim a sonic boom right onto the airfield. A little later the spectators could see him weaving vapour trails before starting his dive, but while he flew back and forth their attention was diverted to the whispering smoothness of the Britannia airliner, the de Havilland Comet with a Sprite rocket-assisted take-off, the Avon powered Canberra with reheat and the Fairey Gannet, a cumbersome naval aircraft with pot belly and gull-like wings.

As the Gannet came in to land, the 110's trail suddenly bent sharply as Derry started his supersonic dive, and then it vanished as he reached lower altitude.

'I shall be with you in quite a short time,' Derry told Farnborough control as he pulled out of the dive. 'It's a little bit bumpy, otherwise conditions are quite good . . . Farnborough 110, I'm coming in now at well over 700mph – coming across the field ...'

The black aircraft, travelling less than 80ft high at little under the speed of sound, scorched past the crowds and then banked to the left.

'I'm doing a turn now, still going very fast, and we're turning away from the airfield and coming round again for a vertical S-climb.'

'Farnborough 110, you have five minutes,' control told him, as the aeroplane banked round towards the spectators from the far side of the airfield.

'I'm coming round again now, still doing 700mph, just a little bit under now,' said John. 'I shall be going up into a climb . . . cloud . . . up to 10,000ft now and rolling round.'

'110, four minutes to go.'

'Thirteen thousand feet, putting airbrakes out, descending. Farnborough 110, I'm coming round now in a steep turn to do three quick rolls over the airfield. How much longer have I got, please?'

'110, you have two and half minutes.'

'Putting airbrakes in now and I'm coming over quite slowly to do three quick rolls . . . one . . . two . . . three – now putting airbrakes out and slowing right up. Farnborough, this time I'm coming round very slowly to demonstrate a manoeuvre at very slow speed to show the power of this aircraft and manoeuvrability at slow speed.'

'Farnborough 110, you have one minute left.'

'Farnborough 110, downwind.'

'Clear to land.'

But in spite of John's searing fly-past and spectacular aerobatics, the crowd's excitement flagged in disappointment after the dive, as the eagerly awaited supersonic booms were not heard. In fact they were scattered over the Blackbushe area a few miles away. Perhaps it was the weather conditions, but no one had much luck with bangs that day. Directing the sound over a specific point was extremely difficult, as the radius is only a couple of miles or so, depending on the angle of the dive.

However, on other days Derry had more luck, even though his task was made harder by solid cloud and he had to be directed by radio. On one occasion he achieved the master stroke of supersonic demonstration flying by coinciding his 700mph fly-past with the arrival of the booms – his theory on the test flight in August when he felt the bangs go past him that it should be possible to get down before them was proved correct.

John's airmanship was at a peak for the displays that week. Though he was tired and drawn, though he was intending to leave the firm, he was able to put aside all mental and physical considerations and concentrate on the job in hand, of giving the most outstanding show within his power.

But WG240 was not always quite so co-operative.

Wednesday 3 September: 'Bloody engines!'

'110, you can come in now,' said control.

'Noise going on bloody things,' muttered John. 'Surge – hell! Now it's gone out properly . . . another run now . . . Farnborough 110, I did not broadcast on that dive . . . Farnborough 110, I'm coming round now for a second high-speed run at over 700mph.'

'110, you have four and half minutes.'

'110, Farnborough, how long? Over.'

'110, two and a half minutes.'

'This blasted engine!'

'110, one minute.'

'110 Farnborough, downwind.'

It had been a frustrating flight, but at least the bangs were heard, in spite of a thick mattress of cloud over most of Hampshire.

Compared to its rival from Gloster, the 110 was putting up by far the more spectacular performance – but the Javelin was nevertheless most impressive. As the crash investigation was still under way it was not cleared for high-speed flying, but Waterton put up an interesting display, including some aerobatics, and the aircraft, looking like an ace of spades against the sky, left an indelible impression on the eyes – and on the ears, with the weird howling from its twin Sapphire engines.

Thursday was the last of the trade days and the intensity of the whole thing tended to tail off – at least until the start of the public performances. John had no success with the supersonic bangs on that day, and the 110 developed problems with the ailerons and elevator. At one point the ailerons jammed and then the elevator followed suit. However, Derry made a neat landing.

'Any bang? Over.'

'No bang, 110,' said control.

'We must have been too close,' remarked John. 'Bags of pressure,' he said to Tony, talking about the controls. 'I could just move them like that, you see, but I couldn't move them to land. Full tailplane landing.'

'Nice landing, anyway,' said Tony.

'George Medal?' quipped John.

'Just the job!'

'Glad I had the ailerons, though,' he went on. 'Full manual on the ailerons is a bit heavy. The ailerons stuck fast, you see, and then the elevator. I could move it, just, but couldn't do anything useful with it.'

The Press, of course, loved Farnborough. There were good pictures and stories to be found, and one reporter stationed himself near Eve Derry as John was starting one of his supersonic dives. He wanted to see if her expression changed, but she took good care to see that it didn't, so he never got the story he was after.

That little incident was on Friday 5 September, the first of the three public days: not the biggest, of course, as it was a working day and tickets were at selectively high prices. But thousands of people were either on holiday, had the day off, or simply didn't turn up for work. Instead, they all turned up at Farnborough.

The test pilots' tent was always a popular target for autograph hunters, and some who went along that day saw John and Eve chatting to Ann Todd and David Lean – *The Sound Barrier* was already a box office sell-out. During the display that day, the two film celebrities were with an Eastern potentate, who was so alarmed at the noise and speed of the 110 that he instantly dropped to his knees and uttered an impromptu prayer.

But on that day John himself had a thought-provoking experience when he met Russell Bannock, who was operations manager and director of military sales for de Havilland, Canada. As the two of them were chatting about the show, John mentioned that although he loved high-speed test flying he would eventually be looking for more long-term opportunities, adding that his brother Duncan had said that Canada was a good place in which to find them. Bannock regarded John as the most remarkable and highly skilled demonstration pilot he had ever seen, and immediately offered him the job as chief test pilot if he decided to emigrate.

John was deeply impressed by Bannock's words and said he would consider it most seriously. Nothing had been signed and sealed with Gloster, so his options were still open.

That morning, before the display, Bannock climbed into the observer's seat and John gave him his first flight in the 110.

However, at high altitude during the afternoon's show, John and Tony had an alarming moment. At one point John noticed 'a terrible crash' when he put the airbrakes out and Tony remarked on an unusual amount of buffet. A few moments later John loosened his seat straps to lean forward and look at the wings – impossible to see unless the straps were undone because of the sweepback. The wire recorder was switched on:

'God streuth! I am glad I haven't looked at the wings before at high-speed, Tony!'

Tony looked across at the starboard wing: 'Hell, they are all over the place!' he said. 'Waggling about.'

'Waggling about like an ornithopter,' observed John.

'Christ!' said Tony, getting worried.

'Never mind,' said John, 'not to worry.' Then to control: 'How long, 110?'

'110, two minutes to go … 110, one minute left.'

'110, downwind.'

'What's the control like today, John?' asked Tony. Earlier in the week John had not been too happy about some of the directions given by control, and he had remarked: 'Can't trust these buggers much.' But on the Friday all was well.

'Jolly good, this control,' he said. 'I am just wondering if the bonk with the airbrakes at high Mach number was anything to do with –'

'110, clear to land.'

'Good,' said John. 'That was about the most complete one we've done, I think.'

What John and Tony had witnessed on that flight was a case of wing flutter, yet its severity would not have been known to them unless they undid their straps and leant forward. Although the wing was fluttering visibly, any vibrations from it were being damped out so effectively by the booms, engines and fuselage that there was no feedback to the cockpit – not even through the control column.

Just what it was that made John decide to look at the wings at that moment will never be known, for he was not able to make out a flight report. But there is no doubt that what he saw worried him, particularly as it could have been happening on previous high-speed flights.

Saturday 6 September, four years to the day after Derry's first supersonic flight in the DH108, dawned unseasonably cloudy and chilly. Eve was the first to awake that morning, and as she did so she had the odd impression that she was alone in bed, so much so that she turned over to see if John was there. It was one of those silly feelings that one gets from time to time and she thought no more about it then. And it merely seemed mildly amusing when the maid, on collecting the breakfast tea cups, pointed at the tealeaves and said: 'Oh look, there's your husband's plane!' Sure enough, there was the crude but unmistakable outline of the 110 in the tea leaves.

John and Eve got up and prepared to make an earlyish start for Farnborough as traffic was certain to be heavy on the approach roads to the airfield that morning, being one of the two main public days. But as they were getting ready, a phone call came through from de Havilland engineer Frank Reynolds to say there was a serious problem with the troublesome starboard engine on WG240: it would not fire up and there seemed no immediate solution. It was a disappointment, but John decided they should drive up to see what the problem was and whether there was any chance of getting it sorted out in time for the display.

They set out from Frensham and, after some delay in the mounting traffic, arrived later in the morning. John parked their car, a powerful Ford V8 Pilot, put the keys in his pocket, left Eve at the test pilots' tent and went over to the ground crew. It was quite clear that WG240 would not be able to fly that day. The engine, which had always tended to run hot, had been stiffening up all week and now refused even to turn, jamming the mobile starting equipment. After some discussion, John decided to fly up to Hatfield to collect WG236 for the afternoon's demonstration as it had been cleared for display flying and been given a thorough inspection that day.

But it was already late in the morning, so he told the ground crew to put the starting gear onto a low loader to be taken up to Hatfield as quickly as possible while he, in the meantime, made arrangements for his number two pilot, John Wilson, to ferry him there in a de Havilland Dove that was used as the firm's runabout.

Because this had been a last minute decision, the first Tony Richards knew about it was when he saw the Dove taxying out. When told what was happening, he looked at it gloomily:

'I wouldn't have minded going along for the ride,' he said.

'Well come on,' said ground crew member Roy Pledger. 'You can just about make it if we hurry.'

The two men jumped into a Ford Prefect, one of the RAE's vehicles, and Pledger drove furiously towards the Dove, both of them gesticulating wildly as the aircraft lined up on the runway to take off. A few moments later, and Tony would have missed it.

The previous few months had been an exciting and fulfilling time for young Richards, both on professional and personal levels: not only was he playing a major role in an advanced flight test programme, but he was also engaged to be married. He didn't want to miss out on the first display of the 110 to the public at the country's most prestigious air show.

Meanwhile, Eve was at the enclosure chatting with some of the other test pilots and their wives. Les and Katy Colquhoun were there; so was Bill Waterton, waiting his turn to fly the Javelin, and Derek Taylor, de Havilland production test pilot who was to demonstrate the Heron. Before the flying started, John Wilson returned in the Dove and joined them.

But as the afternoon wore on at Hatfield, John was getting increasingly anxious and realised that if the starting equipment did not arrive very shortly, the 110 would miss its slot and he would have no chance of flying. He looked at his watch and, just as he was about to call the whole thing off, the low loader appeared. With just moments to spare, the engines of WG236 were run up and it taxied out for take-off.

Back at the pilots' enclosure Eve and her friends were watching the display. The weather had not improved much: it was still on the chilly side and there was a thick cloud layer at about 5,000ft. Shortly before the 110 was due over the airfield there was some minor drama as the ultra-short take-off and landing Prestwick Pioneer damaged an elevator on the ground as the pilot slightly overdid things in a rocket-like take-off – but it was not serious and the aircraft landed safely.

John and Tony had left Hatfield at about 3.15, and a few minutes later were over Farnborough, high above the cloud in brilliant sunshine, climbing to 40,000ft to begin the supersonic dive. A patch of blue sky had broken over the airfield and that day's commentator, Charles Gardner, directed 120,000 pairs of eyes to this spot in the hope that they would see the 110, which at this point in its development was flying with no wing fences: the four temporary wooden ones had been removed, but the two standard metal ones had not been replaced.

Then John put the aircraft into a dive. The crowd quietened, eagerly hoping to hear the sonic booms. The 110 was seen as a bright silver speck against the blue, and the crowd's excitement mounted as they saw two puffs of vapour behind the aeroplane – a characteristic caused by shockwave changes as an aircraft passes the speed of sound. Moments later there was a shattering triple explosion that shook the buildings. A surge of cheering and clapping broke out – then WG236 was seen pulling out sharply as

Derry swept in for a searing high-speed run from the Laffan's Plain direction.

Those with the best view of John's fly-past, which came just moments after the bangs, were those lining the runway barrier fence and several thousand packed tightly on a large mound known as Observation Hill because of the fine view that it gave. Being well away from the mass of cars, it was a much sought after spot and many people had been there since early morning. Once there, it was almost impossible to move until the end of the display.

After scorching past the onlookers at more than 700mph, Derry banked to the left as usual and began his long sweeping turn away from the airfield, at the same time gaining height and losing speed. For a while the aircraft was out of sight and Gardner took up his commentary again, describing the machine and saying that it would reappear shortly when Derry would do some aerobatics.

The crowd was still at fever pitch, for the bangs were the loudest heard that week. As Gardner spoke, WG236 came into view, still turning and approaching the airfield at an altitude of about 500ft. It was flying fast, although nothing like as quickly as the low level run a few moments earlier. The 110's head-on silhouette took on recognisable shape and, as it was over the northeastern edge of the airfield, John prepared to put it into an upward roll.

The end came with appalling suddenness.

There was a brief scatter of fragments behind the 110 while it was still turning and, before anyone realised what was happening, the whole aircraft reared up violently, seemingly surrounded by a momentary shimmer of light. A split second later the sky in front of the crowds was filled with pieces of broken aircraft. Some parts were already fluttering to earth while others were arcing across the sky at speed.

Gardner screamed, 'Oh my God, this was never meant to happen' – but even before he spoke the two Avon engines had torn free and, whistling gently and streaming thin trails of smoke, were soaring in a graceful arc over the airfield towards the crowd.

Appallingly, the cockpit section with Derry and Richards still inside, had been thrown skywards in the violence of the break-up and was now slowly rotating as it tumbled toward the crowd line near the main runway.

As the shattered tailplane, along with thousands of pieces of wing and fuselage, scattered over the northern edge of the airfield and Cove Radio Station, the remains of the centre section – still grotesquely recognisable as booms and inner parts of the wings – soared almost lazily upwards until inverted then righted itself and sank down, seeming almost in slow motion, finally crashing onto a mobile generator near the perimeter fence.

Almost at the same moment, the cockpit section plummeted onto the grass a few yards from the crowds nearest the runway, shattering violently and injuring some spectators who were showered with fragments. They had little chance to move to safety – and some were too mesmerised even to realise the danger. But those on the hill had no chance and Gardner's desperate cry of 'look out!' was in vain. It was only in the final moments they knew that a jet engine was going to hit them and, packed too tightly to move, they were helpless.

The engine, weighing more than a ton, fell into them, gouged a three-foot crater and finally came to rest. The other engine flew over the airfield boundary and crashed harmlessly onto wasteland.

Some spectators vaulted over the metal fence to try to give aid to Derry and Richards. There was nothing to be done: it was over for John and Tony.

A terrible silence fell upon the crowd. There was not a word, not a murmur. In a few unbelievable moments a happy and excited scene had been replaced by devastation as the wreckage lay scattered over and beyond the airfield. People who, seconds earlier, had thrilled to the sight and sound of the 110 were now lying dead, dying, or fearfully injured.

A thin blue haze of smoke rose from the hill.

Eve looked up. 'There's no hope, is there?' she asked quietly.

John Wilson, numbed by what he had witnessed, hesitated, fearful of telling her what he knew must be true.

'No,' said Derek Taylor. 'There is no hope.'

The crowd remained silent and still. Police, ambulances and fire engines converged on the disaster area. A helicopter took off and monitored the rescue operation while police hastily cordoned off the spot with a makeshift barrier of sacking. The task facing the rescuers was dreadful: twenty-nine were dead or dying, some of them children at their first air show, and identification was often difficult or impossible. Another sixty three were injured.

But Eve knew nothing of this. All she knew was that John was dead – and yet in that moment as the aircraft broke up she felt curiously detached, as though it were all happening to someone else, as though it were not real at all. The tears never came. If they had, everything may have been less of an ordeal later on, but at that point it was a blessing, for minutes later it fell to her to break the news to the children, to John's father, to John's sister and to her own parents. But her only wish in those immediate moments after the crash was that the show must go on – anything to end that awful silence.

After the wreckage was cleared from the runway, the show continued to help keep a shocked crowd from panic. Towards the end of the programme it was the turn of Neville Duke in the Hawker Hunter.

'Are you going to climb and do a bang?' control asked him.

'Roger,' replied Neville. It did not occur to him to call off his flight, and he thought afterwards that it would have been more difficult to back down than to have carried on. He had seen friends die in the war and then had flown immediately afterwards. But this was different. This was not war. This was not expected. And John had been a dear friend.

As the last of the shattered fragments of the 110 were cleared from the runway, as the bodies of John and Tony were taken away and the dying were tended on the hill, Duke opened the throttle of WB195, released the brakes and took off. He flew towards Laffan's Plain in the pale sunshine that had broken through and climbed to 40,000ft. There were a few minutes before making his supersonic dive, a few minutes to reflect . . . could John's crash have had something to do with the sound barrier, he wondered?

Then he dived. The needle passed Mach One, and the double boom echoed across the airfield, as John's had done such a short while earlier. It was an extraordinary moment – almost unreal – and some regarded it as unnecessary and irreverent. But most saw it as an inspiring and extremely brave tribute to those who had died, and later Winston Churchill, who was then Prime Minister, commended Neville for his 'characteristic' courage.

After Duke's flight, Eve went into the officers' mess room, desperate to make the phone calls before the six o'clock news. She rang her parents first, fearful that Carol would answer. Carol did answer: 'Is Daddy all right?' she asked.

'Yes,' Eve replied calmly, 'Daddy's all right now.'

It was, after all, true in a way and seemed the only thing to say. Meanwhile, John's brother Hugh, who was at the display with a party of schoolchildren, had joined Eve after giving his charges enough money for the fare back to their school in Oxford. He was shattered at what he had witnessed – yet Eve, almost unbelievably, was still totally in control of herself. Once more she picked up the telephone, this time to ring John's father.

'We lost John this afternoon,' she told him – and that was what she told them all, in just those words.

The young wife of a test pilot, seeing how Eve was coping with the terrible duties she had to perform, came up to her and said: 'If this ever happens to us, we shall remember you.'

Eve did not know who she was. She never knew.

As she made the phone calls, which seemed almost endless and more awful each time, someone offered her a brandy. But she refused, instead drinking cup after cup of tea and smoking cigarette after cigarette. Then, as the show ended and as the last phone call was made, there was nothing left but to go back to the hotel – but she couldn't take the car: the keys were still in John's pocket from the morning, so John Cunningham, who had been flying the Comet at the show, gently led her away and prepared to drive her back to Frensham Pond. There was a police escort, and the crowd, sensing who she was, clamoured to the car in their insatiable curiosity, pressing their faces to every window, pushing, jostling, staring wide-eyed, eager to see what a woman looks like after she has just watched her husband die.

It was terrible for Eve, and she felt the panic of claustrophobia rising within her. But gradually the crowds cleared as the police car led the way and by early evening they were back at the hotel.

In the meantime, Derek Taylor was driving to collect Connie from Sevenoaks, where she was visiting a relative. When she arrived at Frensham she was utterly devastated: the boy to whom she had devoted her life, whom she had loved, adored and indulged, was gone forever.

Next day there were 140,000 spectators at Farnborough, even though it was pouring with rain.

It had suddenly become the circus act with no safety net.

Chapter 11

UNCHARTED SEAS

'Had he lived then, he would have crossed the uncharted seas.'
Wing Commander C.D. North-Lewis

'I do not know a single thing about him that ever displeased me,
and there are not many people of whom one can say that.'
C. Martin Sharp, de Havilland

A flight of Canberra jet bombers passed slowly over the great
Abbey of St Albans, dipping in perfect formation as they flew
over the tower. Thus the Royal Air Force paid tribute to the
two men whose memory was being honoured inside the
ancient building.

The impressive salute in the skies, nine days after the
Farnborough tragedy, was one more expression of the shock and
distress felt, not only by the aviation world, at John Derry's death.
In April the following year, the *Spectator*, looking back, commented
in a leading article: 'The accident had been publicised as nothing
outside a world war has been publicised before or since.' So it
was; newspaper headlines spelt out little else, the world over, for
days afterwards.

Letters and telegrams came in their hundreds to both Eve and
de Havilland. The enormity of the tragedy was acknowledged by
everyone, from Buckingham Palace down. There were telegrams
from the Queen and the Duke of Edinburgh, from the Queen
Mother and Queen Mary. Duncan Sandys, then Minister of Supply,
expressed his sorrow and Lord Trenchard sent a personal letter. It
seemed that no one who had ever met John was unaffected by
his death.

Derry's old commanding officer, Wing Commander C.D. 'Kit' North-Lewis, summed up what many people tried, touchingly, to say, when he wrote from Rhodesia:

'In John was reincarnated that Elizabethan Spirit which has made our country great. A thirst to explore the unknown; to attempt things which man had not tried before. Had he lived then, he would have crossed the uncharted seas: Instead he probed the mysteries of space and speed . . . although he achieved so much fame he remained completely unspoilt.'

There were many letters from complete strangers to Eve. People who had met and admired John whilst working with him, no matter how briefly, paid their tributes:

'. . . in common with all those who knew your husband, those of us in this Unit who met him appreciated greatly his friendly and unassuming personality; just as we admired – with some technical insight – his superb ability as a pilot and, perhaps even more, the unique and highly personal contribution that he was able, with his unusual gifts, to make to the extension of the outer fringes of man's knowledge of a new world.'

This was from the manager of the Shell Film Unit, the group that had taken publicity film when John had made record-breaking flights, including one in July 1950 in a Vampire from Hurn to Lisbon and another from Hatfield to Rome in November 1948.

Another professional in the film world, Anthony Squires, worked with John during the shooting of *The Sound Barrier*. He paid his tribute: 'As long as I live, I'll remember John as one of the finest men I've ever met – brilliant yet generous, fearless yet gentle, always considerate and an inspiration to all those with whom he came in contact.'

Ann Todd, star of the film, wrote, mourning John as a 'Special Person'.

The greatest sense of loss was undoubtedly felt by the people who worked at the forefront of the air industry. Test pilot Neville Duke acknowledged John to be 'the foremost and most knowledgeable pilot in this country in the art and science of high-speed flying.' R.E. Bishop, head of the design department and a director at de Havilland, knew that designers owed a debt to his memory: '(He) has made an immense contribution to the design and development of supersonic aircraft, by his ability as a pilot and by his intelligence in analysing and interpreting what he observed in the air.' Handel Davies, then Chief Superintendent of the A&AEE at Boscombe Down, wrote sadly: 'We at the RAE and at Boscombe Down had come to regard John Derry as the outstanding experimental test pilot of this country and we had learnt to value his advice above all others.' His colleague at the Royal Aircraft Establishment, Group Captain Sidney Hughes OBE, AFC, concurred with his account of the respect in which Derry was held at RAE: 'John was our friend, a comrade-in-arms, as well as a favourite consultant and expert. . . No news travelled faster at Farnborough than information that John Derry would pay us a visit . . .'

The letters poured in, from schoolboys to whom John had been an idol, from ordinary air enthusiasts who had followed his career ('Today's paper brings the terrible news about poor John Derry and the 110. His death is tragic and having so very recently captured the imagination of the whole world and for long having held the admiration and a warmest place in the hearts of those of us who take a rather more than ordinary interest in aviation,' wrote a Yorkshire man), and from air enthusiasts the world over.

Mr Richard Clarkson, a director of de Havilland who had worked closely with Derry, knew him well but found himself in the same difficulty as many of the writers:

'It is difficult in writing about John Derry to avoid the appearance of being too fulsome in one's praise . . . I knew him as a man who was supreme in his profession to which he was devoted with an enthusiasm and singlemindedness of purpose which was, to me, almost breathtaking. An encounter with him was always to me a most exhilarating experience. I was always impressed by his intelligent, thoughtful approach and his remarkable powers of diagnosis; as for his piloting skill and courage, there is nothing I can tell you, I am sure.'

Other tangible tributes were sent to Eve to honour John's memory. The Queen posthumously commended him and Tony Richards for valuable services in the air; American Air Cadets voted him their Airman of the Year and a Derry and Richards Memorial was set up, giving an annual award for outstanding achievements in the air.

Eve faced the lonely walk down the long aisle of St Alban's Abbey, crowded with hundreds of friends, colleagues and admirers at the Memorial Service for John and Tony. Outwardly she was calm; she had to be brave for her dead husband's sake. She put a comforting hand on Neville Duke's arm as she saw the distress in his eyes. She spoke a few words to John's ground crew who had collected £600 for her children when John was killed. They could not hide their tears. Eve bore everything bravely. She watched, dry-eyed, as the two bronze urns containing the ashes of John and Tony were buried side by side in the little churchyard at Knebworth, in the park where John had so often walked in the dawn.

But when the funeral was over, the letters answered and the public ordeal in the past, Eve collapsed with her grief. For three months she could not eat or sleep, seeing over and over again the break up of her husband's aeroplane. At the time, absurdly, the first piece that had come away from the 110 had seemed to her to resemble the leg of a kitchen chair. She could not help but see that chair leg falling away, again and again. . .

She had known when she married John the risks attached to his job: 'I would not have him change his job for the world. It is his whole life and must be mine, too,' she had said in a newspaper interview. But the cruelty of the end, the picture in her mind was more than anyone – even someone as brave as Eve – could bear. Slowly the rawness of the grief lessened and the knowledge that her children needed her pulled her round. Carol, to whom John had meant everything, was heartbroken, although Jo, at six, couldn't grasp the implication of death.

While John's family and friends mourned and the nation slowly forgot the horror of Farnborough 1952 with its death toll of thirty one, questions had to be asked and answered. What had gone wrong with the new de Havilland aeroplane?

An intense investigation into the crash was underway as soon as the wreckage was cleared from the runway. Although the break-up of the DH110 had more witnesses than any other disaster in history, the initial clues were frustratingly few. The Press speculated: Why, wondered several air correspondents, did the aircraft disintegrate at that point, when it appeared to be in a moderate turn and not under any great strain?

Why did it not break up as it pulled out of the dive at great speed? As one newspaper put it: 'The stresses during the "pull-out" may have weakened some part of the machine which did not betray itself to the super-sensitive hands of John Derry.' Others felt that, because the bangs had been so loud, John must have been flying considerably faster than before in his final dive – a false assumption, of course, as whatever the speed reached after Mach One, the intensity of the sonic boom cannot be affected.

The inquest, at Aldershot, a few days after the tragedy included evidence from the Airfield Commandant, Group Captain S.W.R. Hughes.

'I am quite convinced that the pilot had no warning whatsoever of the impending failure of his aircraft,' he told the coroner. He emphasised that Derry's flying never gave one moment of anxiety and described him as 'one of the most experienced pilots in the country'.

The coroner made it clear that spectators knew that there was to be supersonic flying at Farnborough and must have realised the element of risk. He said that he was sure that Derry was not responsible for the crash and the jury agreed, adding a rider to their verdicts of 'accidental death' on the victims, that 'No blame is to be attached to Mr Derry'.

At the Royal Aircraft Establishment, Farnborough, a team of experts led by Dr Percy Walker, head of the Structures Department, was carrying out the official investigation. Because this was no ordinary aeroplane – it was an advanced design engaged in very high-speed flying – the repercussions on the designs of future aircraft were thought to be such that the major technical investigation should be carried out by the top men in the country in collaboration, of course, with the design firm, de Havilland.

Witness accounts and photographs were urgently needed and Sir Arnold Hall, RAE director, put out a public appeal. The response was instantaneous and overwhelming with an eager public anxious to solve the air riddle of the year sending in well over 1,000 letters and photographs. Many of the accounts are touchingly detailed and well intentioned, but the whole of the vast mail was of little use. Only a handful of the pages and pages of carefully penned notes give anything that resemble an accurate report of the sequence – and the photographs only show pieces of wreckage sailing through the air.

Then came a vital clue: the RAE received a cine film taken by Victor Gardner, who was a member of the establishment's scientific department, but on the day of the crash was enjoying the weekend off and pursuing his hobby of cine photography. He was watching the display from a field on the northern side of the airfield, together with his wife and son Richard, who was then five and is now with the Farnborough Air Sciences Trust.

'I still remember it clearly,' said Richard. 'My father was passionate about cine photography and he was filming the 110 as it came round. It was going very fast. Suddenly there were pieces falling everywhere like confetti and my mother pulled at my father's arm saying "look, look". But he shook her off and carried on filming.

'I remember the main part of the aircraft floating down like an acorn leaf and the engines flying across with a strange whistling noise.'

It was an excellent piece of filming – far better than any of the newsreels –and from this it became clear what had happened, although not why. As the 110 was banking to the left and heading towards the crowd, the outer half of the starboard wing broke up. A similar portion of the port wing failed in the same way a fraction of a second later. With only the inner part of its wings left, the 110 underwent a sudden and violent trim change, causing it to rear up so quickly that the cockpit section ripped off under the g forces, while the engines just carried straight on as the airframe tore itself from them. The tailplane broke up as it was hit by debris from the fuselage.

The film showed that all this happened in about one second. It is not surprising, therefore, that not many people were able to give an accurate account of events. Most witnesses thought that the tailplane had broken first – even Oliver Stewart, an experienced observer, got it wrong: '. . . the first sign of trouble was the scatter, towards the inside of the turn, of small fragments which I believe were from the empennage – tailplane elevators, fins or rudders.'

While a small group of investigators was busy sifting through the letters and photographs, another team was examining the wreckage, which had been gathered from a one and a half mile trail, extending from Cove radio station right across the airfield. It was now all piled up in a hangar, the various pieces labelled and photographed. Among this team of three was Fred Jones, a young man who was establishing himself as an outstanding 'detective' in the complex field of wreckage analysis. He had been specially called in for this job and the first thing he did was to spend a few hours alone in the hangar with the ruin of the 110, just getting the 'feel' of the twisted wreckage, a period of contemplation which was important to him.

Meanwhile, Dr Walker kept a file of private notes in which he detailed the course of the investigation and his own thoughts on the progress. He mentioned a visit to Hatfield to see design chief R.E. Bishop and Bob Harper, de Havilland's head of Structures. This was on Monday 29 September, when he saw the second prototype 110, WG240, with its wings 'well dismantled'. He noted cracks in ribs under the skin attachment nuts in seven places. 'Some say this may be the result of overtightening. I do not accept this myself,' he noted. Dr Walker felt that the cracks were consistent with 'heavy suction loads' (caused by the airflow at high speed). 'I inspected firm's load curves for 650mph at 7g pull out. Suction loads are heavy . . . information on transonic and supersonic loads is very scanty and almost negligible.'

On this visit he told Mr Bishop that Sir Vernon Brown, chief inspector of accidents, would soon have to make an interim statement to the Ministry of Civil Aviation and it would be best to base this on conclusions agreed by both de Havilland and RAE. Apparently, Bishop was not so happy. It seemed to Walker that he would have preferred just to say that 'the accident was caused by high-speed flutter'. 'I was not prepared,' wrote Walker, 'to ignore the suction loads and known weakness of ribs. We reached a compromise which is as near the truth as we can probably get at present.'

That preliminary 'compromise' statement, blaming suction loads and flutter as the probable cause of the accident, went to the Ministry on 16 November and it turned out to be a good example of a red herring. It was based on a number of assumptions that simply were not backed up by hard evidence. Flutter had been responsible for a number of disastrous high-speed crashes at that time and this knowledge, combined with the evidence of the Gardner film, which showed blurring on the starboard wing, tended to influence some of the investigators in the early days. But Fred Jones was unmoved – 'Assume nothing – just be certain,' was his motto and to him the only way of being certain was to analyse the wreckage and clear all other considerations from his mind.

Walker's private notes show how unhappy he was about certain aspects of the 110. He was concerned that the suction loads were heavier than was generally appreciated and he was worried that the aircraft had exceeded its design maximum speed of 650mph. 'From the still limited information available it appears that the ribs could not withstand even the assumed design load,' he wrote in his private file, adding that WG236 had not been strength tested as a whole (although de Havilland had tested the individual components) and he felt that, 'It should not have been allowed to fly in the way it has.' Even at this stage he admitted that although the information on transonic and supersonic loadings was inadequate, this may have had little or no bearing on the accident. One of the worries he noted proved to be well founded. He had investigated the wing construction of the aircraft and had noted the unconventional design of the leading edge section ahead of the main spar. This is known as the 'D' nose. Walker had the feeling that at least one of the de Havilland stressmen was more worried than he outwardly appeared about the D-nose structure.

'Doubts such as this can only be settled by a strength test,' concluded Walker.

That is exactly how the doubts were settled for, as Dr Walker mused, Fred Jones had detected crucial evidence on the starboard wing. He found a compression buckle at the leading edge between ribs number eight and nine and he was able to trace the consequences of such a failure by a detailed process of elimination. He was also able, by the same process, to pinpoint this as the first part of the aircraft to fail and to say with certainty that the whole break up had been as a result of this.

To Jones and the team, the evidence was irrefutable and it negated all theories about flutter. He maintained that the buckle had been caused by the aeroplane executing a rolling pull-out, a manoeuvre that combines turning and climbing and puts a tremendous twisting force on the wing. There was nothing uncommon about it, but Derry's tragedy threw a new light on the dangers.

The moment Derry moved the control column to straighten up from his final turn to begin an upward roll, the wing tore off, overcome by the aileron pushing the starboard wing down and the elevator pulling the nose of the aircraft up.

Mr D.T. Jones, head of the RAE accidents department, sent a memo to Dr Walker, telling him that the rib flanges appeared to have failed from a single load rather than a progressive weakening from flutter – in other words, the crash was the result of just one manoeuvre. The investigators were certain that this was what had happened; a strength test reproducing conditions on the fatal day would prove it. On 4 December, de Havilland set up the port wing from a 110 in the 'E' block of their structural test house and carried out a straight load test, without any twisting force applied. It withstood this satisfactorily.

Then they carried out the crucial test – the one that would imitate the twisting loads of a rolling pull-out. The wing failed and the RAE team went immediately to Hatfield to inspect the buckled piece of aircraft. Mr D.T. Jones wrote a memo to Dr Walker on 9 December:

'. . . it appears that the wing failed in a condition representing a rolling pull-out manoeuvre of 4½g and 8.5 degrees of aileron at 650mph . . . from the test result the firm have estimated the combinations of normal acceleration and aileron angle which would produce failure and they find that the wing has about 64 per cent of the ultimate strength required in the design.'

A shear buckle, similar to that of Derry's wrecked WG236, had formed on the wing leading edge between ribs nine and ten. 'The firm ascribe this failure to an erroneous estimate of the allowable stress at that point,' wrote D.T. Jones.

The theory of such catastrophic failure was not entirely unknown in the aircraft industry. Nearly a year earlier, in December 1951, SAAB Technical Note No 5, entitled 'An Empirical Formula for the Ultimate Shear Strength of Wing Leading Edges' by Mr F. Turner, was published and the de Havilland test result on the buckled wing was consistent with the theory in this. But de Havilland did not know of this publication until late in 1952.

The investigation also established that Derry had been flying at about 450mph and pulling 4½g with an 'up' aileron angle on the starboard wing of 7½ degrees – although there was some uncertainty about this last figure.

If, as the investigators now postulated, the wing breakage was not the result of a gradual build up of stress, one immediate mystery was why it had not failed before in the aircraft's 120 hours of flying. Fred Jones was certain that it never reached the crucial combination of forces before, although it had closely approached the single point of stress in previous flights. It only had to do this once before disaster struck.

The design of the wing, said the investigators, was the culprit. Although it conformed to the Ministry's AP 970 requirements, and although this method of a thick gauge D-nose leading edge had been satisfactory on the Vampire and the Venom, it was simply not up to the greater stresses induced on the 110. The RAE team maintained that vertical webbing on the main spar would have prevented failure.

Although de Havilland may not have agreed with all the RAE findings, and they were by no means bound to do so, there is no doubt that before the second prototype, WG240, flew again, the wings were extensively redesigned and these modifications remained when it was developed into the carrier-based Sea Vixen. A member of the RAE investigation team, Mr P.B. Hovell, sent a memo to Dr Walker on 24 March 1953, telling him that de Havilland proposed to incorporate a front spar web, fit thicker wing ribs and to reinforce the inter-spar stringers between ribs eight and eleven.

The final official statement, Service Accident Report No. S.2594, was issued on 17 April 1953 and signed by P.G. Tweedie, chief inspector of accidents, Ministry of Civil Aviation. The document refers to the wing loading tests carried out at Hatfield: 'In the test the structure failed to achieve the designers' aim and was weaker than it had been thought to be.'

The cause of the crash, 'considered to be established beyond doubt', is given as 'structural failure of the starboard outer wing caused by the combined effect of pull up acceleration (associated with turning) and the loads produced by upward aileron (appropriate to straightening out from a turn).' The report mentions the unusual wing design:

'For the type of construction used in the DH110 outer wing it is not possible to predict from general experience and theoretical knowledge the stage of loading at which failure would occur. The design problem is rendered more difficult by the absence of a forward main spar or forward vertical webbing in the outer wings.'

Derry is absolved from all blame:

'It is considered that the pilot was in no way responsible for the accident. There is no evidence to suggest that transonic dives were directly contributory or that power operation of the controls was a significant factor.'

This report, which was never made public, contains an observation: 'This accident emphasises that for future new designs of aircraft structure, the aircraft should not be flown at high speed or subjected to severe manoeuvres until the agreed programme of essential major strength tests have been completed.'

Derry hadn't died in vain – new light was thrown on the stresses engendered by this new breed of fast aircraft and more intensive structural testing programmes were devised.

But with Derry's death, the end of an era was rapidly approaching; disappearing were the days when man and machine would battle it out together to solve the mysteries of flight. Telemetering equipment, then in its infancy, was rapidly developed; increasingly sophisticated computers solved the problems, which before had only found their solution in bravery.

The first British supersonic aircraft had been the strange little 108. More reliably supersonic were the four that followed hard on its heels: the DH110, the Hawker Hunter, the Gloster Javelin and the Supermarine Swift. True supersonic speeds, achieved in level flight, came with the English Electric Lightning and the experimental Fairey Delta FD2, the forerunner of Concorde.

John Derry and test pilots like him made this rapid development possible. He translated the unknown into reality for the scientists and designers on the ground who put his hard earned knowledge into practice. John was widely quoted after that first supersonic flight in 1948: 'We must press on'; that was the key to his whole philosophy.

He was one of those rare people who follow a direct path in life

Right: WG236 on an early flight. (BAE SYSTEMS)

Below: Derry in WG236, which is now fitted with boom stiffeners and under fin extensions to improve handling at high altitude. (BAE SYSTEMS)

Bottom: The second prototype 110 (WG240) on an early flight in its original silver finish. (Aeroplane Monthly Archive)

A rare shot of WG240 in a silver finish. After its first few flights it was painted black to depict its intended role as a night fighter. (BAE SYSTEMS)

Now in its sinister black finish, Derry moves WG240 in for a close-up shortly before Farnborough 1952. (BAE SYSTEMS)

The second prototype 110 resplendent in its black finish. This was how it appeared on the trade days at Farnborough in 1952. (Aeroplane Monthly Archive)

Neville Duke, hero of Farnborough 1952.

FROM THE DERRY FAMILY ALBUM

John and Eve with Carol and Jo and the dogs at Greensleeves.

John, with 'onion seller's' beret, and Eve on board the Hebrides.

The SS Hebrides *in the Western Isles, May 1952.*

John, Eve and Jo on holiday in Cornwall, July 1952.

Friday 5 September 1952, Farnborough. Ann Todd and David Lean chat with John and Eve outside the test pilots' tent.

John Derry and Tony Richards (white overalls) with their ground crew in front of WG240 during Farnborough Week, September 1952. Ground crew: Standing left-to-right – 'Mac' MacKenzie (electrician), Dave Fish (instrumentation), Mr Robilliard (flight test inspector), Roy Pledger (hydraulic fitter), Fred Sykes (airframe fuel system). Kneeling – Tom Carter (foreman), Bob Jones (general fitter).

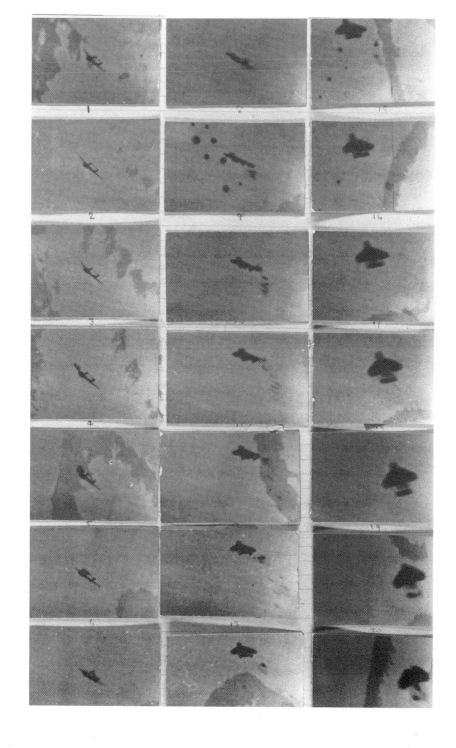

Opposite: stills from the Gardner cine film showing the break-up of WG236. The sequence is arranged in three columns, each consisting of seven frames and starts at the top left corner. Reading downwards, the first three frames show the aircraft banking towards the camera – all is well. On frame four, a slight blurring shows the starboard wing beginning to disintegrate. By frame six the outer part of the wing has been lost, the aircraft starts rolling to starboard (frame seven) and the next seven frames show the break-up of the same portion of the port wing. (The circular blobs on some frames are blemishes on the film.) With the outer parts of its wings gone, the aircraft rears up violently and in the final two frames the cockpit section has broken away and the tail plane is starting to disintegrate. The whole sequence took little more than one second.

Below: John Derry and Tony Richards.

In memory of the few and those that have come after them

PER ARDUA AD ASTRA

*'In memory of the few and those that have come after them.' A tribute by an
unknown artist published in a national newspaper shortly after John Derry's death.*

and, moreover, he was able to do this with none of the personal ambition that harms the lives of others. He was charming, honest, selfless, thoughtful and brave. He was resolute; from a very early age he had made up his mind that he would devote his life to aircraft. That resolution was to be the cause of his death, but not before he had paved the way for safe supersonic flight as we know it today.

Footnote: Seven days after Derry's death, John Cunningham flew WG240 from Farnborough to Hatfield after the faulty RA7 engine number 73 was replaced with engine number 299. Following major structural modifications, in particular to the wings, it eventually flew again on 17 June 1953. Later that month de Havilland test pilots John Wilson and Chris Capper took over most of the test programme and were joined by Jock Elliott, who was to have a long association with the 110's carrier deck trials.

WG240's final flight was on 20 May 1957 when Chris Capper ferried it from Hurn to Christchurch. It spent some time as an instructional airframe at RNAS Arbroath and ended its life at the Royal Naval Engineering College at Manadon, Plymouth, where it was broken up on 5 July 1965 and sold as scrap.

JOHN DERRY'S TEST REPORTS ON
THE DH108

Three pilot's reports are given here. The first and last refer to the two occasions on which an indicated Mach Number of unity has been exceeded. The second refers to a series of flights between these two occasions. During these flights Mach Numbers of about .98 were obtained without loss of control. The purpose of including these pilot's reports is to give a more detailed description of the behaviour of the aircraft, and of the piloting technique necessary, than is given in the body of the main report.

   (a) Type: DH108   No: VW120

      Pilot: J. D. Derry   Date: 6. 9. 48

      Take-off CG: 0.177 SMC   Take off weight: 8,913lb

      Mean flight CG: 0.181 SMC Duration: 45 mins

Dive to High Mach Number

The original intention of this flight was to take pressure-plotting shots with trim flap up and down at varying M. Before this, an attempt was to be made to obtain further film records at M = .96 to match up with those obtained on the previous flight. It was hoped to reach M = .96 in a steeper dive and have a larger elevon angle at the same point.

Accordingly the aircraft was climbed to 45,000ft (using pressure waistcoat and mask) and after being flown level to obtain maximum level speed, ie, M = .85 owing to engine temperature limitations, a dive of about 30° was commenced. The now well-known characteristics at M = .93 – .945 were encountered, followed at M = .95 by the sudden steadying (described in flight report) accompanied by right wing heaviness. At this point the engine was opened up to 10,750rpm but the extra thrust did not increase M further. At this point it was felt that drag had become extremely high and small forward movements of the stick were necessary to prevent M decreasing. It was quite obvious on this flight that the up elevon angle was being decreased gradually in the attempt to increase the dive. Eventually a point was reached at which very small elevon movement caused a sudden, but not violent, nose down pitch. In other words the elevon appeared to reach an angle beyond which a sudden change occurs. The first nose down pitch was over and the aircraft back in a 30° dive before an attempt could be made to hold a steeper angle. The stick was again eased very slightly further forward and this caused a more violent nose down pitch similar to that on the previous flight. In trying to recover to 45° dive the aircraft again recovered to the 30° attitude and a third attempt caused a much more violent nose down pitch which was akin to a half bunt and put the aircraft over the vertical. An immediate pull out was started again in the hope of taking a shot in a steeper attitude before complete recovery. During the pull out through the vertical however, M increased rapidly and M = .97 was indicated at this point. As the aircraft reached a 60–80° dive with M still increasing the stick force rose rapidly until it became impossible to hold the aircraft, which took over and increased the dive angle to the vertical. At this point M = 1.0 was reached and passed.

The engine was throttled right back as soon as recovery became impossible and full strength with both hands failed to make any impression on the aircraft at all. It was noted that M did not decrease below the zero point on the machmeter (approximately 1.04) in spite of power being shut off. Little time was wasted when once it was realised that the elevons were immovable. (It is thought that the elevon angle was up at this point but it is not known by how much.)

The only hope of recovery was then tried and full trim flap applied at once. Almost at once a very gradual recovery began, applying extremely little g and causing, what seemed to the pilot a very slow decrease in M. At M = .98 recovery rate was increasing and the elevons were having some effect. It was thought that the trim flap might suddenly become effective and for this reason it was returned to approximately 4°. At M = .94 the aircraft was nearly level and a sudden undamped oscillation began; this was checked by immediately returning trim flap to neutral. Altitude was noted at this point as 23,500ft. ASI was just under 500mph ASI. (This was not read accurately.)

During the dive at Mach numbers above M = .98 − 1.0 the aircraft appeared to be extremely stable. Apart from the heaviness of the controls there was no movement of any kind, the aircraft being rock steady, in the dive. No buffeting of any kind was experienced in spite of large amounts of negative g at M = .98 and up to 2g at the bottom of the dive at M = .98 and 1½g at M = 1.0 or just below.

   (b) Type: DH108   No: VW120

       Pilot: J. D. Derry   Date: 1.2.49

                                        1.2.49

                                        2.2.49

      Take-off CG: 0.1 77 SMC   Take-off weight: 8,913

      Mean flight CG: 0.181 SMC Duration: 40 min

                                        35 min

                                      25 min

Dives to High Mach Number

Three flights are contained in this report since all three contained almost identical runs.

It is first of all necessary to go back to the previous two flights on which M = .95 was exceeded.

The unstable downward pitching at M = .95 to .96 appeared to be due to forward movement of the stick until the elevon angle was almost 0°. This movement of the stick was not obvious on the first occasion on which it occurred but was investigated at the time and it was found that at M = .95 in a 15–20° dive there was no further acceleration and the stick was allowed to go forward gradually in attempting to steepen the dive. During recovery from M = .92 there was no instability, therefore it seemed reasonable that if the elevon could be maintained at a large up angle during acceleration, the aircraft should not become unstable. This seemed almost certain after easing the stick forward at M = .93 and incurring instability, also by the slight instability at M = .93 with trim flap up 3° (ie, during runs with tufts).

The trim flaps were therefore set to 2° down prior to the runs on these flights and the aircraft set in a constant angle of dive (20–25°) at M = .86 at 44,000ft. The trim tab desynn was set to 2.4 (maximum) and feel-back at 25% (minimum). The aircraft accelerated to M = .96 quite rapidly but a slightly steeper dive (30°) was necessary to exceed this. Altogether nine dives were made, on the last dive the highest M being M = .99 indicated. Film was taken in all these dives but unfortunately in the last dive on the third flight the film jammed. However, film records have been obtained up to M = .97 which was .975 indicated.

Several points which have now come to light completely change the picture of behaviour above M = .95. Firstly at M = .96 the stick can be pulled right onto the stops and gives only 1½g recovery. At M = .98 the aircraft can just be held in a steady dive with full elevon and recovery is made using trim flap. This ineffectiveness of controls was not fully appreciated before, neither was the fact that the elevons can be pulled onto the stops at M = .97. Originally it was thought that the prohibitive pull force at M = .97 to M = 1.04 was due to reaching the maximum power of the servodyne to overcome the hinge moment. However, the elevons can be pulled onto the stops at M = .985 with a 40lb pull. It is now obvious that during the dive to M = 1.04 the elevons were in fact on the stops so that the large stick force obtained then is hardly surprising.

Secondly, these Mach numbers can be obtained in a 30° dive at 40,000ft and consequently power can be effectively used to decelerate.

Thirdly there is no instability similar to that experienced previously at M = .95, if the elevons are kept at a large up angle.

We can now assume that to be true up to M = 1.04 since there was no further instability after the downward pitch on that occasion.

Fourthly, although the elevons become completely ineffective, the trim flap is a good positive means of controlling the aircraft during recovery. On these three flights the most trim flap used was 4° up which gave a 1½g recovery to M = .95 increasing to 2g at M = .93. At M = .99, 4° up trim flap was applied and gave immediate response. It can be used at this point to control the gradual nose down trim change which cannot be held by the elevons when fully up. This nose down trim change occurs at M = .98 but is not violent nor an unstable pitch.

A history of one of these runs is included to give a clearer picture and in order to emphasise the true characteristics as opposed to those which were thought to be present from earlier work. This is interesting in that it lends power to the argument that first impressions are unreliable, particularly when compressed into a very short space of time and therefore repetition of each characteristic, several times, is essential.

ACCELERATION:

M = .86†   44,000ft trim flap 2° down. Trim tab fully down (2.4° on desynn). Aircraft pushed into 30° dive and stick moved back as soon as dive angle reached.

M = .93   Nose down trim change reached a peak (**). Stick force 50lb to hold aircraft at 30°. Elevons can be pulled to stops giving 1¾g.

M = .95   Stick force has eased off to 30lb. Starboard wing becomes heavy but is easily held. Full elevon gives 1½g.

M = .96   Aircraft quite steady and easily held in constant dive. No instability. Very slight high frequency buffet but barely noticeable on some runs.

M = .97   Constant stick force but elevons almost completely ineffective; recovery just possible with full elevon. Throttling back gives deceleration.

M = .98   Further nose down trim change occurs, with full up elevon aircraft can just be held in 30° dive. Trim flap necessary for recovery.

M = .99   Nose down trim change has increased gradually and dive steepens slowly if trim flap is not used. 3°–4° up trim flap gives positive recovery. Throttling back at this point prevents further acceleration and will just cause deceleration if dive angle is not allowed to steepen.

DECELERATION:

Recovery is smooth if stick is held fully back. Instability can be incurred at M = .92 if stick is moved forward of central. With 4° up trim flap and fully down tab, push force becomes strong at M = .85 and trim must be taken off. (Flap and/or tab).

There is no pitching oscillation with 4° up trim flap if stick is held back. The pitching in this case is an indication of approaching instability and occurs at M = .93 with elevons only 2–3° up and trim flap up.

† Indicated Mach number throughout.

**This peak is higher than hitherto owing to down trim flap which has not previously been used above M = .92.

*Full up elevon = 21° Static. Full up trim flap = 10°.

When loaded as in this flight they will be reduced, owing to control circuit stretch.

(c) Type: DH108   No: VW120
    Pilot: J.D. Derry   Date: 1. 3. 49
    Take-off C.G: 0.179 SMC   Take-off weight: 8,917
    Mean flight CG: 0.183 SMC Duration: 40 minutes.

Dive to High Mach Number

This dive was the fourth in the flight and not unnaturally, the last. All the dives on this flight were started with 2° down trim flap. The first three dives were as on previous flight up to M = .97

or so in a 20–30° dive from 44–45,000ft. On the fourth dive everything was normal up to M = .97 and the stick was pulled back as if for recovery. The dive was steeper than the others (35° approx) but at M = .970 there was a check and temporarily no increase in M. As the stick was pulled back almost to the stops M increased to M = .980 and the nose down pitch, now well known, occurred at this point. M increased to M = .99 and just before trim flap was applied for recovery a further steepening of the dive occurred. Trim flap was pulled from 2° down to 8° up (full) but with no effect. The engine was throttled. Negative g increased and the slight roll to port continued. The stick was held on the stops with both hands and because the rolling was steepening the dive, full opposite aileron was applied and this was partially effective in levelling the aircraft laterally. However, the dive was beyond 60° by this time and although recovery appeared in sight the aircraft again rolled slowly but uncontrollably to port until after 90° of roll and considerable negative g the aircraft was in a true vertical dive. There was absolutely no control at this point and all lateral control, which had been effective after all else, had now disappeared. What now happened is hard to believe and indeed was so at the time, but every evolution of the aircraft was quite slow and could be followed and remembered clearly. From a vertical attitude the negative g now increased even more and the spiralling almost stopped. The aircraft now completed the latter half of a bunt and then rolled slowly round at the bottom so that it became level laterally in a shallower dive. During the last part of this extraordinary manoeuvre which took up an enormous loss of height and increase of speed, there came a sudden sharp normal acceleration and the aircraft suddenly began to respond again to the controls although the elevons were, of course, still almost completely ineffective. However, after this 'bump' which was apparently due to the sudden return of effectiveness all negative g ceased and the aircraft recovered from the spiralling into level flight and very shortly into a climb as the trim flaps and elevons became more effective. Although little was seen of the instruments during this performance, at the point when the aircraft began to climb M = .98 was indicated at an ASI of 490mph. At M = .95 in the subsequent climb an undamped oscillation of very small amplitude occurred exactly as on the dive of 6.9.48. Trim flap was progressively reduced and the aircraft levelled out of the climb at 29,000ft at which point the camera was switched off. The main points were:

1. The stick force to hold the stick right back became extremely large but a fairly large elevon angle was maintained throughout.
2. During the outside loop effect there were some signs of buffeting although this was slight and was more of a vibration.
3. The aircraft evidently reached its terminal Mach number with throttle closed since the return of control effectiveness happened shortly after the outside loop, indicating that M was decreasing during the last part of this contortion. The return of effectiveness occurred at about M = 1.0 or even a little above.
4. The remarkable dive was in many ways similar to that of 6. 9.48 but went a stage further, probably because the nose down pitch at M = .98 occurred at a higher altitude; also in the earlier case the trouble began at M = .95 with instability so that more height was lost before the point of loss of control was reached.
5. It is significant that at a stage further in the M range the trim flaps also become completely ineffective and there is an increasing nose down pitch which is completely uncontrollable and finally caused the aircraft to dive beyond the vertical. It is also most interesting that it is in fact almost impossible to dive below 26,000ft or so before recovery becomes possible (providing the aircraft controls remain in recovery attitude) since terminal Mach number is about M = 1.0 at 30,000ft. Since there was some sign of buffeting during the last part of the dive when negative g was largest, deceleration is presumably likely to have been greater than in a 0g dive.
6. The machmeter went right off the calibrated scale but there was little time for watching instruments.

7. The ineffectiveness of the controls does not appear to vary much with ASI, since at 480mph the acceleration caused by 8° trim flap about 10° up elevon and full down tab at M = .97 was not more than 1¾ or 2g.

8. At anything above 1¾g at M = .96, a form of undamped small amplitude oscillation occurs.

9. If any further acceleration is allowed after the nose down pitch at M = .99 the trim flaps also become ineffective and a continuous increase in nose down pitch occurs as M increases without any method of control. Therefore the limit to which the aircraft can be comfortably taken is M = .97 indicated. This point can be reached in dive angles from 20–25° and is not exceeded if the dives are not steeper than this.

It has been realised since writing the report (c) that, since a terminal M was reached at some point during the vertical dive, M must have been constant or decreasing at the moment when the partial bunt occurred and consequently it would appear that this increase in -g was due to returning to the nose down trim change at M = 1.02 or so and not to increasing M. Therefore it would seem that there is a decrease in nose down pitch beyond M = 1.02 approximately.

The much larger normal acceleration which occurred on the deceleration may be due to an increase in ASI of 100mph increasing the stick force to a limiting value at some elevon angle below the stops, so that the maximum elevon power cannot be used.

The solution is confirmed in my report of being unable to hold the stick on the stops after half way through the vertical dive and also in the film record which shows a mean elevon angle of less than 7° during the increase of -v g. It is possible that the stick was not held back so hard when it was realised that the aircraft was going beyond the vertical but this would not amount to a loss of more than 2 or 3°.

HIGH-SPEED FLYING

by Squadron Leader John D. Derry

A Lecture given before the Graduates' and Students' Section
of the Royal Aeronautical Society on 30 November 1950
at 4 Hamilton Place, London W1.

The title of this paper gives only the broadest indication of the line it is intended to take. Other papers with similar titles have been read by those connected with the design or aerodynamic side, but this paper is mainly concerned in conveying the pilot's own view of the problems of high-speed flying.

The paper is divided under the following main headings: –

1. The obstacles to negotiate at high and low altitude.
2. The approach to high-speed investigation and means of obtaining test results.
3. Present and future requirements of research aircraft.
4. Pilot safety measures.
5. Some requirements of a pilot engaged in high-speed research and development flying.

For the most part it is intended only to cover research and development flying. This necessarily entails some reference to combat, which is in itself a separate field.

The problems confronting a pilot who sets out to explore the behaviour of contemporary aircraft at high-speed are considered first.

High Mach numbers and high indicated air speeds are now irrevocably joined in a modern high-speed aircraft. But it is still possible to isolate the effects of pure compressibility from the problems associated with high air loads. It is important for the pilot, as well as the aerodynamicist, to achieve this isolation. To some extent their desire to initiate all research at high altitude springs from the same source. For a given true speed the indicated speed or dynamic pressure is halved at 40,000ft. Also the speed of sound is 100mph slower above 35,000ft.

The effects of distortion and changing lift coefficients are technical problems which do affect the pilot in some degree. But there are other considerations more directly in the pilot's interest.

In the first place, up to now it has been, and will be for some considerable time hence, impossible to break a normally strong research or fighter type of aircraft above 35,000ft. This is a fact, often not appreciated, which makes nonsense of most popular ideas about flying through the 'barrier.' Secondly, control forces are low so that any increase due to Mach number does not immediately give rise to difficulties and at the same time rapid corrections can be made. Power operations and other devices largely obviate such considerations, but at present only a few aircraft in Great Britain have such controls and the problems of manual operation must be considered. A third advantage of more than passing interest to the pilot is the ability to abandon aircraft without encountering the shattering effects of high air pressures. It follows from this that at the higher altitudes a small margin of time exists in which to sum up a situation in which the possibility of baling out arises. It is hoped to show that such a situation is unlikely to occur at high altitude.

Consider what are, in fact, the pilot's main worries during investigation at high altitudes; that is to say above about 30,000ft. Problems not directly connected with speed, for example the effects of altitude on the pilot, can be disregarded for the present.

Experience has shown that compressibility effects produce the following general symptoms: variations of hinge moment, flow breakaway causing buffet, changes in stability, tab and control ineffectiveness, and large unpredictable trim changes. Of these, the last two are the most serious obstacles and have given rise to the popular stories, which have only served to confuse the issue.

As already mentioned, the advent of power controls has brought new solutions to these problems but manual controls are dying hard and a great deal of the early high subsonic work has been completed without recourse to the unconventional. Most of the original reports concerned very high stick forces and tab ineffectiveness; in most cases one following on the other. It is difficult for a pilot to be aware of the stick position or elevator angle and consequently it was not easy to recognise when the high forces were due to high angles.

Power controls have shown that all the available control movement may not be sufficient to cope with very strong trim changes. But they have permitted an increase in the limiting speed. The most troublesome trim change is nose-down, both for manual and power controls. In both cases the final result can be a very steep dive, either because of the inability of the trimmer to relieve sufficiently the stick force, or because of complete ineffectiveness. It is difficult to know when it is due to a large trim change and when it is a case of a small change, plus losing control power. It is obvious then, that a serious nose-down trim change can result in a genuine loss of control.

In practice, however, the onset of the trim change is rarely so sudden that some form of corrective action cannot be taken. Two examples of this form of vice might be of interest; one with manual controls, one with power boost.

The first concerns the Spitfire. It is often forgotten that jet aircraft have not got the monopoly of the high Mach number field. In fact only very few jets have exceeded the limiting Mach number of the Spitfire. Regular tests were made up to M = 0.86 and on one occasion M = 0.92 was reached by Martindale, then of the Royal Aircraft Establishment.

The present illustration, however, concerns the moderate Mach numbers. At M = 0.83 or so, a strong nose-down trim change occurred building up rapidly at M = 0.85 until full nose-up trim was insufficient. At M = 0.86 the aircraft could not be pulled out of the dive with a 150lb stick force. In this case the uncontrolled dive lasted only for a short time owing to the very big drag increase on closing the throttle in fine pitch.

The second example concerns the DH108. In this case the uncontrolled dive resulted from a serious loss in elevon effectiveness which resulted in having to use the full amount of up movement to trim at M = 0.98. Consequently a relatively small nose-down trim change at M = 0.99 was sufficient to carry the aircraft into a dive. Additional trim was provided by trim flaps but these quickly became ineffective and only very prompt action could prevent a vertical dive developing. Unlike the Spitfire there was no big drag increase; indeed no means of recovery existed until the terminal Mach number fell below that at which control was lost. This condition was realised at 30,000ft in the DH108 where the terminal Mach number was 1.0 and a slow recovery became possible. It was completed by 25,000ft at M = 0.95, or so.

These two examples illustrate the worst effects of Mach number and also indicate that even the extreme case is not disastrous. The author is unaware of any crash which can be directly attributed to loss of control at high altitude as a result of compressibility effects. On more advanced aircraft the results of an uncontrolled dive might be more serious, as the extra weight and lower drag might result in the dive continuing until structural limits were reached.

Nose-up trim changes are more irritating than dangerous at high altitude. A strong nose-up trim change with manual controls may prevent further acceleration since an involuntary recovery takes place. The Hornet was one example of this. At M = 0.75 a 100lb push force caused no increase in dive angle. Several modern jets have suffered from large nose-up trim changes. The only dangerous case is at medium altitudes when a sudden or unstable nose-up pitch or rapid trim change may subject the aircraft to high accelerations. At the altitude being considered such a form of vice, at the worst, results in a high g stall.

It has already been remarked that it is impossible to break a high-speed aircraft above 35,000ft. This is because the g loading at which the aircraft stalls is below that at which structural failure occurs. Given powerful enough trim changes with insufficient or heavy control, coupled with instability or lack of damping, an unintentional stall may develop. The possible consequence of such a state of affairs may be as follows.

It is necessary, in combat, to use the aircraft to its limits and g stalls are a common occurrence in fighter aircraft. For this reason the stall must be quite safe and in fact on present-day fighters it is innocuous, giving no more than a slight drop of the nose or one wing and accompanied by considerable buffeting. Reduction of g gives immediate recovery to positive control.

Aircraft with swept wings, however, exhibit the now well-known tip stall before reaching their maximum lift and this results in a rapid and unusually large trim reversal, so that the aircraft tightens suddenly in the turn or pull-out sometimes before the pilot can check it. Although this makes the stall more sudden, again there has been little trouble in stalling and unstalling satisfactorily. For tailless aircraft, or a conventional aircraft with spinning tendencies, it is possible that risk of spinning might exist. Fortunately in most aircraft the g stall is straighter than the normal stall.

A stall, then, is not likely to prove catastrophic, and in practice is rarely experienced unintentionally at high Mach number.

Since stalling has been discussed, it would be as well to mention the characteristics of aircraft with relatively low critical Mach number in which the maximum lift falls off rapidly in this region. The result, as would be expected, has all the symptoms of a g stall with buffeting, wing dropping, lack of control effectiveness and sometimes, instability. Operational aircraft of this type in service for the past few years have been cleared up to this point. This, perhaps, illustrates the absence of alarming behaviour, which is so often referred to.

The only trim change, which has not been discussed is the lateral.

Straight-winged aircraft with relatively thick wings, eg, Meteor and Vampire, experience lateral trim changes or even sharp wing drop in the advanced stages of compressibility misbehaviour. But the more gradual wing heaviness, as it is sometimes called, of the swept-wing types is more serious because it may be the only limiting feature. Because there is usually adequate warning these lateral trim changes are seldom dangerous, although in the latter stages full aileron is often ineffective in maintaining an even keel. If this stage is reached, slightly unusual attitudes can occur and a steepening of the dive is perhaps the most uncomfortable aspect of the vice.

Many swept-wing aircraft are susceptible, in varying degree, to what has become an innocuous but sometimes deciding factor in the ultimate limit. In some cases it has been found possible to raise the downgoing wing by applying rudder towards that wing; that is to say, the reverse of normal corrective action. The effect of yawing or unyawing swept wings at high Mach number can be understood but it remains a new reaction for the pilot to master. Lateral control is bound to be more satisfactory to the pilot and development to this end is in progress. Very large ailerons are an obvious solution.

Of the broad symptoms of compressibility outlined at the beginning of this section all are seen to be at their worst when connected with trim changes.

Individually they amount to little more than a distraction at high altitude, although they can be serious at low altitude.

Variation of hinge moment can result in over-balance of controls or, more commonly partial balance, producing what is known as hunting; an oscillation of the control, usually the elevator, which can be checked by the pilot and, if a serious obstacle, can usually be put right by small adjustments to the control balance.

Buffet comes in the same class although it is often harder to reduce. With very few exceptions buffet comes from the tail, although possibly as a direct result of the wing wake. Buffet can be tolerated provided that it is not of a frequency likely to cause fatigue of the structure. This is difficult to establish and sometimes necessitates the fitting of a vibrograph.

208

Control and tab ineffectiveness have already been discussed in conjunction with trim changes. The difficulty of separating these two causes of vice has been pointed out. In the absence of trim changes the result is obviously much less troublesome but with further acceleration in mind it has to be remembered that quite small variations in configuration can induce changes in effectiveness out of all proportion.

Static stability is the essence of trim changes but manoeuvre or dynamic stability has a direct bearing on the extent to which a longitudinal trim change may be investigated or negotiated. An example of this is to be found in a nose-up trim change coupled with instability in manoeuvre, referred to earlier; a stall at high altitude, but structural failure at lower levels, is a possible outcome of such circumstances.

Summarising the effects of high altitude and high speed it can be said that there is a small element of risk, but that the nose-down trim change which contributes more towards it has to be faced. In the transonic region it cannot be avoided ultimately.

Going on to the pilot's problems at low altitude, it should be explained that the extremes of both cases are being described. There is obviously a merging of the two and in the process of combining the separate effects lies the secret of approaching the low altitude problems with the minimum of risk. The gap between the two is purely arbitrary and as speeds are increased it tends to close.

What are the problems involved when high dynamic pressures are combined with the effects of compressibility? The indicated speeds considered high today are inevitably at moderately high Mach number but with improved design, particularly sweepback, aeroelastic effects can be explored without much interference from compressibility.

By far the most unacceptable of all forms of aircraft misbehaviour is flutter. Under this heading is included any undamped oscillation of control or aircraft with a frequency greater than a half-cycle per second. Below this frequency some control or deceleration is possible before high stresses are reached. Under any other conditions the only possible action is immediate deceleration and a climb; and with existing air brakes this is likely to be too slow! It is quite unsafe to investigate flutter or oscillations in flight unless a condition of indicated air speed and Mach number can be found when damping is neutral or just positive. In these circumstances a limited amount of investigation is possible but in general any attempt deliberately to induce an oscillation at high IAS is very unsatisfactory.

With the present trend for flutter speeds to rise, serious flutter is not a cause for anxiety at high altitude, but the need for a careful build-up in the Mach number-IAS combination cannot be too highly stressed.

Pitching oscillations due to lack of damping are even more unpleasant than control flutter. It has been possible to make useful investigations into this phenomenon because the fall in damping which gives rise to the oscillations has been reasonably progressive. Once again extreme care and much repetition is necessary in building up speed when this type of oscillation is expected. Ideal conditions – absence of turbulent air, failure to operate all controls at increasing speed, and so on, may result in the loss of damping remaining undetected until the point is reached where damping is negative.

This latter type of flutter or oscillation has so far mainly been confined to tailless aircraft, but the possibility of serious loss in damping when big increases in Mach number are possible must not be forgotten. Lack of damping in roll and yaw in fact have been experienced at high Mach number in the United States and under certain conditions of high IAS in the United Kingdom.

A good illustration of a pitching oscillation was provided by the DH108 in which damping was reduced with both Mach number and IAS. During investigation of high M/IAS combinations when the presence of a loss in damping was apparent and, consequently, increases were being made very gradually, a serious state of affairs occurred in spite of all possible care, in which an undamped oscillation built up to +4, -3g at the rate of 3 cycles/sec. The final loss in damping from neutral to seriously negative occurred over a Mach number range of 0.005, a variation which can occur through gusts, apart from the difficulty of maintaining M to such extreme accuracy.

At the same Mach number, however, at lower IAS, it was possible to reach a state of zero damping with a lower frequency, which allowed controlled investigation to be made.

Aerodynamic noise may produce an uncomfortable sensation of speed but may also indicate a flow breakaway. A recent example of this occurred on the night fighter Venom. The canopy had been bulged to provide increased headroom. On reaching M = 0.75 at indicated speeds above 350 knots a roaring noise began. It became progressively worse with IAS and an increase in M at 400 knots and over produced a curious whip crack effect. In moist air at low altitudes the area of high suction could be seen by the presence of a vapour cloud over it. At M = 0.78 the actual shock position was indicated by an opaque area of mist extending several inches at right angles to the surface. A lower canopy improved this but the suction is still sufficient to produce mist under certain conditions at M = 0.82 and above.

Most people have noticed the mist effect on aircraft wings during a high-speed fly past. During this phenomenon the effect of a shock formation described above can often be seen on the wing from the cockpit as a more opaque area of mist in the centre of the cloud. It is also sometimes possible to see the shadow caused by light refraction at the shock but this depends on the position of the sun and other variables. The author's experience is limited to one occasion in a Spiteful at M = 0.83 but the Americans have proved that careful positioning of the aircraft relative to the sun can make the shadow visible from any cockpit position.

It is perhaps unnecessary to point out that in spite of avoiding serious forms of vice there is always a psychological effect from high indicated speeds, at low altitude, due to noise, turbulent air and at present the inability to abandon aircraft, which will always make this side of high speed flying the least pleasant and the most spectacular. As aircraft speeds rise so the sensations remain with, or near, the critical speeds so that in a well-designed supersonic aircraft, 800mph IAS will seem little worse than 600mph IAS on a present-day aircraft capable of 650mph. High speed flying, in its true sense, means flying at, or near, limiting speed. It is probable that the Wright Brothers found 30mph extremely trying.

HIGH SPEED INVESTIGATION

Turning now to the methods used in high-speed investigation, discussion will be confined to the techniques developed over the past couple of years which, it is hoped, will bear little relation to those of the near future.

Straight winged aircraft with moderately thick wings (12–14 per cent) were attaining $M = 0.8$ or so in level flight and this was close to the vice Mach number or to the point at which the drag rise called for a steep dive.

A great deal of work was done on such aircraft up to $M = 0.86$ to 0.88. On the Spitfire, and to a lesser extent on the early jets, very uncomfortable dives were necessary to obtain these Mach numbers. The arrival of the swept wing aircraft at once led to Mach numbers in the 0.86 to 0.90 bracket in level flight. This might seem to be the answer; but it is not. The swept aircraft exhibits normal behaviour up to its level Mach number and consequently its real value for research lies in its being able to attain the 0.95 to 1.0 bracket. And so it is necessary to dive again.

This may seen obvious, but it is mentioned because it does mean that the ultimate work must still be done in a dive. On this fact hangs the framework of all methods of investigation.

It has been shown earlier that it is imperative to build up speed and Mach number slowly. At high altitude this is difficult when controls are sloppy and stability possibly doubtful.

Furthermore the rapid change in the drag results in very large changes in dive angle if a steady acceleration is to be observed. To use the DH108 again as an example. A 30° dive at 40,000ft was sufficient to reach M = 1.0 at full power while at 30,000ft the terminal Mach number is 1.0. Admittedly the latter case is with power off but at this height in a vertical dive the power only represents 15 to 20 per cent of the total thrust.

The region of the drag rise is well indicated to the pilot in a steady dive by a relatively sudden disappearance of acceleration. Below the drag rise the opposite effect results in a feeling that the aircraft is 'running away'. This is one of the main differences noticeable when first flying a jet and is equally noticeable between flying say, a straight winged aircraft of 12 per cent wing thickness and a swept wing version of the same type with a 10 per cent thick wing. In one case the propeller provides a big increase in drag while in the other the variation in compressibility drag rise is responsible. Air brakes have been fitted to alleviate this effect but their use during careful acceleration is undesirable owing to their coarse action.

From the foregoing it is obviously desirable, and possibly vital, to know the dive angle required to obtain a range of speeds at full throttle. Some means of measuring this is necessary; dive angles are always over-estimated by pilots, particularly on aircraft in which the pilot is in the nose. With this knowledge it is possible to set a certain dive angle, which can be held constant with no risk of exceeding limitations. This means that no change in control angle is necessary apart from trim changes and a steady condition of 1g can be maintained. This is most important in certain aircraft where change in lift coefficient or control angle affect compressibility behaviour.

This type of approach was experienced by the author when it was discovered that when the elevator angle was reduced in attempting to steepen the dive, a violent unstable pitching occurred. It was found possible to get over this serious obstruction by keeping the control angle above a certain value. This could only be done by presetting a dive angle to reach a predetermined speed and this method was used on every subsequent run up to these Mach numbers.

Accurate dive angles may be required at low altitude on aircraft which have a limiting IAS near limiting Mach number and which are unable to reach this speed in level flight. In these circumstances a steep dive may be necessary to obtain limiting speed but in doing this it becomes very easy to exceed the limiting Mach number at a lower IAS. To reach limiting IAS without exceeding the Mach number limitation the maximum speed must be obtained as near to sea level as possible.

If it is possible to make a long dive from a medium altitude at limiting Mach number this problem is less serious, but on occasions it is necessary to accelerate rapidly through a much smaller height band and here a previous knowledge of dive angles at constant thrust is extremely helpful, if not vital.

The importance and critical nature of control angle variation at high Mach numbers, coupled with the possibility, due to large trim changes, of over-stressing the tail at a high M/IAS combination, leads to an instrument, previously familiar only to the aerodynamicist, becoming an important source of information to the pilot, namely the desynn.

The coming of power controls has still further increased the case for the desynn since an aircraft where irreversible controls are fitted and feel is largely, or completely, artificial, stick forces are no longer useful in the assessment of stick-free stability and control angles assume as great a significance to the pilot as stick forces did on aircraft with manual controls.

Variation of control angles have been known to alter completely the compressibility vice and by control angles are meant any movable flap or control liable to be used at high speed or Mach number. Furthermore, as has already been seen, the effectiveness may vary greatly over a relatively small speed range. It is important therefore to operate all controls to the fullest possible extent with each small increment in Mach number. It is extremely disquieting to discover that the elevator has become over-balanced only when attempting to change the dive angle, or that a recovery flap has become ineffective during the time taken to apply it. Such embarrassments have occurred.

The importance of repetition in all forms of test flying cannot be too highly stressed, but it applies most acutely to this type of work. Most pilots can find examples of this in their own experience. When a succession of changes is occurring in a very short time and particularly when trouble is brewing, one point is liable to take precedence over all others in the pilot's memory. An incorrect interpretation can be placed on a certain general sensation when no hard and fast symptom presents itself. Such things as stick position may not have been clearly noted, or may even be reported incorrectly, due to unusual forces. This is one illustration, but there are many, of the necessity for repeating any particular phase. It may be possible to repeat at once but if any doubt exists it is often worth while waiting until a more clear, concise idea of what is happening, can be provided by thought and discussions on the ground. There is probably no single aircraft about which conflicting reports have not been given concerning the same behaviour.

REQUIREMENTS FOR RESEARCH AIRCRAFT

It obviously follows from this that improved means of recording are necessary and in fact this is one of the chief requirements at the present time. Auto-observers have been used for some time but the pressing need is for continuous transmission of all instrument readings. This entails a vast amount of work in sorting out the wheat from the chaff in the reduction of results but it means that no change, however small, passes unnoticed and that in the event of an accident there is complete knowledge of the circumstances leading up to it.

Continuous speech recording is a step in the right direction but until the perfecting of a telemetering system is complete, the responsibility for missing nothing rests with the pilot.

In referring to recorders one of the requirements for future highspeed research work has been mentioned, and there are other vital needs for future aircraft.

From the preceding remarks it is clear that the biggest deterrent to a pilot investigating aircraft behaviour is to find himself in a dive. It is essential therefore to have sufficient thrust to negotiate the transonic region in a climb. This not only provides a bigger margin of safety in cases of violent nose-down trim changes and control ineffectiveness, but provides a greatly improved deceleration which has been seen to be very important, particularly under conditions of high IAS. It should be remembered that, from the point of view of aeroelasticity and its allied troubles, high IAS means speeds in excess of 450 to 500mph. A Mach number of 1.0 at 30,000ft is 450mph IAS so that even moderately high altitudes will produce effects which have hitherto been connected with the sea level to 15,000ft region.

The first requirement then is vastly increased thrust. A recent paper by Owner and Hooker[1] gave some interesting figures of thrust needed for level speeds of M = 1.0, in contemporary fighter and research aircraft. At the present stage of development of gas turbines a rocket motor seems to be essential for this work. There does not seem to be any immediate hope of increasing gas turbine thrust three to four times, which is the sort of figure required. The American Bell XS-1 has proved the tremendous advantage of high thrust. In spite of very short endurance, a steady and complete test was made at transonic and supersonic speeds on almost every flight.

Larger air brakes should be included with any increase in thrust and this requirement is equally important in combat aircraft where rapid changes in speed are necessary. The necessity for air brakes of tremendous power follows from the previous mention of steep dives, should such a state of affairs occur with insufficient control.

Reference to the Bell XS-1 leads to an important point in considering high speed research aircraft of the future. In the past, all aircraft have been built to operate in a conventional manner from limited airfields. For pure research machines and possibly, eventually operational aircraft, considerable increases in performance could be expected if landing speeds were allowed to rise and new steps taken to decelerate the aircraft on the ground. Even more unconventional methods apply equally.

Contrary to popular belief, there is a greater degree of safety in flying such an aircraft to transonic or supersonic speeds than more conventional aircraft, which have not been designed with that end in view.

Further requirements, the success of which has been seen already, are power boost controls and movable tailplanes or stabilisers. As already stated, power boost controls require new techniques of flying and testing, particularly when irreversible. Their use appears to be doubly important in view of flutter experience.

The moving tailplane is essential to provide the degree of trim necessary, at the same time overcoming ineffectiveness. Incidentally, incidence changes on the tailplane have been found to influence other characteristics such as buffet, and also to allow varying elevator angles to be used under otherwise identical conditions.

No aircraft has exceeded a Mach number of 1.0 in full control without a trimming tailplane. On the DH108 no investigation beyond M = 0.88 would have been possible without power boost.

The stick forces which a pilot is happy to cope with seem surprisingly low, but his position in relation to the stick, combined with the psychological differences between pulling and pushing, must be remembered. Morgan, of the RAE, in a paper on stability and control[2] presented a table, which gave a very fair idea of this problem. Thus the most a pilot likes to hold is 20lb, although if worried he may hold 100lb for a short time. Research aircraft should have controls which can be deflected to their limit stops under any conditions. This means that the pilot could break the aircraft quite easily, but in the interests of trim changes and ineffectiveness such considerations must not be allowed to cloud the issue. Operational aircraft, in this respect, differ from the research types, but various forms of g restrictors are being developed which will provide a good compromise between safety and manoeuvrability.

The future should provide a more straightforward approach to the speeds, which are now obtained under the most disagreeable circumstances. Naturally any aircraft to reach its maximum obtainable speed in the supersonic region will have to be dived. But given the big increase in thrust mentioned, the intervening region where behaviour is unpredictable will have been negotiated in a climb and the extreme safety measures should no longer be necessary.

Recent experience seems to indicate that the worst pains are over. The unfortunate decision to delay development of a supersonic research aircraft in Great Britain has had far-reaching repercussions.

The unrealistic ideas concerning pilot safety arose not so much from the absence of knowledge of transonic behaviour, as from an incorrect appreciation of what the pilot can cope with in an unconventional aircraft, particularly in relation to take-off and landing.

Although to some extent small airfields are a limiting factor, considerably more progress could have been made in the transonic field by piloted aircraft.

The result of failure to go ahead has resulted in the type of test work described earlier. Ironically, the risk involved has been far higher than would otherwise have been so. Reports on flights on the Bell XS-1 leave no doubt on this matter.

It is to be hoped that lost ground will soon be recovered with these mistakes left behind, and there is no doubt that this country can lead the world in this field. There is a tremendous store of keenness among pilots and scientists. It remains for those in control to use it fully.

A word about tailless aircraft and the pilot would not be out of place. There has been a fierce controversy in this and other countries over the tail. Pilots' impressions of tailless aircraft have, in general, been unfavourable, but it is worth examining the evidence. Unfortunately, there have been several accidents to tailless aircraft and there is no doubt that under certain conditions of low and high speed there are several problems to be solved. Unfavourable conditions arise mainly from a lack of damping in pitch, rather sloppy controls at low speed and high angle of attack on the approach. These are not solely high-speed aircraft problems but they are mentioned to show the reasons for the pilots' apathy to this type of configuration.

To set this in its true perspective the credit side must be viewed. The DH108, which was similar in appearance to some German designs, first flew in 1946 and had a level speed performance which in 1950 was still equal to, or greater than, any other aircraft flying in Great Britain to have exceeded a Mach number of 1.0 although it was only in full control up to M = 0.98. No case of buffeting has been experienced on a tailless aircraft at high Mach number. The true tailless configuration has now been developed into the delta plan form. Several of these aircraft are now flying.

In view of the aerodynamic and structural advantages of this type it is to be hoped that the handling qualities and impressions will be superior to the old tailless configuration.

In all this it must be remembered that in approaching supersonic flight pilots will have to accept new standards. Some are already accepted. Therefore unfavourable impressions should not be too readily accepted at an early stage.

SAFETY MEASURES

The pilot safety factor is increased by various means of protecting the pilot from indirect effects of high speed. Indirect because there is no physical effect from simply flying fast in a straight line. At 40,000ft where IAS is low, there is no impression of speed, and at low altitude, but for air noise or the view of the ground, the passenger has no way of judging his speed in smooth air. The physical effects come from normal acceleration, measured in units of gravity of g's and from the low atmospheric pressure at high altitude. Turns and pull-outs give steady values of positive g, while bumps or oscillations of the aircraft controls give a sharp rise and fall in g, both positive and negative. This latter effect is uncomfortable and, due to lack of headroom and so on, may cause injury but, being instantaneous, has no effect upon the blood stream. Sustained g, however, causes the blood to flow away from the head and the heart is unable eventually to maintain sufficient pressure, resulting in temporary blindness and finally unconsciousness. Blacking out, as the initial blindness is called, occurs at 4½ to 5g after 6 to 8 sec on the average man. Recovery is almost immediate on reducing g but the accumulative effect of many applications of g, such as in combat or aerobatics, is fatiguing. Unconsciousness occurs only if further g is applied after the pilot has completely blacked out. This is a most unlikely contingency.

For some years before the 1939–45 war it was possible to black out at low altitudes. The Schneider Trophy race was an example of this in 1930. Only recently, however, has it become possible to black out at quite high altitude. This is due partly to the increase in indicated speeds possible at high altitude, but more particularly at high Mach numbers, to the improvement in maximum lift with Mach number allowing stalling g equal to, or in excess of, 'blacking-out g' above 30,000ft. It is essential now, therefore, to provide g-suits for work on research aircraft and, in the near future, for fighters as well. The g-suit inflates with air under g, squeezing the legs and stomach and preventing the blood from pooling. It also gives support to the stomach. A very uncomfortable feeling in the pit of the stomach can be produced by g combined with high altitude due to a form of air lock. The chances of this are reduced by the suit.

Negative g has not given rise to much trouble since it is rarely experienced unintentionally. However, as described earlier, the author was subjected to -3g in the DH108 for several seconds and up to -4g instantaneously in a Vampire. This is considered the limit that can be withstood without such unpleasant effects as eye blood vessels bursting (-3g and over causes small white flashes before the eyes and beyond this a red-out occurs). It seems possible, however, in the light of development of rocket powered aircraft with vertical climbs and so forth, that it will be necessary to apply negative g more frequently in the future. If so, a remedy for the effects is essential. Negative g is much more uncomfortable and *demoralising* than positive. A well fitting, tight harness, is vital. This applies in bumps and oscillations when sharp increments of g are applied. Strapping-in well cannot be over-emphasised for high-speed flying.

A discussion of high speed is not complete without reference to physical problems at low atmospheric pressures, since it has been shown that all high-speed investigation starts under such conditions.

Until quite recently there was a curious idea that test pilots were in a better position to suffer the discomforts of very low pressures than their Service companions. In consequence, even now, some research machines have no pressure cabin.

The maximum altitude that can be withstood in reasonable comfort with no pressure cabin and a normal oxygen mask is 42,000ft. Unconsciousness will occur at 45,000ft after a short time. The use of a pressurised mask and waistcoat increases these limits to 44,000ft and 47,000ft. However, morale becomes extremely low under these conditions and sometimes the pilot climbs up bent on carrying out a full programme to find himself curiously apathetic to the whole affair and even losing height without pressing on to the extent planned. This state of affairs, although obviously most unsatisfactory, was tolerated in the absence of pressure cabins. But now that the ceiling of fighter and research types has risen well beyond 45,000ft the pressure cabin is vital to the success of the aircraft. This means that devices such as pressurised masks or pressure suits are only used in emergency when the cabin pressure fails. In the event of this happening the pilot is subjected to rapid decompression or a height change of 30,000ft in about one second. At the heights being discussed the immediate effects of decompression are not serious, but bearing in mind what has been said concerning maximum heights without pressure it is obvious that, if at 47,000ft or above, there is only a very short time in which to descend to a safe height. The pressure mask and waistcoat permit failure at 50,000ft provided that a descent is started within 10 or 15 seconds. Above this height a full pressure suit is needed to provide for an emergency. The pressure suit, which covers the whole body, will permit a pilot to be exposed to an almost infinitely low pressure. When this type of apparel is fully developed the worst problem of the altitude aspect will be over.

On this question most harmful statements have been made in various Press articles. It is a problem, which, if respected, can be safely negotiated.

At all heights and under any condition it may be necessary and must be possible to abandon the machine. The author has never had this experience and is therefore unqualified to discuss it at length, but all pilots have strong views on the subject. It is physically impossible to bale out without assistance at speeds of over 500mph and, except through nothing less than a miracle, the chances of getting clear away from an aircraft at 400mph are remote. These speeds are, of course, indicated air speed, since this is the measure of air *force*, which will be experienced. It is possible to get clear at 600mph at 40,000ft when IAS is only 300mph! Obviously then it is extremely desirable to be ejected from modern aircraft which are flying in excess of safe 'baling-out' speeds almost all the time. At present, in some cases, 550 to 600mph aircraft are being used without ejection seats, but all future designs will have some means of freeing the pilot mechanically from his aircraft.

The ejection seat has been used both in experiment and emergency and has proved itself very successful. However, all live ejections have been made at speeds considerably below the present capabilities. The fastest live ejection was made experimentally at a *true* speed of 505mph. This represents, however, an indicated speed of less than 450mph at the height at which the ejection was made. Since speeds up to 650mph indicated have been reached in this country and up to nearly 700mph indicated in the United States, it is apparent that a vast increase in safe ejection speed is necessary. It seems unlikely that the tremendous effect of air loads on the human frame when exposed at 600mph and over will allow the use of the ejection seat, eventually requiring a detachable cockpit or fuselage section, which will be decelerated before the pilot leaves it, either manually or by further ejection. This method is applied to the Douglas series of high-speed research aircraft, the D-558-1 and 2 and, although untried in practice, would appear to be quite straightforward provided that there is sufficient height in hand and some form of stabiliser for the detachable portion. It is fairly certain that there can never be any completely satisfactory means of leaving an aircraft at very high indicated speeds below, say, 3,000ft. There are plenty of miraculous escapes on record, particularly during the war, at all kinds of heights and speeds, but they are, nevertheless, the exception and cannot be allowed as evidence in making the decision concerning methods of abandoning aeroplanes.

Baling out at high altitudes means low or moderate indicated speeds, but requires emergency oxygen and a delayed drop to 15,000ft or so before opening the parachute. At altitude above 20,000ft damage to the parachute may result from the higher terminal velocity attained by a body. It is an advantage, anyway, to drop to 20,000ft as quickly as possible to avoid discomfort from cold. A portable oxygen bottle is now always carried on the parachute. Development work on high altitude baling out has recently resulted in an automatic ripcord operated by an altitude switch. It is then simply a case of waiting! All development in this field must lead to the jettisoning of a compartment which rapidly decelerates and which maintains pressure and contains oxygen supply.

TEST PILOTS

Much nonsense has been heard and talked of in the past about test flying, but few people outside the actual design teams have much idea of the requirements of a test pilot. In dealing with high-speed research, particularly, where the smallest change of trim or barely perceptible stick movement may tell a whole story, it is essential for the pilot to have a sound knowledge of what is actually happening to the various parts of his machine under all conditions. The author considers it essential to have an overlapping in the spheres of knowledge of pilot and scientist. This may suggest agreement with recent suggestions that fully trained aerodynamicists or engineers should be converted to test pilots, but this appears to be the wrong way to do it. A considerable amount of theory should be understood by the pilot and he should be trained in it. That is precisely what the Empire Test Pilots'

School course is doing, and doing extremely well. After such a training it is up to the pilot to maintain an up-to-date knowledge of all theory that concerns his work. The specialised problems of mathematics and engineering are not required by the pilot. He and the scientist must speak the same language but not necessarily the same dialect.

The test pilot must be first and foremost a pilot, with the necessary temperament and keenness on flying itself. In the air he must be determined and patient. He must try everything more than once. Many convincing examples have been experienced of the false impressions, which can be registered when several things are happening in a very short space of time. Such incidents must be repeated until they can be fully analysed by pilot and auto-observer results. Contrary to popular opinion, the test pilot must possess a good fear! As an experienced test pilot of the past said, 'fear is the pilot's governor'. A complete absence of fright will result in poor test results and often in catastrophe.

It is important that he should keep as closely as possible in touch with similar types of work, not only throughout the country, but the whole world. Rivalry between firms and national security have to be respected, but exchanges of information and experience between pilots is tremendously valuable. The pilot must always be up-to-date in his particular field, both on the practical and theoretical side.

REFERENCES

1. Owner, F.M. and Hooker, S.G. (1950), 'Power Plant Requirements for Future Aircraft.' Presented at the Fourth World Conference on Power, London, July 1950
2. Morgan, M.B. and Thomas, H.H.B.M. (1945), 'Control Surface Design in Theory and Practice,' *RAeS Journal*, August 1945

DISCUSSION

K.G. Rendle (Graduate): What would the author regard as a dangerous landing speed?

Squadron Leader Derry: There was no difficulty in landing an aeroplane fast, provided that there was an unlimited length of run; the Americans had runs of 12 or 13 miles. It was true to say that it was much easier to land an aeroplane fast than slowly, at stalling speed, if the undercarriage and tyres were strong enough; indeed, inexperienced pilots could be seen landing much too fast because it was easier than to land slowly. There was nothing at all in touching down; the whole problem depended on means of stopping the aircraft after it had touched down.

Brakes were inadequate to cope with much higher landing speeds than were normal today. He was not criticising them, for they were extremely good for the job they had to do at present. The tyres also would not withstand much increase of landing speed although without the use of brakes they would withstand quite a lot more than with brakes. There were such things as the tail parachute which had been seen operating on the Avro Delta and gave reasonable deceleration which should effect a 30 per cent reduction of landing run. Again, the use on aerodromes of arresting wires, such as were used on the decks of aircraft carriers, was a possibility.

Thus it was difficult to estimate what might be considered as the maximum landing speed, but given a suitable aerodrome, it was possible to land quite happily at 200mph.

A Speaker: At what Mach number did flutter occur, and how was it stopped when once it had started?

Squadron Leader Derry: There was no positive way of stopping it, once it had started. It would stop itself, however, if one decelerated quickly enough; in the paper he had mentioned one serious case of flutter, and that was stopped by decelerating.

As to the Mach number at which flutter occurred, there was a damping loss in the DH108 at a much lower Mach number, but it eventually became negative at high indicated air speeds at a Mach number of about 0.87 or 0.875. It was possible to fly at 0.87 with zero damping, but an increase of 0.005 would exceed the limit. Zero damping could be tolerated for research purposes if the point at which it would become negative were known. It was not satisfactory to accept zero damping except for limited investigations. It must be avoided if any further use were to be made of the aeroplane.

D.J. Adams (De Havilland Technical School): Could the author throw any light on the DH108 crashes?

Squadron Leader Derry: He was unable to say much about them, because the results of the enquiries had not been published. He would like to see the results published officially, because there had been a lot of doubt about the causes, and that had given the aircraft an unnecessarily bad name. The fact that tailless aircraft had crashed had gone against them; there were a lot of things to get right, but the aircraft were not so bad to fly and they could give a magnificent performance – he was talking of high-speed aircraft, and did not wish to become involved in the transport argument.

P.T. Fink (Graduate, Imperial College): Would the author give an opinion on the nature of the artificial feel which a pilot would like to be given in aeroplanes which had irreversible power controls.

Squadron Leader Derry: He had not flown with fully irreversible controls. One could not get feel back from irreversible control; feel could only be produced by means of a spring, and it was difficult to arrange without involving a too positive neutral position, so that an unnatural force was needed to initiate a movement. Artificial feel brought about a different technique of flying. The first thing that was inclined to result was flying on the trimmer.

In this connection doing away with the trimmer would be a good step forward. The old form was a wheel, and the latest form was a switch on the stick to operate the movable tailplane. The ideal would be a fully trimming device working off the stick, which meant that the aircraft would trim itself. But that stage had not been reached yet.

Mr Irving: How was stability affected by inequalities such as walking over wings when wearing hobnailed boots? He also invited comment on the problem of a damping loss.

Squadron Leader Derry: The cause was not known exactly so it was difficult to give an answer. He felt that the chances of repeatability were fairly good in the case of the DH108, because the wing was not a laminar flow wing and small changes of section should not be expected to make much difference. There might be small local differences, but they would not amount to much at the Mach number at which loss of damping occurred. But there were cases of poor repeatability, as, for example, the Vampire; one Vampire varied a good deal from another at high Mach number, although not in a sense which would cause any serious trouble, there being small changes in hinge moment, stick force and the feel of the elevator.

One particular characteristic which was very critical to something – it was hard to tell what – was the wing drop. Production aircraft, some of which suffered wing drop at high Mach number did not repeat at all well; one wing would go on one flight and the other wing on the same aircraft would go on another flight. That was obviously very critical, and the whole thing was dependent on small changes in yaw and possibly changes in profile. There was experience of wing drop on all aircraft; but it did not always repeat.

Stalling on high-speed wings was another problem. There must be very small changes in the profile of the wing, for they were cured by putting on the thinnest possible application of filler.

Mr Dynall: Was it the author's opinion that dog-fighting was likely to occur again in the future, and what was the effect of it on the pilots?

Squadron Leader Derry: If two fighters were in the air and were shooting at one another, there was bound to be some sort of dog-fight. The idea that there would not be any more dog-fighting had resulted rather from the thought that that state of affairs would not arise so much in the future, that fighters would be escorting a bomber and would stay with it, or that they would be attacking a bomber and would not bother with the escort, so that there would not be big fights between fighter forces. He believed there would be dog-fights in the end, but they would occupy much more space than formerly, for with higher speed the aircraft would have to travel greater distances to turn round. They would also occur high up, for dog-fights could not be prolonged in a jet at fairly low altitude; if an enemy wanted to get away he would then climb and, if he were caught, he would be caught at high altitude. Probably there would be less tendency to turn and more tendency for one man to use his higher critical Mach number or higher limiting Mach number, if he thought he had got it, and he would get away in a dive while his opponent was turning inside out in the effort to catch him.

A Speaker: Would there be any difficulties in flying supersonic aircraft?

Squadron Leader Derry: There would be difficulties and pilots would have to get accustomed to new methods of flying. One of the arguments about the tailless aircraft was that it was not a normal aircraft and that it behaved in an unusual way. But pilots must become accustomed to aircraft behaving in an unusual way, and one of the problems would be to get used to different behaviour at high speeds, and particularly to an altogether different feel of the controls.

The biggest problem perhaps of supersonic aircraft would be to fly at subsonic speeds, and particularly at the comparatively low speed of landing. The landing speeds were bound to increase; but the present trend to low aspect ratio with sweepback was not as bad as all that for landing speeds. The delta wings illustrated had quite a low wing loading. There were other reasons for higher landing speeds, but he did not think that anything above 200mph would have to be accepted. That might horrify some people, but he did not think it should. Certainly a new set of rules for the air must be found, because the aircraft would not be able to cruise around at low speeds. From his little knowledge of the theoretical research, which had been going on, there should not be a great deal of difficulty in flying at high subsonic speeds. Apart from cruising conditions, he felt that the whole idea of having to poise oneself at about 0.9, take a deep breath and rush madly through to 1.5, or whatever it was, was quite false. The aircraft would not be able to cruise in the transonic region; it would be either supersonic or subsonic. But from the research point of view there was not much doubt, particularly from what the XS-1 had done, that the change from subsonic to supersonic speeds could be quite gradual. It depended on the trim changes, among other things; but in any aircraft, however well designed, there was bound to be a trim change. There was no reason to suppose that it would be better to encounter the transonic region in a rush than to do it gently.

A.C. Campion (Graduate): Had the author seen flying saucers?

Squadron Leader Derry: He had not; but he had seen an interesting thing which might have led many people to believe that they had seen flying saucers. It was a shooting star; viewed from the very high altitude at which he was flying, and apparently because of the rare atmosphere at that height, the star seemed to be much bigger than it would look from the ground. Although he was not much nearer to it than when on the ground, relatively speaking, it had looked surprisingly big, and quite close.

J. Wingate (Student, Fairey Aviation Co): Was there any marked change in the noise of the engine when flying at about the speed of sound and was there any danger resulting from the noise?

Squadron Leader Derry: He felt that the speaker was perhaps confusing what were called ultra-sonic effects from high frequency engine noise with supersonic aircraft speeds. The noises in aircraft came through the aircraft, where the air was pretty well stationary, so that it was unaffected. He had heard stories that pilots had sometimes encountered suddenly a curious silence, but he could not understand that, because the propagation of the sound waves from the outside of the cockpit to one's ear was through air which was stationary, or very nearly so.

The noise from jet engines was not so great as at first expected.

Nevertheless, it was a good thing to wear helmets and to protect the ears, not only in order to pay attention to the radio, but because it could be shown medically that continued flying with the ears exposed to sound would gradually reduce hearing.

JOHN DERRY'S DIARY OF HOLIDAY IN THE WESTERN ISLES, MAY 1952

Went aboard in Glasgow dock 1015. Pleasant little ship. No longer carries official passengers but wardrooms and cabins nicely fitted. Ornate, slightly Victorian woodwork which always seems at home in a ship.

Moved off 1030. Dock dirty and full of flotsam. Purser remarks on cleaner water we shall soon be sailing in. Says suicides float in Macbrayne's dock. I think of contrast between Glasgow and the scenery we shall soon be seeing. Glasgow, by being so ugly and dirty, with its black, slab-faced tenements, makes the hills and woods seem still greener and softer. Almost within minutes, it seems, we are looking up at the thickly wooded slopes above Bowling or at the gently sloping fields on the south bank. It is hard to believe that Glasgow is set amongst so much beauty.

Purser is amusing and pleasant. Looks like a bank clerk but carries an assurance and a boisterous humour that belie his appearance. Wears a neat, blue suit but puts on nautical officer's cap with white cover when on deck or bridge and looks completely different. Thoughtful and charming. Highly efficient.

Rest of officers met at various times during day. Very good crowd. Captain and 1st Mate from Isles. Delightful speech, a joy to listen to, especially Mate. Strong sense of humour amongst all.

Sailed down to Greenock for loading. Shipyards. Noise of riveting astonishing. How do they fare inside the hull? The rusty appearance of the plates makes the hulls look like wrecks until one sees a finished one beside the yard, with neat white superstructure and shining hull. Half sunk tug. Clever captain.

[John and Eve did some shopping in Greenock and then sailed again in the afternoon, going up on deck in the evening to watch the Isles slipping past.]

Out on deck and on bridge while sailing down past Holy Loch, Cumbraes, Arran and, when almost dark, round the Mull of Kintyre. Change in wind and slight swell but nothing much. Ship notorious for rolling, Purser tells, and Eve tries to look calm!

Have bought a beret for deck, much to Eve's amusement. Probably look more like an onion man from Brittany, but it does its job.

Saw guillemots and gannets on way down Firth. Sight of mountains behind Holy Loch (Beinn Thor) half visible through cloud gives foretaste of tomorrow's scenery.

Friday, 16th May: Up at 6am to be on deck while passing through Kerrera Sound. Quite narrow, steep slopes on either side, but fertile between base and sea. We slide up the Sound in absolute peace. Only a ship (and not all ships) can pass on its way without disturbing anyone. In the flat, calm Sound we seemed to move effortlessly through the mist. The hills beyond showed faintly. Mate remarks on poor viz. but it is pure charm to me. Early morning mist just above the water, the hills slightly veiled and smoke from early fires curving into a thin layer across the houses. Oban looks pleasant.

[He comments that it would probably be crowded with tourists in the summer, and remarks:]

The peace of these islands and the ship cutting between them surely cannot be equalled. I can feel fatigue and worry soaking out of me. We lie on deck going through Sound of Mull. Sun is beautiful, quite warm. I am in shirt sleeves.

Duart Castle typical, tall, narrow with clustered chimneys. Even when deprived of its arms and men it seems to guard the Sound. Solid and stern. Lot of castles on Mull. Lord of Isles. Plenty of stories. Should like to visit one day. Passed Tobermory during lunch. Early meal hours give one false sense of time, but agreeably so. Tea every two hours. Eve delighted. So am I!

1400, we steam down Coll and turn into the little bay of Armagour. No pier, we anchor in bay. Island is flat at this point, and looks scrubbed by a giant brush. Reminds me of Iceland. No trees, mostly rock. Nevertheless, rocky coast with little islands looks welcoming in the warm sun. While leaning on rail watching boat come out for cargo, I realise I can see the bottom clearly. Beautifully clear – I am tempted to swim but do not. I shall answer the call of that clear water before we leave the Isles.

Men from Coll in boat speak Gaelic to each other. Village is handful of houses and toy-like church on high ground above. Is there a Minister or does one suffice for Tiree also?

On to Tiree. Much more civilised. Pier and many houses, very flat, but with sandy coves with silver sand. Sea over it is pure green. The water beneath the pier reminds me of some half lit cathedral.

We go ashore and walk along the coast. New born lambs, springy turf and many birds, but masses of junk. Probably left over from Service and also washed ashore. Generally untidy near village. Wreck of smack in harbour. Eve upset. Many birds. Dunlin, oyster catchers, one turnstone flying, shellduck, eider, Arctic terns, greater black-backed, hoodie crows, curlew. Watched gannets diving, wonderful 'peel-off and knife-like plummet'. Story of The Brothers.

[He was disappointed, however, in Tiree and glad to sail on to Skye through the Sound of Canna. He spent a lot of the journey chatting to the Captain and Mate and enjoying their colourful local stories.]

Captain sounds very slightly Scandinavian as well as West Highland. 'O' is 'ou' in some words and intonation typically Scandinavian now and again. Mate is a really delightful person, the best of a very nice bunch. He is from Skye and I am refreshed to find that he still appreciates the beauty of the Isles and does not take them for granted.

Saturday 17th May. Called at 5.30 entering Loch Dunvegan. Did not call me at 3am because viz. nil at Pooltiel. Eve disappointed to have missed thunderstorm during the night.

Sailed up to Dunvegan. Loch very narrow here. Castle stands on north side amongst rhododendrons and spruce. Nothing beautiful about castle but, like Duart, has imposing personality. Sides of loch steep and hills close on south side where river runs into loch. North side thickly wooded. Went ashore at 6 am, walked around castle and up small hill above harbour. Azaleas and rhododendrons wonderful, latter not completely out but one completely white bush 15ft high. Azaleas scarlet, yellow and pink, magnificent. Sweet scent mixed with morning scent from spruce and birch. Shrubs growing everywhere but also broad sides with heaped rhododendrons on either side.

Found an owl after investigating excited blackbird and thrushes chattering wildly. Seemed to have long tail and wingspan of short-eared owl, but ears only just visible and wrong type for short-eared. Can long-eared retract ears? Possibly tawny owl, but tail and wings seemed too long.

Looked down on *Hebrides* lying at pier. Sounds of unloading came up to me, carrying on morning air. Weather dull and viz. poor. Cuillins invisible. Picked azaleas and rhodes for Eve. She was amused to see me carrying them. So were the crew. The beret completed the picture!

Sailed at 7am for Uig. Difficult turning round in narrows. Fascinating watching method of turning. Skilled business with rocks all round. Arrived Uig after breakfast. Wide bay surrounded by hills with mountains behind. Village looks very new, spread round bay a mile wide. Used by holiday makers. Several new houses and other building. Disappointing village but glens lovely. Bought pc's and sat by broad rapids in thickly wooded glen. All trees have light coloured bark, whatever sort. Must be effect of salt. Have not noticed before. Bird-song in glen, warblers and chaffinches. In fields on way back to ship sound of corncrakes and whitethroats. Could not see crakes or flush them. On way into Uig in morning met *Loch Carron* on way out. Motor ship neat and smart. Four women passengers. Much prefer *Hebrides*. To be part of crew, or anyway amongst them, and to see everything from their point of view as well as ours is important part of doing this trip properly and not as pleasure cruise which is only like being in an expensive pub.

Sailed from Uig about 1430. Becoming very warm, clouds cleared. Took mattresses onto poop and sunbathed. Slept two hours. Gulls nearly stole our tea when I went to call Eve up. In spite of unpleasant nature of herring gulls you can't help liking them when they come and sit beside you. Crew say they are offered rewards for black-backed gulls because of chickens and lambs lost. No doubt gulls need keeping down but afraid offer will be abused due to ignorance. Fulmars, particularly when immature, look quite dark on top. They are grand gentle birds, and what splendid aviators! Curiously, in spite of the reward, none of the crew carries a gun. Lots of talk but I have suspicion sailors do not really like shooting gulls which follow for hours. There can be something comforting about them and old superstitions probably still cling. Fulmars coming right up to ship between Uig and Loch Skipport. Puffins, guillemots and razorbills. Possibly petrels.

Came into Loch Skipport at 1500. As we moved slowly into Loch I knew it was, for me, by far the most beautiful place we had yet seen. The loch twists and turns, with low cliffs surmounted by heather slopes on either side. Here and there small islands, also about 100ft high with domes of heather and peat grass. As across the Minch, in the loch it was flat calm, not as much as a ripple.

As we rounded a small promontory the harbour came into view. A little pier nestling against a steep hill of rock and grass. Around the loch lay one or two small crofts, one of them particularly in the traditional Highland style. Little more than the door breaking the walls. Hens and sheep wandered in the surrounding moor. We tied up and unloading of grain and tar barrels began.

The Skipper suggested I might like to borrow a boat. I was delighted. He spoke to a clearly commanding person who stood watching the unloading. Mr McLeod is Harbour Master. He is also butcher, grocer, organiser and a kind of unofficial sheriff. Very shrewd. Looks out of corner of eye and appears shy. Very quiet spoken but mischievous and probably a terror to all. A real Highland clansman if ever there was one. All workers are his relations! He provides boat which boys bring over. Eve not keen to go, does not trust me! Captain worried, feels responsible, fusses, says boat is large for one but I take him across a little bay and persuade him I can manage. As he walks back to *Hebrides* I see his face continually turning in my direction. He was waiting when I returned 1½ hours later. I rowed up to head of loch. Beyond the pier the loch narrows and then opens out into along stretch almost landlocked.

Surely there can be few places more peaceful and more beautiful than this loch on a windless summer night with the sun sinking and the mountains a mile or two south of the loch taking on their mantle of pink and mauve. Against the sun is a shepherd, wandering down with his dog to collect his sheep. The silhouette is perfect. Smoked and let the boat drift on the stream. Absolute silence but for an occasional curlew calling and, of all things, a cuckoo. What extra urge drives him on beyond the safe fields of England, where nests for his mate abound, to this wild land where he must run the gauntlet of crow and peregrine, and where small birds' nests must be hard to find? Does he join his mate elsewhere? If not, what chance is there of finding one here? But he has his mate. Together they flew over the loch, a lone pipit chasing them gallantly. A merganser took off and flew past me. I hope to see red throated divers here but not yet. The 2nd purser saw two from the lorry on its rounds with the cargo.

Up the loch herons stand at regular intervals amongst the rocks and seaweed like silent sentries, their necks stretched up, beaks raised, to observe my passage. Now and then they fly with heavy wings low across the water. It is not difficult to see why they have earned a place in Highland superstition. An old woman sits outside one of the crofts, with black shawl she looks like part of the scene as she stares down the loch.

From the head of the loch the masts of the *Hebrides* and the smoke from the funnel rise above the rocks. She looks to be land-bound on all sides. I tie up again at the pier with the Captain's help. The lorry returns and we have tea with the Purser and Chief. He has a bee in his bonnet about subsidies to the natives. Surprisingly he is teetotal. The 2nd Mate tells a good story. Much amused by the one about the pail.

Eve and I smoked a last cigarette on deck at 23.30. Almost midnight sun; light to the north, reflection in water of hills. Hard to tell where water line is. Ripples tell of incoming tide.

On way over to Skipport saw one shark and two others in loch. Basking sharks have squarish fin. Do much damage to nets, but men say they eat plankton mostly.

Old McLeod says he believes I come from one of the English towns. Is this a derogatory reference to London? Family sit around on form, only old man makes conversation. No one else speaks unless spoken to. But he is wise enough and has a sense of humour.

Sunday May 18th. Awoke at 6.30 without a call! Went straight out for a walk. Beautiful morning, cloudless sky. Headed through mountains and ploughed through bog after bog. The Mate said this was a dry island! Climbed half way up Heckler (1,800ft). Bog and springs remain up to top. Rock slippery and tufts of peat between. No good for climbing with rubber soles. Splendid view from point reached of north and west of island. West absolutely flat like south coast of Iceland. Villages here and there and large inland lochs. Many small lochs passed during climb but few birds about. Saw what seemed to be two divers or Gt crested grebes on one loch at long range. The beauty of this spot is on and around the loch; the moor and mountains are wild but poor for walking and not particularly unusual.

Beauty of loch even more striking after returning from walk. Met crofter's wife going to milk her one cow. She asked if I liked the loch and obviously realised I was English, or anyway from foreign parts. She remarked, astonishingly enough, 'I'm a stranger here myself -just married the postman here'. I said, 'Are you from the mainland or another island?' 'No', says she, 'I'm from Boisdale'. Boisdale is 10 miles from here and there can be few more than 100 people between the two!

Got back a bit late for breakfast. All astonished at my early rising on Sunday morning. Like Eve, they think I'm mad.

While I was walking wind got up, coming down from mountains, apparently orographic, for pressure is very high. When I returned to ship small gale blowing across loch. Crew and locals (Mr McLeod) confirm nature of wind. We went ashore in morning and sat on lee of bank overlooking loch and pier. Warm there and glorious. Started to sketch ship and loch. After lunch ashore again while *Heb* went out to anchorage to let *Loch Broom* in to load cattle. Eve upset by handling of cattle. Don't like it myself, but clearly cows won't go down gangway if asked kindly. Nevertheless, it does seem a bit rough and rather spoilt peace of the loch. Mostly Highland cattle. On board they are packed tight to prevent falling and trampling. But here again one wonders if these people should not be forced to use separate stalls for each beast, although cost of transport would go up. Horses more comfortable (only 7). *Loch Broom* took 200 cattle, smaller ship than this. We have about 100 for Kyle. Three dealer farmers from Durham came aboard for tea. Real Jordies. Cheery and very tough. Having a good time away on buying trip but not keen on Uist. Take cattle for two years and then re-sell for a fat profit. Surprised how cattle can be reared on peat grass here. These three had a leak right in front of us on the hill. They clearly had not seen Eve. Much laughter.

Visited *Loch Broom* for tea and shown Diesel engine. No headroom but clean. Crew of *Loch Broom* not a patch on ours. Captain looked scruffy. Our Skipper a real winner. Says he doesn't like to anchor with cattle aboard because of lack of draft.

During afternoon wind changed to west then up came low stratus covering hills and finally down to sea.

Sailed for Kyle 1800. Last sight of McLeod standing expressionless on pier. Would not take money for boat. Pleased to meet Eve though we feared her dress might shock (Sunday).

He must have missed church. Very smart and good taste in his tie and shirt. Notice he also runs bus service and owns pier sheds!

Left loch looking less attractive in mist but still a place to remember always. Ran into clear weather five miles out but then into fog. Nice to be on move again. This is a wonderful holiday. Always changing and so devoid wondering about best place to go which makes ordinary holidays liable to friction. Crew help to make ship a pleasure to be aboard.

Saw two more mergansers or goosanders before sailing. Porpoises near ship this morning when water was choppy. They porpoise exactly in formation. Noticed that there were no guillemots or razorbills to be seen on way back across Minches. Although ocean birds they seem to keep near land. Probably because of breeding. Fulmars disdain to take scraps from boat and make gulls look like urchins scrambling with evil manners for bread. They do not seem to fish much for all their low flying. Saw sandpiper flying over loch this morning. Long pipe on wing then ripple after alighting. Phalarope!

At 2030 we ran into fog and after sailing as near as he dared to Canna the Skipper decided to head back into the Minch until a clearance came. It is astonishing that this ship, 580 tons, has no radio and no D/F, never mind radar. This ship had radio when carrying passengers but for some obscure or mean purpose it was taken out. The Captain is helpless in these tricky waters without it and cannot navigate accurately with variable tides and streams. At least a D/F loop would seem vital. *Loch Broom* had this and will soon have radar and it is purely a cargo vessel. We used mileage counter which is his only resort.

Monday May 19th: Awoke at call 745 to find ship passing Loch Portree but only base of cliffs visible. Viz. good along sea at this point but fog patches very bad. We cruised up and down Minch all night and then found a clearance around north of the island. Saw *Loch Nevis* coming out of Portree. She is faster and went ahead. After breakfast passed us again having called at Raasay Island. We follow her in fog and see her turn suddenly at buoy in narrows off Salpay. Tricky entrance to Kyle, especially in fog. Straining eyes to pick out buoys and lighthouses.

[The fog lifted soon after entering Kyle and John and Eve went ashore and took the ferry to Kyleakin where they walked and had lunch. They spent the afternoon there and then took the ferry back to Kyle, rejoining the *Hebrides* in time for tea. John made some notes about the senior crew members.]

We are latterly much impressed by Chief who, in spite of some querulousness and surliness, is a most kind person. Very upset by treatment of cattle. Purser says RSPCA (cruelty) man at Kyle worse than anyone. Chief was on armed merchant cruiser during war in Navy. 2nd Purser inclined to be unpleasant with cattle and generally rather a poor character. 2nd Engineer fancies himself with the girls and is always dressed for the kill when we spend a night alongside.

After tea I did some sketching. Improving slowly. It is very enjoyable. I shall keep it up. Later went for walk along cliffs by myself. Very lovely walk with well made path along cliff side. In one spot oak wood stretches down to sea with boulders and green dry turf amongst the trees.

[He reached a little pebbly cove, which was fringed with turf, and when he tasted the water it was only just salt.]

Saw 2 goosanders amongst the rocks, then swimming out into loch. On way back to Kyle met two boys running down path. Watched them out to cove. Afraid they might suspect or know about goosanders' nest. I cannot wait to see but hope they will not disturb it or take eggs. Egg collecting is, I hope, dying out. It has been a deplorable business. Many keen naturalists relate with understandable pride that they have a hundred different eggs or so. Undoubtedly it is a skilled affair and many keen bird watchers collect eggs in all innocence. But we cannot afford to let everyone take an egg collection, quite apart from the abuse the hobby suffers at the hands of thoughtless and ignorant youths, and even grown-ups. We should have a few organised collections and try to let the hobby fade away. It is lessening but should be discouraged in schools. Common garden birds are one thing but rare birds nesting in these remote parts must be protected.

Walked back along cliff. It is a beautiful evening. To the west I can see the Red Hills, the conical peak of Ben na Carlich. The other Ben near Carlich rears straight out of the loch opposite me. At the other end of the loch to the East is a hive of small peaks. They become alive with colour as the sun sinks and we are in shadow. I walked back through ex-Admiralty camp. It is squalid and awful.

There are squatters in the better huts but many other huts are empty and broken down. Old buildings half pulled down scar the ground all round and disused latrines stand with gaping doors. Barbed wire and rusty iron work lie everywhere.

There is no doubt that deserted military camps breed squalor, not least by reason of slap dash occupation by squatters. It would be better if the Government were to recognise the squatters and organise the camps properly making rules about gardens and outbuildings and cleaning up and knocking down all unused buildings. The camps are a blot on our landscape. They have no place here, particularly by these beautiful lochs. Much can be done without turning out the squatters who may be breaking the law but must live somewhere. Theirs is only a small part of the responsibility. The making of a slum is there before they arrive.

[When John arrived back at the ship he and Eve changed out of their 'deck gear' and walked to the nearby Lochalsh Hotel for a drink. But they felt the atmosphere there was out of tune with the mood of their holiday and didn't stay long.]

It is dull and not part of the Highlands in this lounge. We are glad to get back to our snug vessel down the steep gangway to sit on deck as the light dies, or go down to the warm saloon. Only lamps in cabins while we are alongside. No standby generator. Eve and I have separate cabins and feel like a guilty couple in each others!

Birds today include great northern diver just off Kyle close to ship on way in. Also one off Babay. Winchats on road out of Kyleakin.

Watched human divers building pier for fishing boats near our quay. When they put on their gear and check their lines and fittings I am reminded of our own business. The check over the gear is the same and in both it is swift and thorough, for with both the diver and airman our lives depend upon the equipment. Should like to go down in suit. Must be cold for the hands which are bare. Large uprush of air after descent must be due to deflating suit to balance weight.

When telling steward, who is keen on birds, about great northern divers, second steward, Alec, thought I was talking about men. He said he had seen them close in. Said I thought they were shy. He said, 'Well they are building a pier'. Much laughter.

Tuesday 20th May: Called at 4.50am by Mate as I had asked so that I might see our passage through Kyle Rhea and Sleat Sound. We slipped away at 5.00am with the mountains clear of mist but sky overcast. Lovely villages further up Loch Alsh. Balmacana, view down Sleat Sound. Sailing between wooded slopes of Skye and Invernesshire. Clouds now covering tops. High peaks showing faintly through mist. Mate tells of deer swimming to island. Even to Mull. Apparently cases in paper also. Most interesting. Purser has seen them across Rhea. Cloud coming down as we sail round Sleat Point. Only about 50ft. Poor viz. until about 10 miles from Outer Isles when a sudden lift reveals South Uist hills dark and beautifully coloured against the blue sky with the dull cloud line above their peaks. Loch Boisdale is wider mouthed loch with fewer islands than Skipport and head of loch opens to flat country to the west coast. In every way it is much less attractive than Skipport. Village lies behind piers. Very unattractive. Pub and two shops, some new wooden council houses, very ugly, for some reason cannot be painted by owners or tenants. Have orange doors and green windows, same in Skye.

Visited Carding Mill where raw wool is combed on vast machine then sent out to crofts for spinning. Some cloth half hand, half machine woven, some 100% hand. New effort by Highland Industries to encourage old crafts. Potteries as well on mainland. Saw very nice tweeds in little showroom made from old mission hut. Also delightful scarves and pottery from Skye. Miss Shand runs this part of the organisation and visits outlying crofts to find women to weave. Old women easier to persuade but young women beginning to value it more. Great shortage of wool because farmers waited to sell to mainland at higher prices during wool boom.

Miss Shand says Eriskay lovely island. Original of *Whisky Galore*. Those who have experienced it say that if you are offered whisky round here, it still carries 'Export Only' label. Rumoured that many cases were buried by men too drunk to remember the spot! Islanders drunk for weeks! Ship had whisky for States, ran aground in convoy 1943 off Eriskay. Cases disappeared even after Customs men arrived!

While on hill above village heard beautiful song from a bird I couldn't spot. Sounded somewhere between a thrush, nightingale and lark. Miss Shand says hen harriers here. Saw a bird I took to be a buzzard crossing loch as we entered but flight unusually jerky. Possibly harrier. Many fulmars in part of Minch opposite here. Sitting on water in flocks and flying alongside ship. Kittiwakes joined us on way back. Look very small after herring gulls.

We sailed after loading cattle. Cattle loading certainly leaves much to be desired, particularly when loading to lower hold which is necessary on this trip with 140 beasts, some for Mallaig, some Kyle. This lower deck hold should not be used. Very poor ventilation from fans and sail ventilator when at sea and only fans when at anchor as we are tonight. Heat and lack of air shocking in lower hold. Disgraceful that railwaymen at Mallaig should be allowed to refuse to unload until morning. The alternatives (1) Condemn lower hold and ventilate and check on all ships (2) Insist on unloading at any time of day or night. This cattle business has sickened me but it is not fault of ship's officers. Captain does what he can but is in hands of organisers and railwaymen. Some of the hands unnecessarily rough with cattle but mostly of low intelligence, brought up with beasts and probably have had similar treatment themselves and know no better.

Beautiful evening sailed from Loch Boisdale 18.00. Can see

Skye, Rhum, Eigg, Canna and Lewis. Best viz. yet but Cuillins still in clouds. We see three sharks quite near ship off Uist. They are very large, tails waving about away behind fins. They seem to be almost motionless and rolling.

Glorious sunset when between Rhum and Skye. Sun just above horizon in clear patch with one or two streaks across it. Clouds above coloured pink and grey. Uist visible against horizon. Skye hills very soft in this light.

[Derry records that they anchor off Isle Oronsay until 5 am the next day and that Eve gets up early to see Mallaig, which was their first port of call, and to see how the cattle in the lower hold had fared. He didn't wake, but they were both up and about when they reached Kyle at 9 o'clock as the sun was breaking through the mist.]

We decide to go ashore for a stroll along the cliff. I casually ask Skipper time of sailing and he (equally casually), 'Right away, I think, aye'. This after definite plans to take on water. However, we are used to change of plans now and the delightfully non-committal way it is all decided. We find that all transport up here is the same although perhaps not as bad as appears at first sight. I enjoy it, it gives one a feeling of detachment. Only snag is arranging when and where we are to leave ship to get back for Saturday flying. Will ring Jack to find if really necessary.* Would be nice to complete trip. Train journey from Mallaig, though picturesque, will be tiring.

[They sailed from Kyle and arrived at Portree, which they found lovely, after lunch.]

I go for a climb. I always like to get up on a bit of high ground so that I can see as much of the surrounding country as possible and also enjoy a climb thoroughly. I climb to Beinna Greine behind Portree after skirting Portree Loch at low tide in hope of seeing waders, but only herons, gulls and crows. The climb is longer than I thought but I reach lower peaks in 50 minutes from the ship. I

---

* 'Jack' is Jack Arthur, who was secretary to the test pilots at de Havilland.

am always deceived by Scottish hills. They look like smooth unbroken slopes or cliffs until one is half way up when an unending series of ledges, colls and small valleys opens before the final climb to the peak. The time for a climb is always twice what I expect, but I never seem to have learnt my lesson. The truth is I am so attracted by these hills that subconsciously I banish the question of time only to find that I have to hurry on my return. Nevertheless it is thoroughly enjoyable.

After some casting around I found a reasonably dry way to the hill except near the top. I found a beautiful little brown burn from which I drank gratefully. There were no little mountain ash bushes by this burn as there are near Loch Skipport, but the orchids and other wild flowers are plentiful amongst the springy turf where there is no heather. From the top I looked down on Portree Loch, part of the village and the headlands on either side. To the north I could see the Storr and the peculiar pillar of rock known as 'the old man of Storr'. To the south at long last I had a splendid view of the Cuillins, their jagged summits still showing streaks of snow. To the west it was hazy but I could see Loch Emzort Beag and to the south-east I could see the channel back to Kyle. A lovely view and well worth the climb. I tried to sketch it but have no practice in this sort of thing.

Got back to ship easily but only just in time. Eve has gone to look for me and so we blow the hooter for her. We have to leave Portree at high water for when we docked the bows were aground when we tied up. Any tightening on the rope caused us to roll and not pull into pier. It is a tiny pier for a busy village. *Heb* can only get her bows alongside even when aground. I congratulate Skipper on his skill. He says only a few Skippers with sufficient local knowledge, for this company has no mercy if they make a mistake in this tricky business. The *Heb* draws 12½ft at present load. She has lines and keel of yacht. Nothing to protect hull if aground, so even greater care necessary.

We sail out of Portree at 1620 passing MS *Loch Nevis* sailing in. Long chat with Chief. He is first class person but takes a bit of knowing. Half his apparent complaining is dry humour. He has had plenty of sea-going experience on armed merchant cruisers.

Back in Kyle. I phoned Jack but not in, speak to Joan and ask for cable. Changed and we crossed to Kyleakin in ferry for drink and to see if there is a Ceilidh. There is not but we have our drink at King's Arms before last ferry goes. Kyleakin is really a neat attractive little place. Kyle is very dreary. It is a lovely evening and the view up and down Loch Alsh is lovely, very peaceful. I can hear eider ducks making their peculiar howling out on the loch. They seem plentiful around these islands.

We give Captain a glass of whisky and have long chat. He was convoy pilot in Islands during war. He is most amusing. Used to be wild character so they say and then suddenly quietened down after some incident. Has many amusing phrases, 'cool, calm and collective' is one.

Thursday 22nd May: Eve's birthday. Sail at 7.00am for Loch Maddy. I hear sounds of sailing from my bunk. Have not bothered to get up early but intend to see dawn during trip back tomorrow morning from Maddy. Weather at Kyle and up Raasay Sound very dull with low cloud on hills but breaking to south and glass is very high (30.6 inches). This cloud, though extensive, is evidently formed over land masses like Skye at night but owing to amount of moisture from fogs and lochs it becomes thick and covers wide area. Soon clears when sun gets up. As we sail north round Skye many breaks appear and suddenly we come from under line of cloud into clear blue sky.

The hills of Skye slope out of a crystal sea. Everything is aglow. The light and shade of the hills is breathtaking. What a difference the sun makes in these Islands. Admittedly this trip would lose a lot of its fascination in dull weather. T'would be better stormy.

We passed by flock of guillemots on water near Holm Island. Flight of fulmar reminds me of an owl. Even appearance from quarter view has something of the owl family. There is unlimited scope for study of herring gulls in flight. Pure beauty, but they land very clumsily compared with gannets and cormorants. We have seen two gulls with only one foot. How do they lose them? Do basking sharks bite off or take whole bird sometimes? What other fish?

From Radha Huish we can see mountains of Sutherland, must be 70 miles. We sail into Loch Maddy about 13.00. Once again the strange enchantment of these Outer Isles with their sea lochs and islands. One reason for their beauty I think is the actual banks of the lochs which shelve up steeply for 50 or 100ft but not more. In the Inner Isles there is a more progressive sloping and there is a feeling of being shut in.

At loch mouth there are two rocks (Maddys, dogs in Gaelic). Curiously these rocks have Skye formation (pleating, the Mate calls it), whereas the Outer Islands themselves, although only 1½ mile away, are totally different with the smooth scrubbed formation. The Maddys look like cliffs which have had the mainland collapse behind them and have themselves toppled backwards through about 40 degrees, so that the grass at the top now slopes to the water facing east while the pleated cliffs look upwards to the west. (The story round this peculiar rock formation is evidently much discussed in these parts. Presumably Outer Isles are a later addition and are possibly volcanic, with pleats caused by land between Outer Isles and Skye collapsing). So these two lone outposts are separated by 40 miles of sea from their nearest kin. Two golden eagles nested in Maddys a few years ago.

We go ashore and wander a short way round the edge of the loch to a bank sheltered from the fresh westerly. Here we find an excellent spot with no seaweed and deep clear water so that every detail of the sea bed can be seen. I dive in, it is cold but no worse than I expected.

I had two dives and some brisk swimming, then lay stark in the sun to dry, it was marvellous. I am very glad I swam and also glad I waited and did not swim off ship. Skipper was not too happy about it anyway. We lay for 1½ hours before going back to tea.

I received wire on arrival from Jack. Great disappointment to find I was required Saturday. Although date expected back, somehow I had convinced myself it wouldn't be really necessary. Now we must leave ship tomorrow at Mallaig. After tea Father rang thru' a wonderful surprise, phone from Jack 110 not ready. * OK for Monday now. We can stay aboard and complete the trip. I have rarely been so pleased. The weather seems to get better and better.

[By way of a small celebration, John and Eve spent the evening having a small party in the pub at Mallaig with the Mate and Purser. His notes return to daytime events.]

On way into islands at lunchtime saw several flights on fighters steering SE leaving trails. Probably US or RCAF Sabres. Mate had often seen trails but did not understand. Strange how people can accept such peculiar sights without question. Master of *Loch Broom* SnRNR, and nicer to speak to than look upon, says they were going over one flight every six minutes on previous night until 10pm. We see destroyer on ASK patrol. Must be large numbers of them – one group coming over. Enough of aeroplanes.

After tea I was sketching ship from poop deck. As sun got lower the grass covered islands in centre of loch took on an amazingly lush vivid green, which stood out against the brown of heather and rock on other islands and on the headland. The colour of the loch became a very vivid blue. If anything, the evening is more splendid than the morning on these outer isles.

We sailed from Loch Maddy for Kyle at about 2200 carrying a load of rather tipsy farmers returning with their purchases. The pub has done great trade. The bar is spit and sawdust but satisfactory and unpretentious. Draught beer is grim. All drink Scotch. God knows how they afford it but maybe cattle sales were bi-annual excuse. At Loch Boisdale they were hiding in corners and passing round the bottle. Eve came across a chap drinking and leaking at the same time. He was undisturbed at seeing her. This is what the Skipper would refer to as 'continuous movement'.

---

* 'Father' is Eve's father who used a shore telephone line to relay the message from Jack Arthur to say that the DH110 wasn't ready for weekend testing.

After leaving the loch I see the sunset I have been waiting for. Gradually deepening to a fiery red with Harris darkening to matt black in front of the sun; its peaks a perfect silhouette. Behind us the cliffs of Skye lie bathed in the last glow and in the pastel blue-grey to the east, the merest pencil line marks the change in shade between the Cuillins and the eastern sky. All their fiery redness is going. They are wispy and soon gone.

The sea is calm. Two or three fulmars sweep and plunge in our wake and the hills of South Uist begin to lose their hard outline as the light goes. But still Harris makes a bold stern line in front of the last orange and green of the sky. Below in the saloon the farmers shout at each other and two of them wrestle on the ledge at the stern end of the saloon where they are sleeping.

We enquired about buying salmon in Loch Maddy, but George Taylor, the Purser, said difficult. Season has begun. Our best way is to arrange a poaching expedition with gaff. Wish we had thought of it before, would have been great sport at Loch Skipport. Charge for fishing is 3 guineas a day! Poaching better value.

Donald, 2nd Purser, is from Loch Maddy. He talks of being caught fishing. Gillie did not object providing fish not taken away! All fish property of Duke. Donald has come right out of his shell now. Appears as a highly intelligent individual. Should have gone to University but after national service decided to take job straight away. Educated at Portree. Never saw train until national service. Told about Portree. Bonnie Prince C. came to Uist from France, thence to Skye. Stayed in pub at Portree and later less commodiously in cave up the coast.

I was cynical about 'Over the sea to Skye' when I realised distance from Kyle, but distance from Uist another matter. Must be debatable whether Prince C. should have stayed after Culloden in view of trouble his followers got into. Should such a leader stay to face music even if he loses head? Highlanders do not seem to resent him leaving their bloody moors after Culloden for comfortable Paris.

We sit on deck until sunset has faded to gentle green then turn in. I arrange for call at 3am to see dawn. We take look at horses and cattle. Fairly comfortable, though bottom hold seems pretty warm. This time we shall not be at anchor. The buyer of the horses comes down to speak to them and quieten them before he turns in. This is an unexpectedly thoughtful move for one of these hardbitten Highlanders.

Friday May 23rd: Mate calls me at 3.15am. We have tea, then up on deck. Just light. We are steaming past Longay and Pabay. Applecross Forest begins to show firmly against pale yellow sky. As light increases Cuillins and all Skye hills warm with roseate tint. I settle down to scraperboard sketch of sea, hills and sky to east.

[John records that they docked at Kyle at 4.15am and unloaded quickly before slipping away.]

As we slide easily away from Kyle sun is up behind hills of Loch Alsh. Now visibility better than ever before. To west the Cuillins visible through the deep trench of Loch Alsh, to the east the hills bordering Loch Long and Loch Durch pile one behind the other, each a subtler and more elusive pastel blue than the one ahead of him. As we turn into Kyle Rhea all the glens and all the hillsides spring suddenly into life, the hills bathed in light, the lochs sparkling. The sun is above the towering skyline.

When we reach the narrows of Kyle Rhea and I go up on the bridge, Skipper is ayeing and giving his orders in his musical way. 'Very bad currents here' says he, 'Aye, very bad'. Indeed it is so even to my unpractised eye. The water is actually boiling like a river beneath a slowly opening lock gate. Small whirlpools make gaping twisting holes and the smooth water is circled with streaks of turbulent eddies.

I have never witnessed such a tide current, it runs at 7 knots says the Skipper. Steering is difficult; we must keep bow on to avoid strong yaw. The wheel twirls this way and that, the steering engine clatters, stops and clatters again.

The Second Mate shows me spot where he shot golden eagle when he was a shepherd on Ben Spiel. Although my answer is that of any naturalist, that there are not enough of them to be a serious menace to sheep, I can see well enough the view of the shepherd beneath the crag where lives this mighty bird; his lambs may be small percentage of the country's total but they are his charge. The Bird Society must feed the eagles if they wish to save them. I would dearly like to watch an eyrie. Cairngorms probably still best.

[John then catnaps as they sail on to Mallaig and he and Eve spend the morning sunbathing on mattresses on the deck as they cross the Minch to reach Castle Bay, Barra.]

We get view of all islands with high ground and splendid view of Cuillin. I get much enjoyment from continual study of maps. Also use Skipper's charts. Most valuable to pick out landfalls and various peaks apart from learning accurate geography of islands. What pleasure is denied to any traveller on land, sea or air who does not carry a map.

[He describes the approach to Castle Bay and the small castle stronghold of the McNeils.]

The pier is surrounded by fishing boats. When we enter the bay there is no sign of life anywhere. Even after our siren has echoed round the bay, nothing seems to stir. And then suddenly the fishing boats have moved and we see that they are moving away from the pier in pairs and fours, roped together. Soon the pier is clear and with the usual skill we come alongside. The first line to be thrown ashore is caught by a Husky dog who worries it continuously for about 10 minutes.

There is nothing in particular about the village, but somehow it is attractive and comfortable. Like most of the other villages we have seen there are many Swedish type houses (still with these ghastly orange doors); the houses themselves fit quite well into the scene and are no doubt admirably suited to this part of the world.

We walk along a road which runs out of the village to the north west between the hills. In the outer part of the village are many fairly new stone houses, but the stone and thatch crofts they have displaced still stand near them. One is driven to picture the island with nothing else but these little huts. Some are still inhabited, the thatch securely held with skilfully tied rope and fish net. Usually an old crone is sitting outside. At the door of one of the broken down crofts sits such a one, leaning on a stick, a black bonnet on her head. Perhaps she would prefer to live in this little old house with her memories, rather than the modern building which is strange and uncomfortable to her.

There is a fine new school here with big windows and clean healthy appearance like a new hospital. The sound of children singing comes to us as we pass up the road. We climb to the top of the pass above the village and then up the first part of the hills on our left. As we breast the top of the first rise, the most spectacular view of the whole trip is before us. We are looking down on the Atlantic Ocean, two or three miles distant. But it is not the baleful grey Atlantic one might expect. It is rich blue with white rollers tumbling in to spread themselves quietly on the pure silvery white sand. Lush grass is growing on the sand dunes behind the beach, and away up the coast fertile fields stretch back to the rocks and heather of the hills guarding the east coast lochs. This is a scene with Mediterranean colours, but somehow fresher for being amongst these quiet little islands.

The sands on the small islands are equally white and fine. We begin to think at once of bringing the children here for the summer holidays. The sands are perfect and practically to ourselves. Maybe no other children to play with. But we could visit many different parts of Barra and also small islands like Vaternish with their sheltered coves. This is a really enchanting island, from its fishing boats to its silver sands and exciting views across to the small islands and rocks to the south.

While we sit on the hill a crofter comes by with three bullocks for the *Hebrides*. We tell him she is in and at that moment the siren sounds warning us to return.

We follow the man and his cattle. He has a fearful job with them on the unfenced road. They are into every croft and up every slope. Without his dog he would be done. It is the best working dog I have ever seen. He uses very few commands and the dog does the rest. We can see him look round for the best route to cut off the cattle before he dashes round behind several cottages to appear at exactly the right point at the right moment, never making a false move. We help to drive the cattle over the last ½ mile through village. Crofter says no dog trials on island.

Now that we have seen many cattle loaded and unloaded treatment seems less harsh, in fact most men are very good. One young deckhand very bad, warned by older men but needs good hiding or a kick from a horse.

We sail from Castle Bay at 1510. They have a very smart blue and white lifeboat. She always lies at anchor and does much work in winter.

Four Fireflys, probably from a carrier, make an attack on the harbour while we are in Castle Bay. They would not get away with such flying in wartime.

We sail across the Minch in warm afternoon sun. Trawlers are dotted along the horizon. As we pass loch mouth I see what appears to be a lone goose flying past. Does not come close enough for recognition. Donald says geese nest on west coast of these islands. We saw four or five rough-legged buzzards while walking from Castle Bay. Thought they were common buzzards at first but when they came overhead saw very bright plumage and almost white tail.

We enter Sound of Mull in evening, with last view of those glorious Outer Isles showing their peaks over the horizon. As we sail down Sound sun sets and we have beautiful sight looking west with Rhea lying on the sea beyond the Sound. Ben Nevis and many inland peaks are clear cut and take on their roseate hue once again. As Eve says, the hills to the west near the sun have the colours of burnished copper. A good description.

The Mate tells amusing stories of Macleans and MacDougals. Also of Lady Island where Maclean lost his wife. Rescued by MacDougals.

We reach Oban in very good time at 10.30pm. We finish our bottle of Scotch with Mate, Purser and Donald.

BIBLIOGRAPHY

Barker, Ralph, *The Schneider Trophy Races* (Chatto and Windus, 1971)

Burnet, Charles, *Three Centuries to Concorde* (Mechanical Engineering Publications, 1979)

Duke, Neville, *Test Pilot* (Grub Street, 2003)

Lithgow, Mike, *Mach One* (Wingate, 1954)

Matthews, Henry, *DH 110 – Prelude to the Sea Vixen* (HPM Publications, n.d.)

Rance, Adrian B. (ed), *Sea Planes and Flying Boats of The Solent* (Southampton University Industrial Archaeology Group in association with Southampton City Museum, n.d.)

Sharp, C. Martin, *DH – an Outline of de Havilland History,* (Faber and Faber, 1960)

Thomas, Chris, *The Typhoon File* (Air Britain Historians, 1981)

Waterton, W.A., *The Quick and the Dead* (Frederick Muller, 1956)

INDEX